The Hidden Magic of
Walt Disney
World

3RD EDITION

Over 600 Secrets of the Magic Kingdom, EPCOT, Disney's Hollywood Studios, and Disney's Animal Kingdom

SUSAN VENESS

Adams Media
New York London Toronto Sydney

Adams Media

An Imprint of Simon & Schuster, Inc.

57 Littlefield Street

Avon, Massachusetts 02322

This Adams Media trade paperback edition October 2020

ADAMS MEDIA and colophon are trademarks of Simon & Schuster.

For information about special discounts for bulk purchases, please contact Simon & Schuster Special Sales at 1-866-506-1949 or business@simonandschuster.com.

The Simon & Schuster Speakers Bureau can bring authors to your live event. For more information or to book an event contact the Simon & Schuster Speakers Bureau at 1-866-248-3049 or visit our website at www.simonspeakers.com.

Interior design by Michelle Kelly
Maps created by Joe Comeau

Manufactured in the United States of America

1 2020

Library of Congress Cataloging-in-Publication Data has been applied for.

ISBN 978-1-5072-1256-1
ISBN 978-1-5072-1257-8 (ebook)

Contents

Foreword

Magic flows out of the tricks you don't see. It is the magician's way of weaving what is right in front of your eyes with something subtle, something hidden. It is a blending of your expectation of what *should* happen with the delightful surprise of something far more creative.

Disney magic is even more elusive. Some say it's in the attractions, some say it's in the atmosphere, and some credit the can-do attitude of the Cast Members. But nearly everyone who visits the parks agrees: The magic is there; they just can't quite put their finger on where. And like the magician's, Disney's magic also lies in the sleight of hand, the hidden detail.

My first visit to the Magic Kingdom was as a child. While it was great family fun and the delight in exploring a "whole new world" was already apparent, my childlike viewpoint did not see any further than that. It wasn't until my next visit in 1989 that I really understood the magic. Settled in my seat during the preshow for the Living Seas at EPCOT, I was fully immersed in watching the movie about how the seas were formed and what their future might be. When the show ended, a set of doors leading to a ride vehicle, the Sea Cabs, opened with a great, satisfying *whoosh*. I was stunned! There was more to this than a film? I was also going to take a ride? Where would it go?

The answer should have been obvious, considering that the pavilion contained the world's largest aquarium. But it wasn't. The park experience was so overwhelming; it was almost impossible to do more than just allow Disney to move me from one attraction to the next, taking in only what was directly in front of me.

Those open doors with an adventure waiting beyond were a defining moment and began my fascination with Disney's flawless ability to add just a bit more.

My Disney obsession translated into yearly vacations. I quickly became an online Disney travel specialist, ultimately becoming a full-time researcher, professional travel writer, and guidebook coauthor, specializing in Orlando and Walt Disney World.

Ongoing research for the guidebook and other writing deepened my knowledge of (and love for) the parks. The more familiar I became with them, the more I began to look around for the smaller details, and the more I looked around, the more I realized how often the details that seemed hidden were actually right in front of my eyes.

Often, I didn't know what I was looking at. Sometimes I knew what I was looking at, but I didn't know why it had been placed there or what it was for. Things had clearly been done for a reason, and I couldn't bear not knowing what that reason was.

Increasingly, I began to feel the real magic of the parks could be found in the details and it became a personal mission to seek them out. Some jumped right out at me (the lanterns in the window in Liberty Square were clearly a reference to Paul Revere and his midnight ride) while others, like the unexpected For Rent sign in a window, left me totally perplexed.

What started as a diversion became a passion, and I began to visit the parks at every opportunity, specifically looking for their hidden gems. I no longer saw the attractions as rides, but instead as opportunities to seek out the details, thus viewing the story in a whole new way—a more complete and satisfying way.

The kernel of an idea formed, and within a short time I began writing and researching in earnest, with an eye toward creating a companion guide to the other Disney writing projects my husband, Simon, and I were already doing.

Further inspiration came in the form of my brother, Chip. As young adults, we had taken a vacation together at Walt Disney World, and although I was already a serious Disney fan, the parks held limited appeal for him. In fact, he was bored. But, in 2006, his wife expressed an interest in visiting Walt Disney World. She had never been, and they had a few days to spare.

We invited them down to our home for a visit and planned a few days at Walt Disney World. Chip was willing, but uninspired. I decided to show him the parks in a whole new light, and as we toured Epcot and Magic Kingdom, I pointed out the wonderful Imagineering jewels scattered all around. We talked about the backstories, we stopped and listened, and he opened his eyes wide.

In a thank-you email, he told me it was the best time he'd ever had in the parks, and that everyone should see them from that perspective. I agreed.

Whether you are a die-hard Disney fan, a casual visitor, or a guest who suspects there is more to it but aren't sure where to look, let *The Hidden Magic of Walt Disney World, 3rd Edition* be your tour guide. Allow it to slow you down long enough for the magic to catch up. It's all there—and now you know where to find it!

Introduction

How can you tell if something in a Walt Disney World park has a story? Ask yourself this: Is it there? If the answer is "Yes," then it has a story. In short, nothing is placed in a park or attraction without a reason, right down to the smallest details. And while those delightful bits of "hidden magic" may not be the stars themselves, they are certainly what makes the parks shine brighter.

The first edition of *The Hidden Magic of Walt Disney World* was filled with details that were, for the most part, easily recognizable by everyone, even if the viewer didn't know exactly what they were looking at, or simply didn't know there *was* something to look at. While the reference to Henry Wadsworth Longfellow's poem may not spring immediately to mind, two lanterns in a window are still recognizable as lanterns, and the viewer is left to wonder what those physical props represent.

The second edition of the book served to update what was new in the parks, and what had been removed, but it also dove deeper into the attractions' backstories and more elusive details. The reimagining of Mickey's Toontown Fair into Storybook Circus turned that area into a catalogue of Disney's early animation history, and with it came a barrage of hidden magic.

Now, fifty years after Magic Kingdom opened, Disney's theme park storytelling has changed profoundly. The hidden and not-so-hidden details are far more subtle, but also far more expansive.

Pandora—The World of Avatar at Disney's Animal Kingdom represents a big shift in the way Disney's lands are created. In keeping with the message of eco-awareness, the land is, on the surface, the outcome of a great battle between the nature-based lives of the Na'vi and the exploitation of the Resources Development Administration. Scratch the surface a bit and you've got a battle between humans and nature. Dig a bit deeper and it becomes a cautionary tale. Peel away another layer and Pandora becomes a metaphor for Earth.

Disney's Hollywood Studios has two new lands, each aligned with the park's theme of entertainment. First came Toy Story Land, which moved the stand-alone attraction Toy Story Mania! into the larger story of Andy and the playground he has set up in his backyard.

Star Wars: Galaxy's Edge, based on the blockbuster movies, books, comics, video games, and television spin-offs, is absolutely filled with references to the franchise, with nearly every element touched by some aspect within the Star Wars canon.

But this drive toward ever-increasing additions of hidden magic doesn't end with the lands or attractions. Dining outlets have also become canvases for further storytelling in a way they simply were not in the parks' earlier years. From the resurrection of the Society of Explorers and Adventurers in Magic Kingdom's Skipper Canteen to the exotic travels of Disney's Imagineers, memorialized in Tiffins and Nomad Lounge in Animal Kingdom, restaurants have become immersive attractions in their own right. Space 220, coming to EPCOT, will take place-making to an even greater degree. And you're going to want to explore it all.

As you tour the parks and attractions you'll find each of the hidden details listed in the book in the order in which you'll encounter them, with specific details highlighted in bold to make it easier to find them at a glance. Bear in mind, the parks are ever-changing, so if you come across a detail in the book that has been removed or isn't working, simply move on to the next thing. And remember, some attractions are dark, so pass the time in the queue by refreshing your memory on what you'll look for once you're inside.

Let *The Hidden Magic of Walt Disney World, 3rd Edition* act as a friendly tour guide, opening your eyes to the backstories, the hidden elements, and the wonderful world that Walt Disney and his Imagineers created.

And now, let's begin the journey where the World began…Disney's Magic Kingdom.

The Magic Kingdom

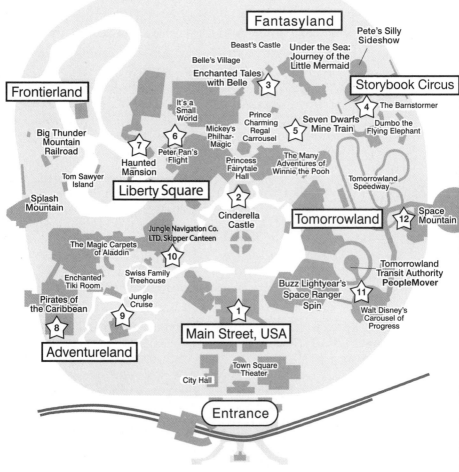

Fantasyland

Pete's Silly Sideshow

Beast's Castle

Under the Sea: Journey of the Little Mermaid

Belle's Village

Enchanted Tales with Belle 3

Storybook Circus

Frontierland

It's a Small World

The Barnstormer 4

Prince Charming Regal Carrousel

Seven Dwarfs Mine Train 5

Dumbo the Flying Elephant

Big Thunder Mountain Railroad

Mickey's Philhar-Magic

7   6

Peter Pan's Flight

Princess Fairytale Hall

The Many Adventures of Winnie the Pooh

Tomorrowland Speedway

Haunted Mansion

Tom Sawyer Island

Liberty Square

2

Splash Mountain

Cinderella Castle

Tomorrowland

12

Space Mountain

Jungle Navigation Co. LTD. Skipper Canteen

The Magic Carpets of Aladdin

10

Tomorrowland Transit Authority PeopleMover

Enchanted Tiki Room

Swiss Family Treehouse

Buzz Lightyear's Space Ranger Spin

11

Pirates of the Caribbean

Jungle Cruise

Walt Disney's Carousel of Progress

9

1

8

Main Street, USA

Adventureland

Town Square Theater

City Hall

Entrance

Seven Seas Lagoon

1. **Main Street, U.S.A.:** On the *Partners* statue, the ring on Walt Disney's outstretched hand is an Irish Claddagh ring, symbolizing his Irish heritage and his commitment to his wife, Lillian.

2. **Cinderella Castle:** The front of Cinderella Castle faces south, which means there is never a time when the sun is directly behind it, nor are there any nearby buildings that could cast a shadow, so every photo comes out fabulous.

3. **Belle's Village:** A special tribute to Walt Disney and animator Ub Iwerks's 1927 cartoon co-creation Oswald the Lucky Rabbit can be found embedded in the walkway outside Enchanted Tales with Belle.

4. **Storybook Circus:** Just after you enter the queue for Barnstormer, turn around and look at the back of the attraction's sign. It was once the original sign for Wiseacre Farm, when Storybook Circus was still Mickey's Toontown Fair.

5. **Seven Dwarfs Mine Train:** The figures for Bashful, Sleepy, Happy, Grumpy, and Doc, seen inside the cottage at the end of your mine ride, once made their home in Fantasyland's long-gone Snow White's Scary Adventures.

6. **Peter Pan's Flight:** December 27 is circled on the 1904 calendar in John's room, and it's the date the stage play version of James M. Barrie's story *Peter Pan* opened at the Duke of York's Theatre in London, England.

7. **Haunted Mansion:** Pay attention to the music as you wind your way through the attic. It's a slow, eerie, twisted rendition of the "Bridal Chorus," better known as "Here Comes the Bride."

8. **Pirates of the Caribbean:** A rock formation on the left-hand side, just as the pirate beach comes into view, looks like an evil skull with teeth.

9. **Jungle Cruise:** While you're in the queue, listen for a swingy stanza from Cole Porter's song "You're the Top," which includes the cheerful compliment, "You're Mickey Mouse!"

10. **Jungle Navigation Co. LTD. Skipper Canteen:** The books lining the walls to the secret meeting room act as little time capsules capturing snippets of Disney history, from television to movies, attractions, and homages to Imagineers.

11. **Carousel of Progress:** A notice attached to the final scene's corkboard reads, MARTY CALLED WANTS CHANGES. It is a reference to Marty Sklar, former vice chairman and principal creative executive at Walt Disney Imagineering.

12. **Space Mountain:** A panel labeled "Collision Prevention Control" includes a list of Traffic Codes. If you know your major Floridian roads you can work out which location each code refers to using the hints about their current status.

Chapter 1

The Magic Kingdom

Touring Disney's Magic Kingdom is like taking a world journey. The park has a distinct flow, from the Small Town America of Walt Disney's childhood memory, to Europe, the New World, the American West, Mexico, the Caribbean, the Middle East, into Space, and finally, to the cartoon world of Walt Disney's imagination.

But there are other ways of looking at the Magic Kingdom as well. We will explore it from three distinct perspectives—the Show, the Facts, and a historical time line of exploration—giving a sense of the thought and detail that went into creating an all-encompassing world filled with the gentleness of fantasy and the fascination of fact.

Main Street, U.S.A.

Every aspect of Walt Disney World focuses on the Show, which invites guests to suspend reality and become part of a fully immersive theatrical experience, but Main Street, U.S.A. also tells the Facts about the making of the Magic Kingdom more vividly than any other area of the park. These elements combine seamlessly, creating a sense of Hometown America as Walt Disney remembered it from his childhood home of Marceline, Missouri. Main Street allows guests to immediately feel a sense of familiarity and, at the same time, experience excitement and anticipation for the grand adventure that waits when we venture beyond the boundaries of home.

It all begins when you set foot on Magic Kingdom property. From the perspective of the Show, the turnstiles are like the entry to a grand theater. As you pass under the train station, you see posters representing Coming Attractions, building the excitement for what's in store. Then, walk into the theater represented by the train station's exit, breathe in the smell of fresh, hot popcorn, and enter the Show. That's when the magic really takes over.

Imagine That!

Walt Disney Imagineering, also known as WDI, is the creative heart of Walt Disney Company. Imagineers—a combination of imagination and engineering—design and create each element of the theme parks, water parks, resorts, and shopping districts, from the technology that runs them to the stories, shops and restaurants, music, ambiance, and entertainment guests experience.

Town Square

The best blockbuster movies take your breath away, putting you firmly on the edge of your seat from the very first scene, and Town Square achieves this in high style. Although Cinderella Castle almost pulls you down Main Street, Town Square sets the scene for the experience to come, moving you through Hometown America and out into the World of Walt Disney.

What's more down-home than mailing a letter rather than sending an email? Magic Kingdom's town square remembers this communications throwback through the **green mailbox** on a lamppost in front of Tony's Town Square Restaurant. You'll find a second mailbox in front of Main Street's Arcade, and yes, you can really send a letter from each.

A cute reference to the theme of Tony's restaurant is found in front of the restaurant, where **Lady and Tramp's paw prints** are enclosed in a heart etched into the pavement.

Imagine That!

It isn't just lands and attractions that tell a tale. Smaller scenes around the parks also play a supporting role within the larger story, such as the time period along Main Street, U.S.A. Imagineering props fabricator and set dresser Eric Baker explains: "It helps tell the story a bit better if it's a vignette-type thing, and it makes it more interesting to look at. One of my favorite things when I was a kid going to Walt Disney World was looking at the animated windows on Main Street. They had little animated figures, and that was just the coolest thing in the world to me, so I like doing little vignettes that help tell a story."

There are many historical dates scattered around the square, including on The Chapeau's pink hatbox sign, marked

No. 63. When prefaced by the number 19, it becomes 1963, the year the movie *Summer Magic* made its debut. Within Magic Kingdom's story, the shop was owned by Nancy Carey, the main character in *Summer Magic*. Another reference to the movie survived, and we'll see it when we reach the Emporium.

While you're in The Chapeau, look for the **old-fashioned crank telephone** just inside the right-hand door. There was a time when phones had a party line, meaning up to twenty homes in the neighborhood were on the same telephone line and could hear each other's conversations. The chatter here is riddled with gossipy conversations, compliments of nosey neighbors. Pick up the receiver and listen.

Fascinating Fact

Though the results of their labors will be appreciated and admired by millions, Imagineers are not allowed to sign their work. Instead, they sometimes place little symbols of themselves, often in the form of initials or birthdates, cleverly disguised to blend into the environment's theme. You will see many as you tour the parks.

As you cross Town Square from right to left, take a look at the plaque on the left-hand side of the landscaping just beyond the flagpole. Each of the Disney parks has a **dedication plaque** with quotations from the executive who opened the park. Here you'll see Roy O. Disney's opening-day comments. Take note of the date, though. Magic Kingdom opened on October 1, 1971, but the official ceremony didn't take place until October 25, once the park was fully functional.

To the left of the dedication plaque is a bench featuring sculptures of **Roy O. Disney and Minnie Mouse**. They are honored here as the supporting actors to Walt and Mickey.

Take notice of the **sepia paintings** in the Chamber of Commerce, to the left of City Hall. They are reproductions of original concept art for Main Street, U.S.A.

Also note the **date for the Chamber of Commerce**. It's 1871, exactly one hundred years before Magic Kingdom opened.

Magic Kingdom's opening year, 1971, is honored through the **Engine Co. 71** designation on the **Fire Station**.

Main Street

On the windows to either side of the Emporium's front door are the words **"Osh" Popham, Proprietor**. Ossium "Osh" Popham was the postmaster in the Disney feature film *Summer Magic* starring Burl Ives and Hayley Mills. Signs inside the Emporium indicate the store was **established in 1863**, a nod to the movie's debut one hundred years later.

The window above the confectionary across the street, labeled "Hollywood Publishing Co. Manuscripts & Melodramas," memorializes **Marty Sklar**, who, over the course of fifty-four years with Disney, served as Walt's speech writer, put Walt's vision for EPCOT Center into words, and became creative head and executive vice president of Imagineering, Imagineering Ambassador, and a Disney Legend. Before his death in 2017, Marty attended the opening of every Disney park, worldwide.

As you walk down Main Street, the "movie credits" roll in the **upper windows** above the shops. In between Roy O. Disney's window at the beginning of Main Street and Walt Disney's window at the end of Main Street are the names of the **cast and crew** who brought the Show to life. Take time to stop and read them to honor these creative women and men.

Main Street's **second-story windows** actually perform a three-part function. At their most basic, they are advertisements for the town's services and business proprietors, from mortgages to dance lessons to interior decorators and so on. As representations of rolling credits, they are the companies involved in creating the Show. In reality, they are the names of Imagineers and designers, artists, and bogus land-purchasing companies that held instrumental roles in the creation of the Magic Kingdom. You will find some of these key people in other areas of the park, and in other hidden magic.

The Emporium Gallery next to the Emporium has a sign over the front door that reads, **Established in 1901**, the year Walt Disney was born.

Pay attention to the **Emporium Gallery's mural**, on the back wall. The faces are real people, and they are an example of a hidden Imagineer "signature."

Fascinating Fact

Orlando is best known for Walt Disney World, but it's also known for the frustrating main strip of Interstate 4, which has long had a far more grumpy and far less happy effect on theme park visitors caught in traffic jams. So what happens when you combine something classically Disney with that most notorious of roadways? Pure magic. Almost.

In 1999, Disney planned to amp up the excitement for the return of Magic Kingdom's beloved nighttime parade from its stint in Disneyland by bringing some of the parade elements, including the iconic Elliott float from the movie *Pete's Dragon*, down I-4 and through the toll gates for Magic Kingdom. But at 16 feet tall, Elliott was a big dragon, and he wouldn't fit under one of the highway's bridges, so a rerouting took place, and as he wound his (rather slow) way toward Magic Kingdom and Main Street, U.S.A., traffic was held up along another highway. Did people complain? They did not! It may have been the most celebratory traffic jam in the history of Orlando. Main Street Electrical Parade had come home!

Now that you have reached the far end of Main Street, look at the upper window above the Plaza Restaurant, facing Cinderella Castle. There, you will find **Walter Elias Disney's window**, the director of the Show. His window reads: "Walter E. Disney, Graduate School of Design & Master Planning— We specialize in Imagineering." While the director's name always comes first and last in the credits, the sentimental version of this placement dictates Walt has been given an eternal view of the castle.

Below Walt's name are the names of his **master planners**—Richard Irvine, John Hench, Howard Brummitt, Marvin Davis, Fred Hope, Vic Greene, Bill Martin, and Chuck Myall—who were instrumental in designing the Magic Kingdom.

As you transition through the Hub area, step beyond the embrace of Hometown America and enter Old World Europe as represented by Fantasyland.

Before you head into one of the park's lands, pause in the Hub for the obligatory photo in front of the *Partners* statue of Walt Disney and Mickey Mouse, taking note of the ring on Walt's outstretched right hand. It isn't a wedding ring worn on the wrong hand, it's an **Irish Claddagh ring**, symbolizing Walt's Irish heritage, and his commitment to his wife, Lillian. The symbols on the ring are a crown, a heart, and two hands encircling the heart, representing loyalty, love, and friendship, respectively. In life, Walt wore a Claddagh ring purchased during a trip to his ancestral homeland.

Fascinating Fact

Claddagh rings aren't just symbols of affection, they are also an indication of the wearer's relationship status. Traditionally, when worn on the left hand with the bottom of the heart pointing away from the wearer, it indicates the wearer is in a lifelong relationship or engaged to be married. When worn on the left hand with the bottom of the heart pointing toward the wearer, it indicates the wearer is married. Placing the ring on the right hand with the bottom of the heart pointing toward the wearer means the wearer is in a relationship, but not necessarily lifelong, and placing the ring on the right hand with the bottom of the heart pointing outward means the wearer is available. Walt's devotion to Lillian is well-known, so it is an error on his part that his Claddagh ring is positioned on his right hand with the heart pointing outward.

Walt's tie also holds a bit of hidden magic. Sculptor Blaine Gibson "dressed" Walt in a special **tie bearing the initials STR**, in remembrance of a tie Walt often wore, which was monogramed with the initials of the residential community Smoke Tree Ranch in Palm Springs, California. Walt and Lillian had a vacation home there, which they sold to help finance the creation of Disneyland. When the park proved successful, Walt and Lillian returned to Smoke Tree Ranch and purchased a second home. One of Walt's Disneyland investors, fellow Smoke Tree Ranch resident Donald Sherwood Gilmore, then-chairman of the board at pharmaceutical manufacturer The Upjohn Company, is honored with a window on Main Street, U.S.A. in Disneyland.

The baseball theme of Casey's Corner is obvious, and if you know your obscure poets you'll make the connection between the restaurant and Ernest Lawrence Thayer's poem "Casey at the Bat," in which Thayer recounts the dismal Mudville game during which mighty Casey struck out. Take a closer look at the baseball on the left side of the "C" that forms **Casey's Corner's sign**. The number on it, 1888, refers to June 3, 1888, the date the poem was published in the *San Francisco Examiner* newspaper. What's the Disney connection to the poem? It's the 1946 animated short *Casey at the Bat*, a musical recitation retelling of the story, later released as part of the *Make Mine Music* video.

Fantasyland

Welcome to the quintessential Disney experience, the epitome of all Walt dreamed of in family entertainment. Fantasyland brings the tales gathered by the Brothers Grimm to life through the graceful charm of European castles, knights, and ladies fair. It is the embodiment of childhood fantasy that has been passed down from grandparent to grandchild throughout the ages.

The Show element is fairly obvious: You have entered the cinematic world of the Disney classics. A more history-based story line brings you out of Hometown America into the charm and gallantry of medieval Europe. Billowing tents, heavy brick, and hand-blown glass windows evoke a feeling of long-ago kingdoms and quaint villages created through childhood imagination.

Fascinating Fact

Each time you pass from one land to another, the landscaping, ambient sound, and architecture change subtly. For example, when transitioning from the Hub to Adventureland, the architecture and landscaping along the front of the Crystal Palace change from Victorian to more colonial style, the design elements on the bridge crossing into Adventureland become more primitive, and the landscaping takes on a more jungle-themed look. What else is special about the transition from Crystal Palace to Adventureland? It's symbolic of the British Empire spreading its influence into Africa.

Cinderella Castle Celebrating Fifty Years!

Ever notice how easy it is to get a fabulous **photo of Cinderella Castle** no matter what the season or time of day? That happy reality is not by accident. The front of the castle faces south, which means there is never a time when the sun is directly behind it, nor are there any nearby buildings that could cast a shadow.

You could be forgiven for thinking Cinderella Castle looks like two castles in one. The bottom is heavy and relatively unadorned in the manner of a **medieval fortress** while the top is much more delicate and fairy tale–like, as would be common for a **Renaissance palace**.

If you have a sharp eye, you may notice the **Disney family coat of arms** standing guard over the front and back entrances to the castle.

In the mural scene inside the breezeway, where the prince has placed the glass slipper on Cinderella's foot, you'll find two Disney Imagineers. The man standing to the far left is **John Hench**, and the man directly behind the prince is

Herbert Ryman. Hench and Ryman were the lead designers of Cinderella Castle.

Imagine That!

Discovering backstories, small details, and hidden references is what this book is all about. Why are these secret gems so appealing? Alex Grayman, art director, Walt Disney Imagineering, explains: "We like to layer in extra things for people who are going to pick up on them. We get it, and a lot of guests eat that up. The more people know about these little things, the deeper they're going to be connected. We respect where we came from, we acknowledge it, we love it, and we live it. It's fun if you're a guest who 'gets' it. You feel special because you know what it means, and 'those people don't know.'"

Unless fortune favors them in the most dramatic way, most guests will never sleep in the suite inside Cinderella Castle. Those who do are in for an enchanting experience, starting with a bit of hidden magic. A simple but elegant **grandfather clock** stands in one corner of the small reception area, with its hands permanently set to 11:59 p.m. Although it all began to unravel for Cinderella when Prince Charming's castle clock struck midnight, this thoughtful stoppage of time ensures unending royal treatment for the suite's guests. You'll see the wooden door leading to the reception area in the breezeway under Cinderella Castle. It's relatively simple, with two elaborate "E"-shaped metal designs on the left side of the door.

Pass through the breezeway and you're in Fantasyland proper. But we're not done with Cinderella Castle yet. Walk to the area near Cinderella's fountain and look up at the square, middle portion of the castle where the smallest turret is located.

You'll see six **stained glass windows**—three on one boxy corner and three on the other—that tell Cinderella's story. They're meant to be viewed from inside the suite, but as you're standing in Fantasyland and you view them from right to left, you'll see them in order. The story (first window) starts with the Tremaine family home, then proceeds to an invitation to the prince's ball, which Cinderella attends. The third window indicates the clock has struck midnight. The next set of windows show Cinderella's lost **glass slipper**, her mouse friends Jaq and Gus bringing her the key to unlock the room she's held captive in by her wicked stepmother, and finally, the prince's castle, indicating she has found her happily ever after.

Fascinating Fact

Forced perspective is a technique used to trick your eye into thinking something is bigger, taller, closer, or farther away than it actually is. Imagineers use this technique throughout Walt Disney World to make the most economical use of space and materials. Many of the buildings you see are built, for example, to an 80/60/40 scale, meaning the lower level is built to 80 percent normal scale, the second level to 60 percent, and the upper level to 40 percent, giving the illusion of greater height.

As with all transitions from one land into another, the themed elements change. As you pass Beast's castle on the way into the village, notice how the light fixtures and the wall along the bridge change from somewhat rustic to more refined.

Belle's Village

No self-respecting village would be without a pub, and Gaston's Tavern pays homage to this tradition, as well as to a few important people. See those barrels behind the counter?

Trois Blondes Bier remembers the three blonde girls in the Disney animated movie *Beauty and the Beast*; **IgerBock** references Bob Iger, CEO of Walt Disney Company from 2005 through 2020; and **Staggs Ale** honors Tom Staggs, chairman of Walt Disney Parks and Resorts from 2010 through 2015, then chief operating officer from 2015 until his departure from the company in 2016.

Although Cast Members staying in character will tell you the portrait on the back wall in Bonjour! Village Gifts is an ancestor of Magic Kingdom's vice president, **Phil Holmes**, you and I know it's really him. The adage "a picture is worth a thousand words" applies here, as there are several wonderful details hidden within the portrait. Tributes to attractions and lands Holmes has been involved with include **Aladdin's lamp** from the Magic Carpets of Aladdin, a **red apple** from Snow White's Scary Adventures, and **peanuts** from Storybook Circus, all of which sit on the table in front of him. Over his left shoulder is a **strip of wallpaper** with the pattern used in the Haunted Mansion, while a **golden statue of Donald Duck** sits on a shelf over his right shoulder. This award is given to Cast Members who have been with the Walt Disney Company for forty years. Just below Donald is a **blue book** with a spine that reads, *Terre de Fantasme*, which translates to "Land of Fantasy," or "Fantasy Land." The open book on the table features a **map of Magic Kingdom**, and Phil sports a **large ring** on his right hand, another symbol of his forty years of service with Disney.

In keeping with Belle's love for reading, the **open book** to the left of Phil Holmes's portrait is the story of "Beauty and the Beast" in French.

Imagine That!

Christopher Lucas, actor, speaker, and author of the book *Top Disney: 100 Top Ten Lists of the Best of Disney, from the Man to the Mouse and Beyond*, shares his most magical memories: "People often ask me when or how my love of Disney began. A lot of it comes from my grandmother, who helped to raise me and my brother and was a big Disney fan herself. Nana took me to see my first movie, Disney's *Robin Hood*, at Radio City Music Hall in 1973. Her dream was also to take us to the newly opened Walt Disney World, but as a low-income family back then, traveling from New York City to Florida was a very expensive journey.

"Nana scrimped and saved enough to take me, my brother, and my cousin to Walt Disney World for one day in the summer of 1976. We all had fun enjoying the magic together for the very first time. I can still recall Nana's shock and amazement while riding Pirates of the Caribbean, when she saw the little hairs on the leg of the pirate above our boat as we passed under the bridge. She yelled in a voice loud enough for all to hear, 'Wow! Walt Disney didn't miss a thing!'

"As we were leaving the park after the fireworks, I held my grandmother's hand as I looked back at Cinderella Castle, never knowing if I'd ever take in that view again. I also spotted a balloon seller holding a bunch of red Mickey-ear balloons, and I begged Nana to buy me one. Unfortunately her budget was tight, and she had to gently tell me that there was no more money left to get me a balloon. I rode back to the hotel on the monorail as any pouty seven-year-old would, disappointed that I didn't have a balloon even after Nana gave us all the happiest day of our young lives.

"I am blessed that in the decades that followed I was able to live my dream of being an actor and writer, including doing some jobs for Disney. I returned to the parks many times after that initial visit. Nana never made it back, for various health reasons.

"My grandmother passed away in January, 1999, at age eighty-three. During her funeral services I held my emotions in check. I tried to be strong, not shedding a tear publicly, even though I lost the person I loved more than almost anyone else.

"Shortly after her burial I was scheduled to shoot something at Disney-MGM Studios. We wrapped early one day, so they gave us passes and allowed us some extra time in the parks. I headed to the Magic Kingdom and spent the afternoon and evening there, by myself, having a blast.

"At the end of the night, just before passing under the Main Street Railroad station, I looked back to take in that stunning castle view that never grows old. At that moment a little boy came up to me with his mother and said, 'Mister, do you want my red Mickey balloon? Mom says I can't take it home, so you can have it.'

"I took the balloon, thanked them both, and after they walked away I broke down, sobbing more than I ever have in my life. So much so that I had to sit down on the ground right there on Main Street. All of the wonderful memories of Nana, her love for us and for Disney, came flooding back. The stoicism I showed at the funeral was gone. Walt's Kingdom and the magic of the red balloon helped me grieve in a positive way.

"Everyone has their own special, personal connections to the parks, of course. For me it will always be that castle, those balloons, and yes, the pirate's hairy leg.

"You were right, Nana. Walt didn't miss a thing."

A special tribute to Walt Disney and animator Ub Iwerks's 1927 cartoon cocreation **Oswald the Lucky Rabbit** can be found embedded in the walkway outside Enchanted Tales with Belle. Look for a section of the pavement about 20 feet from the Enchanted Tales with Belle sign, where two cracks come together to form a sharp point. Then look for a small round stone and two elongated stones. They form Oswald's head (facing Maurice's cottage) and ears (pointing toward Seven Dwarfs Mine Train).

Enchanted Tales with Belle

Mementos from Belle's childhood abound inside Maurice's cottage. A **portrait of Belle** as a child, sitting with her mother while reading a book, is clearly a treasured possession. Notice the shelf to the left of the portrait. The **teapot and cup** on the shelf bear a striking resemblance to characters Belle will meet when she enters the Beast's enchanted castle.

The book on a table near the fireplace is open to the story of a young maiden and Le Prince Charment. But it's not the story of Cinderella and her prince; it is *Le Songe d'une femme* (The Dream of a Woman) written by French author Remy de Gourmont. This is the book Belle reads in the Disney animated movie *Beauty and the Beast* when Gaston asks her how she can read a book with no pictures. However, as you can see in the book on the table, and in the book she holds in the movie, there is most assuredly a picture. Oops!

The **torn corner of Belle's book** wasn't done by a naughty tourist. Instead, it remembers the scene in the movie when Belle is sitting on the edge of a fountain reading, with a flock of sheep around her. One of the sheep takes a bite out of her book, so the book here in Maurice's cottage is post-bite.

Fascinating Fact

In the animated movie, Belle points to a page in the book and says it's her favorite part because it's "where she meets Prince Charming." While the picture is of a prince and a maiden meeting, the text on that page indicates the maiden has already met the prince and cannot stop thinking of him. The book is a curious choice for Belle, as Remy de Gourmont's writings, including *The Dream of a Woman*, are not exactly family-friendly. Even stranger? The original publication of the story of *Beauty and the Beast* was in 1740, but *The Dream of a Woman* was not written until 1899. Double oops!

The **growth chart** you see on the wall as you proceed through Maurice's cottage indicates Belle has lived here for quite some time, since it starts at twelve months and continues until she turns eighteen. This presents a slight continuity problem with the movie, as the opening scene indicates Belle is new to the area and the villagers don't quite know what to make of her. But it's a lovely touch, and one many parents will relate to if they've charted their own children's growth on their walls at home.

Look at the shelf to the left of the **enchanted mirror** in the workshop for a **wood carving of Belle dancing with the Beast**. Maurice used this carving as a model for the **music box** featured in the Castle Dining Room in Be Our Guest Restaurant.

Under the Sea: Journey of the Little Mermaid

You'll find a memorial to the *Nautilus from 20,000 Leagues Under the Sea* in the queue for Journey of the Little Mermaid, and it is a doozy! Just before you reach the water fountains at the entryway into the indoor part of the queue, you'll see ropes wrapped around the railing. Stand on the left side of the ropes, where the wooden beam is broken, and look at the rockwork on the other side of the water. Near the waterline you'll see a carving that doesn't look entirely natural. It's the *Nautilus*, with the front of the submarine pointing to the left. You can also spot it by looking for two vertical cracks in the rockwork that point directly to the top of the sub.

Ariel didn't know her eventual fate as she sang about wanting to "be where the people are," but a foreshadowing of her destiny in the form of a **statue of Prince Eric** sits just beyond her on the right-hand side of her grotto.

After you exit the attraction, look to the right at the two rocks on the left side of the water (ignore the rock closest to the fence). There is a hidden Mickey as the character **Steamboat Willie** here, but it's going to take some doing to see it. First, stand back a bit and look at the rock in front of you. You can see a faint outline of Mickey's left foot and leg, with the beginnings of his shorts, and a button. Now look at the rock behind it, which juts out to the right. Mickey's right foot, leg, and his shorts with the other button will become obvious. Above the shorts, his left arm extends to the rock on the far left. The top of the rock above his arm creates an optical illusion, and while Mickey's left ear (just above his shoulder) is easy to make out, his head looks a bit squashed. But stick with it, and you should be able to make out his face. Just above his left ear you'll see a rock that stands up a bit. That's his hat. Allow your eye to retrace its path and you should see the entire Steamboat Willie.

To keep within the flow of each land, we will pass by Seven Dwarfs Mine Train for now, returning here after our visit to Storybook Circus.

Storybook Circus

Storybook Circus takes its inspiration from the animated film *Dumbo*, with a circus theme that lends itself to whimsical reimaginings of beloved Disney characters. While it remains primarily children's territory, it is the perfect showcase for some of the lesser known Disney characters who blazed the cartoon trail in Disney series such as the How To and Pixar animated shorts, Silly Symphonies, and the animated anthology *Melody Time*. In fact there are so many references to animated shorts here it could rightly still be called Toontown, which was one of the area's former names.

Dumbo the Flying Elephant Celebrating Fifty Years!

See that clock on the faux ticket booth to the left, indicating the FastPass+ return time? It's a **Citizen watch**. Why? Because in 2018, Citizen became the official timepiece for Walt Disney World. You'll also see the name on the Main Street, U.S.A. clock.

Paintings along the base of the attraction help tell the story, but there are two worth noting. Look for the painting of the **pink elephants**, a nod toward the scene when Dumbo hallucinates after drinking a bucket of champagne. Another painting shows storks dropping **babies in diaper-shaped parachutes**. Where are they headed? To Orlando, Florida, of course!

Fascinating Fact

As we look ahead to Walt Disney World's fiftieth anniversary, let's also look back at Disneyland's fiftieth, which was the year Dumbo the elephant actually did fly.

As part of the promotional campaign around Disneyland's major milestone, one of the Dumbo attraction's ride vehicles was donated to the Smithsonian Institution. But how do you move an elephant from California to Washington, DC? It isn't easy.

Dumbo was loaded onto a railway car for the cross-country journey, and after a minor glitch during which his car was accidentally shunted to an unspecified siding and the little elephant appeared to be lost, he was found again and arrived safely just outside his final destination. But this was Disney, and Disney doesn't skimp on dramatic entrances. Dumbo was flown into the city underneath a helicopter and arrived in time for the big ceremony.

He still lives there today and you can visit him in the Entertainment, Sports, and Music section of the National Museum of American History. Don't have time for a visit to the Smithsonian? You can see a photograph of Dumbo, dressed in his jaunty purple hat and blanket, on *Smithsonian Insider.*

The Barnstormer

When the circus comes to town, the posters go up! Here in Storybook Circus, posters to the right of the entry to the Barnstormer advertise Goofy's circus acts Aquamaniac, Tiger Juggling, Bear Wrasslin', and, of course, Barnstorming. **Aquamaniac** refers to the animated short *Aquamania* (1961) in which Goofy goes boating and ends up in a waterskiing race with an octopus on his head; **Tiger Juggling** is a nod toward Goofy's disastrous hunting adventure *Tiger Trouble* (1945); and **Bear Wrasslin'** is a reference to Humphrey the Bear, who appears in several Disney animated shorts, including his first appearance as a hibernating bear harassed by amateur photographer Goofy in the 1950 short *Hold That Pose.*

Just under the banner on the Barnstormer billboard you'll see the words **An Acrobatic Skyleidoscope**. Skyleidoscope was the name of an "aerial spectacular" on and over EPCOT's World Showcase Lagoon from 1985 to 1987, featuring ultralight seaplanes, jet skis, and various power boats.

Pay attention to the white seagulls at the upper right-hand corner of the sign too. They certainly put longtime visitors in mind of the logo for the attraction **If You Had Wings**, which made its home in Magic Kingdom until 1987 when its sponsor, the now-defunct Eastern Airlines, faced financial hardship and declined to renew its contract.

Just after you enter the queue for Barnstormer, turn around and look at the back of the attraction's sign. It looks pretty chopped up, doesn't it? That's because it was once the original sign for **Wiseacre Farm** when Storybook Circus was still Mickey's Toontown. Clever, isn't it?

The **skis in a barrel** to your left as you exit your plane at the Barnstormer are a nod toward Goofy's penchant for getting into trouble on skis in animated shorts such as *The Art of Skiing*, in which he debuted his trademark yell, and which led to the popular How To shorts. The life-saving ring buoy behind the skis also has an interesting name. "Yah-Hah-Buoy" sure sounds a lot like Goofy's yell.

A giant green bottle of **airsickness pills** can be found sitting in front of the Second Aid crate on your right-hand side after you disembark your plane at the Barnstormer. On the label is a picture of stylized captains' wings with a circle in the center that contains a star. Former If You Had Wings attraction sponsor, Eastern Airlines, used Big E Captain Wings badges from 1927 to 1991, which bear a striking resemblance. But the real gem here is the brand name of the airsick pills. They are **How to Fly** brand, recalling the title of the book Mickey Mouse reads in the 1928 black-and-white animated short *Plane Crazy*. In its testing phase, the cartoon did not garner the attention *Steamboat Willie* enjoyed when it was released later that year, but *Plane Crazy* was, in fact, Mickey's debut cartoon.

The green gas can to the left of the airsickness pills is yet another reference to a Disney animated short. The sticker on the front indicates it is fuel supplied by **Pedro Empresa Gasolina**, referencing the character Pedro, the brave little airplane in the animated short that bears his name. Pedro is part of the compilation *Saludos Amigos*, which came from the good-will tour Walt Disney and a handful of his animators made to South America in 1941. José Carioca, Donald Duck's parrot friend in Gran Fiesta Tour at Mexico in EPCOT, also made his debut in *Saludos Amigos* in the short *Aquarela do Brasil*. The two went on to costar with rooster Panchito Pistoles in the animated movie *The Three Caballeros*.

Carolwood Park

If you arrive at Storybook Circus by train (or if you're just wandering around the area), look for the luggage along the left-hand side. Go up the second flight of stairs and spot the hat box that reads, **Ten Schillings and Sixpence Ltd**. In the original *Alice's Adventures in Wonderland* stories by Lewis Carroll, illustrator Sir John Tenniel drew the Mad Hatter with a card tucked into his hatband, which stated, "in this style 10/6," indicating the price of the hat in question. The cost? Ten shillings and sixpence.

A big red suitcase to the right of the hatbox reads, **Red's Amazing Juggling Unicycles**. It refers to the 1987 Pixar animated short *Red's Dream*, featuring a lonely red unicycle that dreams of being a circus juggler.

The name you see inside the train station clock is **Carolwood Park**, a tribute to the one-eighth scale model railroad and steam train Walt Disney built for his backyard and named the Carolwood Pacific Railroad. There are also pictures of Walt playing with his backyard train on the wall to the far left of the stroller rental counter at the front of Magic Kingdom.

Casey Jr. Splash 'n' Soak Station

As you're splashing and soaking at Casey Jr. Splash 'n' Soak, pay attention to the numbers on the back of each circus car. The elephants' car number is **71**, referencing Magic Kingdom's opening year; the monkeys' car number is **82**, honoring EPCOT's opening year; Hollywood Studios' opening year of **89** is on the giraffes' car; and Disney's Animal Kingdom's opening year is remembered by the **98** car filled with camels.

A tribute to animator Ward Kimball, one of Walt Disney's Nine Old Men and the creator of the crows in the movie *Dumbo*, can be found on the red circus car the monkeys have taken over, with a painting on one side featuring **clowns brandishing fire hoses**. The clown in the middle has the distinction of the trademark round glasses Kimball wore. Why does he get special treatment here? Because he was part of the Firehouse Five Plus Two Dixieland band in Disneyland, which included Disney Legend Harper Goff and animator Frank Thomas, also two of Walt Disney's famous Nine Old Men.

You'll see other references to the **Firehouse Five** on the wall to the right of the front entry to Big Top Souvenirs and to the left of the shop's exit near Pete's Silly Sideshow.

And now, let's backtrack a bit to keep the flow of the lands.

Seven Dwarfs Mine Train

There is no doubt about it: The Seven Dwarfs' mine is incredibly scenic. Along with adding dynamic movement to Fantasyland, the highly landscaped mountain takes the area to a new level of realism.

When you enter the queue, the first thing you see is the Dwarfs' cottage. **Picks, shovels, and axes** hint at the hard work they do, but smaller details flesh out the story too. **Weathered metal straps** hold parts of their fence together, all the wooden elements look **hand-hewn**, and the end of each **wooden beam** holding up the roof of their cottage hints at their coexistence with nature and the forest's animals. Even the texture of the mountain goes from crumbling dirt to hard-packed dirt the farther you go in.

Imagine That!

Not all hidden magic is visual. Dave Minichiello, director, creative development at Walt Disney Imagineering, points out one of the audio hidden gems in the Seven Dwarfs Mine Train attraction: "The queue has a surprise song in it, originally written for the film, called 'Music in Your Soup,' which we've recorded in instrumental version and added to our queue area. All the music in the queue area is instrumental, and we wanted to give it a feel that it was played by the Seven Dwarfs." "Music in Your Soup" was originally intended for the animated movie *Snow White and the Seven Dwarfs*, but ultimately was never used.

Just as you're entering the mine for some dig, dig, digging, notice the beam over your head that reads, **Vault**. In the movie *Snow White and the Seven Dwarfs*, Doc and Dopey are seen throwing bags of gems into the vault as they finish up the day's work.

See that **key hanging from a peg** to the right of the vault's door? Also in the movie, Dopey hung the vault's key on a similar peg, an ineffective move considering anyone could grab it and open the door. Equally ineffective for keeping gems safe, the door to the vault you just walked through is literally always open.

The **two vultures** perched at the top of the first lift hill are a sentimental nod to the former Snow White's Scary Adventures attraction. They once made their home there, but have moved and are now keeping watch over the mine.

The **cuckoo-style clock** inside the mine featuring little characters hitting an anvil with their hammers is taken directly from the animated movie *Snow White and the Seven Dwarfs*, and it signals the end of the Dwarfs' workday. In the movie and in the attraction it inspires them to sing, "Hi-ho, Hi-ho, it's home from work we go," and is the cue for your mine car to start its wild journey toward their little cottage and the end of the ride.

Disney loves to recycle, and the **figures for Bashful, Sleepy, Happy, Grumpy, and Doc**, seen inside the cottage at the end of your mine ride, also once made their home in Fantasyland's long-gone Snow White's Scary Adventures. In their former attraction, they were in a main room playing musical instruments, just like they are here, while Snow White was in the kitchen accepting the poison apple from the evil queen, who was disguised as an old hag. What about the Sneezy, Dopey, and Snow White figures? They were purpose-built for Seven Dwarfs Mine Train.

The Many Adventures of Winnie the Pooh
This attraction debuted in its original form in Tokyo Disneyland as Pooh's Hunny Hunt, but the appeal is

international. Children everywhere find it impossible to resist the cuddly cubby, here in a retelling of the animated short film *Winnie the Pooh and the Blustery Day*.

The most prominent feature outside the attraction is the giant tree you pass when entering the queue. Pause to look at the **mailbox's flag**. It's a flyswatter dipped in honey.

Just after you enter the queue, watch for the giant book page, titled "Chapter I," with a map reminiscent of the Hundred Acre Wood. See the spot titled **Poohsticks Bridge**? It refers to a game Winnie the Pooh plays with his friends in A.A. Milne's book *The House at Pooh Corner*. Each player drops a stick over the side of a bridge and into a river, and the player whose stick appears on the downriver side of the bridge first is the winner.

Fascinating Fact

Hartfield, East Sussex, in England, is home to the bridge A.A. Milne wrote about, introducing the game of Poohsticks. It was originally called Posingford Bridge, but was renamed Poohsticks Bridge in honor of Milne's popular stories. Although it has since been rebuilt, visitors still seek it out for their own gentle competitions.

When your ride vehicle enters Owl's house inside the attraction, turn around and look behind you. You will see a picture on the wall showing Mr. Toad from *The Wind in the Willows* handing the **deed** to his house to Owl. Many WDW guests were unhappy to see Mr. Toad's Wild Ride make way for the Pooh attraction, so the Imagineers gave a nod to Toad's popularity and a subtle stamp of approval by having Toady give the deed to the current owner.

Imagine That!

Inspiration comes from many places, including the target audience. Imagineer Eddie Sotto recalls, "When I was involved in Tokyo Disneyland, we wanted to create a Winnie the Pooh attraction that would be beyond anything that had ever been done. The Hunny Pot–themed ride vehicles were wirelessly guided without tracks, allowing them to go backward, spin, and roam freely through the show. It was stunning, but there was still something missing. How did that relate to the story we were trying to tell? We then surveyed little kids and asked them what they would most want to do in a Winnie the Pooh attraction. The answer we got, loud and clear, was to 'bounce in the forest with Tigger.' We then spent the next several years developing a magical effect that would allow each vehicle to actually 'bounce' with Tigger."

It's a Small World Celebrating Fifty Years!

Possibly the best-known attraction in Walt Disney World, it's a small world has a simple, childlike style that is a real departure from the more traditional artistic renderings used by the Imagineers. Artist Mary Blair's unique style appealed greatly to Walt Disney, as it does to young children who, in spite of the all-too-catchy tune, insist on ride after ride.

Fascinating Fact

Ask people what the most recognizable classic Disney attraction is, and the answer will probably be, "it's a small world." That level of international recognition led to the inspiration for the Global Choir, a wonderful tribute during Disneyland's fiftieth anniversary, because, after all, the attraction's song is known worldwide. Or is it?

Disney was betting the lyrics to the Sherman Brothers' classic tune were known around the world, and with that in mind they had video snippets created in several countries, featuring different cultures singing segments of the song, many in their own languages. Those segments were then stitched together, with an introduction by Richard Sherman and ending with an astronaut on the International Space Station, and a promotion for Disneyland—and world peace—was born.

On the heels of that success, an event years later gathered together a group of children from across the globe, chosen for their contributions toward making the world a better place. Dressed in silver ponchos to represent EPCOT's Spaceship Earth, their costumes underneath would "transform" them into planet Earth when the ponchos were removed, and it would all be highlighted by them singing the Sherman Brothers' iconic tune. Problem was, they hadn't rehearsed the song, but when the video rolled they had to sing. And sing they did! It really is a small world, after all.

Want to see the Global Choir video? You'll find it on the Disney Parks *YouTube* channel under "it's a small world" 50th Anniversary Global Choir.

Most of the whimsical figures in the attraction are based only on the Imagineers' creativity, but there are two characters that were taken from literature, specifically the book *The Ingenious Gentleman Don Quixote of La Mancha*. Just after you enter the Spain section of your journey, look to the left and you'll see **Don Quixote** and his comrade **Sancho Panza** in "small world" doll form. Quixote is in front riding a horse while Panza is behind him on a donkey.

At the end of your ride you'll be wished a "**farewell**" by name. Is it magic? More like MagicBand (or your admission card). Each band or card has a tracking device that indicates individual guests' locations, and this attraction makes the most of it.

Peter Pan's Flight Celebrating Fifty Years!

The queue for Peter Pan's Flight underwent a complete reimagining in 2014, expanding on the story by taking guests into the Darling family's home—and adding more hidden magic.

When you enter the indoor portion of the queue you'll walk through a hallway with **Neverland-themed paintings** on the walls. The second painting (on your left) depicts the mermaid lagoon scene from the animated movie *Peter Pan*, with the addition of a rather special gal with trademark flowing red hair, being splashed by another mermaid. Although a scene similar to this takes place in the movie, including a mermaid with long red hair, this isn't her. How do we know? Pan's redheaded mermaid had brown eyes, but Ariel from *The Little Mermaid* has blue eyes.

The third painting, this time on your right, features Captain Hook and Mr. Smee in a rowboat, with the crocodile in hot pursuit. Look closely at **Captain Hook's ship** at the far left of the painting. The scrollwork just above the crocodile's tail forms the letters "M" and "D," a hidden reference to Marc Davis, who animated Tinker Bell in the original 1953 film.

When you reach Nana sitting in the Darling family's backyard, listen closely and you'll hear **crickets chirping** and the clip-clop of **horse hooves** on the cobblestone street beyond the brick wall.

On the bottom shelf of the stained glass cabinet containing the Darling children's books and toys is a **chess set**. Chess fan

Marc Davis, who also animated Mrs. Darling in the movie, gets a hidden mention everywhere, doesn't he?

December 27 is circled on the **1904 calendar** on the back wall of John's room, just beyond the hat stand holding his top hat and umbrella. It's the date the stage play version of James M. Barrie's story *Peter Pan* opened at the Duke of York's Theatre in London, England.

The time frame for this interactive queue is clearly post-Pan. The children have already had their first adventure with Peter, as evidenced by the **alphabet blocks** in Michael's bedroom and the **framed silhouettes** of Peter and little **sketches of Neverland** in Wendy's bedroom.

The stacked blocks to the right of the little red wagon are arranged with **A, B, and C blocks** at the top, recalling the opening scene of the movie, when fastidious Nana is picking up after the children at the end of the day. She rearranges "BAC" to read "ABC."

Take note of the **blocks scattered on the floor** to the left of the building-block castle. If you reassemble six of them, assuming the "&" represents the letter "S" and the upside-down "U" represents an "N," what word can you spell out? You'll find the answer in Appendix: Solutions to Hints, Solution 1 at the end of the book.

As you've been walking past the Darling children's bedrooms you may have seen **Tinker Bell's magical pixie dust trail** that periodically moves from room to room. Tink gets stuck in a treasure chest, falls into the water pitcher, spins the globe, and tips the toy boat in John's room, and in Wendy's room she tips a painting, fiddles with balls of yarn, checks out her image in a hand mirror, then flies into a dresser through a keyhole.

Fascinating Fact

Tinker Bell flying into the dresser drawer through the keyhole is an obvious reference to the time the little pixie got stuck in the keyhole of Wendy's dresser drawer the first time Wendy met Peter Pan, but longtime Walt Disney World fans will also recognize it as a throwback to an adorable interaction guests used to experience at the former Tinker Bell's Treasures gift shop in Fantasyland. The first guests to enter the shop could "wake up" Tinker Bell by releasing her from a wooden box on a shelf behind the cash register and watch her pixie dust trail fly around the room. When she wasn't flitting about, guests could see her by peeping through the keyhole in a special sewing table drawer next to the shop's door.

If you're in Michael's room when the **shadow effects** occur on the bedroom wall you will become an honorary shadow, and that means you can interact with the animations. Stand very still and hold your hand up, and a butterfly may land on it. Then, when the bells drop down, you can interact with them too. On their own the bells play the opening notes of "You Can Fly." Try hitting them individually and see if you can play the tune. Hint: They're not in order!

And now, exit the attraction and pass under the **transition area** to your left; this moves you from Fantasyland into Liberty Square. In keeping with the theme of the Show, you are now undergoing a scene change. The transition area is darker, symbolic of a fade-out; the music and ambient sound change; and when you emerge on the other side, you find yourself in Early America. Turn around and look at the back side of what was a Tudor home in Fantasyland. It has become the upper story of a colonial home.

Liberty Square

Passing into Liberty Square, you have entered the New World. The footbridge over the river between the central Hub area and Liberty Square symbolically takes you across the ocean to the East Coast of the United States, while the transition area near Peter Pan's Flight takes you from London into colonial America. It didn't take long for the colonists to begin their westward trek, and it won't take you long to cross into Frontierland, but there is much to discover in the New World if you take the time to look.

What is the meaning of the plaque on the wall at the end of the small alley to the right of Columbia Harbour House and to the left of the round turret near the door with the number 26 on it, with four hands, each grasping its neighbor's wrist? It is the symbol of the mutual insurance company that spun off from the **Union Fire Company**, founded in 1736 by Benjamin Franklin and four of his friends, also known as Ben Franklin's Bucket Brigade. At that time, only those who paid for protection could expect the fire department to show up if their house was burning down. Franklin's organization was staffed by volunteers who came to the aid of all. Those with an insurance policy would affix the four-hands symbol to their home and would receive compensation for fire damage to their property.

It's a bit of unintentional hidden magic, but those who are curious about the **sprinkler system** used to saturate relevant Fantasyland and Liberty Square buildings before the nightly fireworks show will see evidence of how effective they are by the downpour they create in the alley where you see the Union Fire Company symbol.

Liberty Square's doors each have a **two-digit house number** on them, and if you put "18" in front of the number you have the year that style of house was popular.

See the lanterns in the second-floor window of the round turret to the left of house number 26? They represent the **two lanterns** hung in Boston's Christ Church steeple in April 1776, to warn Paul Revere the British soldiers were arriving by sea.

As you pass by house number 24 you'll see a **rag doll** in the window to the right of the door, and when you round the corner to house number 22 there are **primitive wooden toys** in the lower window. You would be correct if you guessed they're representative of the time frame associated with their door number. In colonial times, cloth dolls with drawn-on faces were used not only as playmates for girls, they were also a means of teaching the necessary skill of sewing. Carved wooden toys (here hiding a set of cameras) taught boys the skills of building and hand-carving.

Walk around the corner of the same building and look at the upper window on that side. The country folk may not be up, but they certainly are armed! During the Revolutionary War, the townsmen would place their **rifle in the window** to indicate they were home and ready to answer the call to arms.

The building number you see above the door at Hall of Presidents is **1787**, which reflects the time setting for the building's architecture.

Though it is often overlooked as just another part of the landscaping, Liberty Square Tree, the centerpiece in this area, has **thirteen lanterns** hanging from its branches; each lantern represents one of the original thirteen colonies.

See that **book-shaped sign** on the corner of Ye Olde Christmas Shoppe? Ichabod Crane is offering music and voice lessons, tying the shop to its former theme as the home of a musician. It also ties to Sleepy Hollow, the quick-service dining outlet directly across the pathway, and the unfortunate legend it's based on.

Haunted Mansion Celebrating Fifty Years!

Haunted Mansion is filled with fascinating details. In the first edition of *The Hidden Magic of Walt Disney World* we looked at the mansion before it underwent a major reimagining. In the second edition we focused on new hidden magic, especially relating to the ghostly bride's story and the new attic scenes. This time we'll delve deeper into the mansion's backstory, and discover more hidden magic inside and in the interactive graveyard.

Prior to the attraction's reimagining in 2011, there was no official backstory. Now, the story of the **ghostly bride**, whose name is **Constance Hatchaway**, takes front and center. In the new story, the terrible temptress marries Ambrose Harper, Frank Banks, the Marquis De Doom, Reginald Caine, and finally poor George Hightower, in quick succession and with wildly successful results...for her.

When you near the mansion's front door you have the choice of detouring through the interactive graveyard or going straight in. For the full array of hidden magic, you'll want to take the detour.

When you enter the graveyard, the first things you see are comical, if somewhat suspicious, **busts**. They memorialize the Dread family, but they also contain a hidden message. Take a quick photo of each one, making sure you can read their epitaphs and identify the small icon at the top of each plaque. Then, as you make your way through the queue, see if you can solve the riddle of who killed whom. You'll find the answers in Appendix: Solutions to Hints, Solution 2.

Fascinating Fact

Many Disney fans know the tombstones for Grandpa Marc, Francis Xavier, Brother Claude, and Master Gracey refer to Imagineers Marc Davis, X Atencio, Claude Coats, and Yale Gracey, but what about the less obvious Imagineer names?

Good Old Fred refers to Fred Joerger. He and Walt Disney established WED Enterprises' model shop, where Fred created miniatures of sets and props that would be used as references for the full-sized versions in the attractions.

Dear Departed Brother Dave is model maker Dave Burkhart who, among other things, helped bring the Haunted Mansion to life.

Cousin Huet remembers Cliff Huet, instrumental in creating the Haunted Mansion's interior design.

A Man Named Martin pays tribute to Bill Martin, architect for many of Magic Kingdom's buildings, including the Haunted Mansion.

Uncle Myall is better known as Chuck Myall, the Imagineer who designed the Haunted Mansion and acted as master planner, designer, and overseer of construction for the entire Magic Kingdom park.

Good Friend Gordon sings the praises of Gordon Williams, head of WDI's audio design, including the sound effects in the Haunted Mansion.

Wathel R. Bender pays its respects to Audio-Animatronics pioneer Wathel Rogers, lead programmer for Magic Kingdom's animatronics.

Mr. Sewell refers to Bob Sewell, head of WDI's model shop.

And finally, the tall grave marker etched with the name **Harriet** stands as a fond homage to Disney Legend Harriet Burns, cocreator of the Haunted Mansion. Her epitaph is a direct reference to her role as the "first lady" hired in a creative capacity by Walt Disney Imagineering.

Watch for references to the **number 13** as you make your way through the graveyard and the mansion. If you're paying close attention in the graveyard you'll notice there are thirteen stops on Ravenscroft's pipe organ, plus thirteen books on each shelf and thirteen stylized writing quills above the books on Prudence Pock's crypt. One of the books even has the number 13 on its spine.

The **raven** you see on Ravenscroft's pipe organ is known as a "recurring" character, an entity that makes several appearances within the story. Originally the raven was going to narrate guests' journey through the mansion, but the "ghost host" idea proved the winner. This is your first sighting as you make your way through the mansion, but it was actually the last raven to be added, having only arrived when the interactive queue was created.

The **creepy skulls** on the pipe organ, just below the raven, mimic the skulls floating out of the pipe organ in the ballroom scene inside the mansion. Be sure to watch for them just before your Doom Buggy leaves that room.

Listen closely and you may notice **Captain Culpepper Clyne**, currently pickling in brine, occasionally sings a rather tortured variation on the song "Drunken Sailor."

The decomposing composer crypt isn't just an interactive touch-sensor experience. All of the **musical instruments** combined play a portion of the Haunted Mansion's famous song "Grim Grinning Ghosts."

Prudence Pock's crypt has another spooky secret. The square blocks on either side of the top of the bookshelf are fairly obviously faces, but turn the corner and stand back a bit while looking at the portion of the crypt where her magical poetry book is located, and you'll see another **monstrous face**. The design above the arched window is a set of eyes and eyebrows, the window is a mouth, the square slab below the window is a tongue, and the small details at the bottom are teeth.

As you near the end of the interactive graveyard, look down at the pavement. Those indentations aren't all just pock marks in the mud. Some of them are **footprints and paw prints**. To whom do they belong? The mansion's caretaker and his dog, and you'll see them in the graveyard scene near the end of the ride.

Sharp eyes will notice a flat panel at the bottom right-hand side of the gate leading into the mansion's mausoleum. What's that all about? It's a **doggie door** for the caretaker's pup.

The ghostly bride's wedding ring can be seen in the pavement in the small fenced-off area just after you leave the graveyard. Look at the ground where the brick wall juts out. The right-hand corner at the bottom of the square pillar points directly to the ring.

You've wandered into **Master Gracey's mansion**, ignoring every indication you're making a bad decision, and that miscalculation is confirmed while you're standing in the lobby with the portrait of a man over the fireplace. It will be obvious when he transforms into a skeleton, but what's less obvious is that he is the **phantom of the manor**, and it is his voice you hear in the stretch room, and as your ghost host narrator during your time in the mansion. You'll encounter him again when you reach the piano room. Sort of. It's his shadow you're seeing as the **ghostly pianist**.

Imagine That!

The Sea Captain painting in the queue leading up to the boarding area has a fascinating history. Part of the original concept for a walk-through haunted mansion included an opening scene featuring the Sea Captain, who regaled guests with a spiel about the spooky house they had entered. As he spun his tale of terror, he slowly liquefied until he was nothing more than ectoplasm on the cold, uncaring floor. Problem was, it took forever to get through the narration, and theme park attractions don't succeed when only a few hundred people can see them each day. His memory remains, not as a pile of jelly but as a prominent painting, forever immortalized as a Haunted Mansion fan favorite. Even better? If you recall the Sea Captain's crypt in the graveyard, it was also a nod to the original concept and was leaking water at an alarming rate!

While it's important you don't ignore the ghost host's comments once you reach the stretch room, it's even more important not to misunderstand his words, as many do. He isn't saying "ghosts" when he refers to the **framed portraits** above you and mentions the paintings have captured their subjects in their former mortal, corruptible state. He's actually saying they're "guests," and it's a foreshadowing of what's about to happen to *you*.

The story of the ghostly bride is based on one of the paintings in the stretch room. When you are asked to move to the dead center of the room and the paintings begin to stretch, notice the one of a **woman sitting on a headstone** holding a rose. She is the ghostly bride, and the ill-fated

George, now resting 6 feet under with an axe in his skull, is just one of her victim grooms.

Before you exit the stretch room, the ghost host challenges you to find a way out of the mansion, an indication that, while in reality you'll be sitting in a ride vehicle making your way through each room (as he acknowledges in the boarding area), within the story you're on foot, looking for an escape route. It's a tie-up to the Imagineers' original concept of a **walk-though haunted house**.

Clacking door knockers in the Corridor of Doors are an effect that was inspired by the original black-and-white 1963 movie *The Haunting*. In the movie, during which a psychically sensitive woman is struggling to stay sane amid the eerie goings-on in a haunted house, one of the doors had a repetitive, muted booming sound; the doorknob moved as if someone—or some*thing*—was trying to open the door; and there was a tight, stretching sound as the door expanded and contracted.

The detailing of the Haunted Mansion's corridor doors mimic the movie's door as well, with a triangular section in the middle and two squares with round elements above. They look like a **monster's face** when seen from below.

What is that big book on the pedestal in front of Madame Leota's table? It's the **spell book** from which she is reading when you hear her conjuring up the mansion's ghosts.

Another creepy detail? The book is turned to **page 1313**.

The most iconic scene in the Haunted Mansion is the **ballroom scene**, where ghosts are throwing a "swinging wake." Much of the mansion's backstory centers on the happy haunts, but for the first half of the ride you don't actually see them, though you do have indications all along that they're there. It's only after **Madame Leota** summons them that they appear in their ghostly "physical" form.

As your Doom Buggy nears the end of the ballroom scene, don't forget to look for those **creepy skulls** you saw on the Ravenscroft pipe organ in the queue. They're here, wafting out of the ballroom's pipe organ.

Once you reach the attic the results of the ghostly bride's marriages are laid out on full display, with hints that all is not well. Notice the **champagne glasses** in the first scene, in front of the elaborate marriage certificate sitting on the table to your right. One of the glasses is lying on its side, a spooky symbolism that the person who drank from it is also lying in repose.

Diamonds may be a girl's best friend, but not if you're Constance Hatchaway. In her case, it's all about the **pearls**. Notice how she starts with one simple strand and ends up with five—one for each husband—by the time she's married her last victim...uh, groom.

Pay attention to the music as you wind your way through the attic. It's a slow, eerie, twisted rendition of the "Bridal Chorus," better known as "**Here Comes the Bride**."

This is one busy bride! She's been married five times, with each **wedding date** depicted in its corresponding scene. Her first marriage occurred in **1869**, as seen on the lacy book propped up on a table in the first scene on the right-hand side; she remarried in **1872**, the date featured in the center of the banner in the second scene; and in **1874**, **1875**, and **1877** she had the dates engraved on her wedding portrait frames.

It's not entirely clear why there is a massive wedding cake in the attic, or how it has stayed fresh for so long, but one thing is certain: If you look closely at the **cake topper** you'll notice the groom's head is missing.

The final **wedding portrait** is the one that ties the attic scene directly back to the Haunted Mansion's stretch room. Constance, newly married to George, is holding a rose. Remember the painting you saw in the stretch room, of the woman sitting on George's gravestone, holding a rose? This is her, brought to life. Well, perhaps not to *life*...!

Before you leave the attic, watch for the **coat stand** in the final scene on your right. Although their heads are gone, each of the ill-fated grooms are remembered here by their hats hanging on the stand.

That **broken window** you see to your extreme right when your Doom Buggy turns around and descends the roof backward hints at how you met your demise. Did you fall through the window—or were you pushed?

Now that you've hit the ground, not only can you see the **ghosts in their ethereal forms**, you can also see them as they were in life. There is only one answer to that conundrum: The Haunted Mansion had room for one more...and you're it!

Before you fell off the roof you were simply observing ghosts inside the mansion, but once you're in the land of the non-living, the **frightfully ominous music** has changed. It becomes upbeat party music, as if your arrival is the reason for their swinging wake.

Fascinating Fact

Many of the tombstones in the graveyard feature the expected epitaph RIP (rest in peace), but many are inscribed with *Memento Mori*, which is Latin for "remember you must die" (literally "remember death"). Although Disney's version opts for a rather nondescript round face flanked by wing-like swoops instead of the traditional elaborate skull with fancy wings or a bone, the tombstones still harken back to a time when many believed mortal life was merely a prelude to "true" life in the afterworld. Here at the mansion, however, it's fair to say it's a nudge to "remember (your recent) death."

The **Hitchhiking Ghosts** are icons of the Haunted Mansion, but have you ever wondered where they're hitchhiking to? Listen carefully to the ghost host's narration as you turn the corner heading toward the unloading area and come face-to-face with Gus, Ezra, and Phineas, because he gives you a clue. You've been chosen to round out the one-thousand-ghost quota and they're going to follow you until you return to fulfill your destiny.

Finally, in keeping with the lesson in US geography, once you leave Liberty Square (the East Coast), you symbolically travel with the pioneers as they make their way westward into unknown territory and you make your way into a new land.

Frontierland

As you pass into Frontierland from Liberty Square, you are symbolically crossing the Mississippi River and journeying west. The transition is gentle but obvious. Building materials in Frontierland are rough-hewn and there is a sense of excitement in the air, as if a gunfight could break out at any moment. It's the land of Davy Crockett and Buffalo Bill Cody, where anything could happen!

You can easily see **Harper's Mill** from the streets of Frontierland just by looking across the water, but its namesake is somewhat less clear. While it is true one of Tom Sawyer's closest friends was the minor character Joe Harper in the book *The Adventures of Tom Sawyer*, and the handwritten sign for the mill indicates it's named for Joe's father, it's hard to overlook the fact that the name on the mill is extremely prominent and it faces Frontierland rather than facing inward, as it would if it were geared toward visitors to the island. Because it practically forces itself upon the story of Frontierland, isn't it more likely to be a hidden tribute to one of the creators of that land, Disney Legend Harper Goff?

Pecos Bill Café gives a nod to the Disney animated short story and, more important, serves as a transition out of Frontierland into the Mexican end of Adventureland. Take a look at the roof of the café. Notice how the front area is pure Wild West saloon, but when you round the corner it takes a Spanish Mission–style turn, common in both California (represented by the Train Depot near Splash Mountain) and Mexico. It also blends harmoniously with the Caribbean theme as you move farther into Adventureland.

Before you leave Frontierland, notice the tiny **Chinese Laundry** building squeezed between Town Hall and the Spanish Mission–style building (really the far-right end of Pecos Bill Café). It may be small, but it represents the enormous role Chinese immigrants played in establishing the Wild West.

Having reached the West Coast and the train station at the terminus of the transcontinental railroad, you can't miss the two mountain ranges reaching skyward.

Splash Mountain

Splash Mountain technically represents the Deep South (the states of Georgia, Florida, Alabama, Louisiana, and Mississippi) and should be painted deep clay-red to represent

Georgia's soil. However, a little creative color mixing went into blending it more harmoniously with Big Thunder Mountain, thus maintaining the theme, at least visually. Shortly after you enter the queue and pass under the bridge, look at the top of the silo-shaped building on your left. A certain mischief-maker is up there, acting as a weather vane.

In 2020 it was announced that the attraction would be rethemed to focus on the 2009 film *The Princess and the Frog*, which will move the ride's depiction from Georgia to a Mardi Gras celebration in New Orleans, Louisiana.

Big Thunder Mountain Railroad

Big Thunder Mountain Railroad has become a true Disney classic, in part because it's a terrific coaster the whole family can enjoy and in part because of its exceptional theme. You are embarking on a tour of Big Thunder Mining Company—through the Mining Office, Explosives Magazine Room, Foreman's Post, and Ventilation Service Room. Along the way you can blast a mine shaft, pump air into the mines, and check out the miners' progress deep beneath the ground before you set off on your own journey.

Notice the name on the Pay Rates sign, to the right of the barred window in the Mining Office. The paymaster here is **G. Willikers**.

There are two signs on the wall just after the Mining Office. Check out the name of the proprietor of the Big Thunder Mining Mountain Company Store. Apparently it is owned by a Greek man by the name of **Costas A. Lott**. Or maybe it's a nod toward the expense of Disney's reimagining of the entire queue in 2012.

Crates in the rafters of the Explosives Magazine Room contain dynamite from **Western River Explosives**, and while the dynamite was contracted by **Lytum and Hyde** (an obvious warning!), the brand's origin is somewhat less obvious. It refers to Western River Expedition, a never-built boat ride once intended for Frontierland.

You will find a tribute to Imagineer Tony Baxter here too. The **portrait in the rafters** as you make your way through the explosives section is meant to be the founder of the mine, Barnabas T. Bullion, but it's really Baxter, designer of the original Big Thunder Mountain Railroad. There is a second tribute to him on the back of the Assay Report information board. Look for **T.W. Baxter** on the Automatic Train Break diagram.

The wooden name plates attached to the door of the Fusing Cage, just after you enter the Explosives Magazine Room, honor several Disney Imagineers.

- **Little Big Blaine** (Blaine Gibson, sculptor)
- **Matchstick Marc** (Marc Davis, Disney Legend)
- **Jolley the Kid** (Bob Jolley, Big Thunder Mountain Railroad designer)
- **Buckaroo Burke** (Pat Burke, show set designer)
- **Calamity Clem** (Clem Hall, concept artist)
- **Skittish Skip** (Skip Lange, rockwork designer)
- **Wild Wolf Joerger** (Fred Joerger, rockwork designer)
- **Mama Hutchinson** (Helena Hutchinson, figure finishing)

Just before you enter the Ventilation Service Room you'll see a diagram of the entire Big Thunder Mountain complex. Under the drawing of the highest peak you'll see the words **Rainbow Caverns**, a reference to Rainbow Caverns Mine Train, an attraction that ran through the Living Desert in Disneyland from 1956 to 1960. The mine shaft diagrammed underneath Rainbow Caverns is **Shaft #71**, remembering the opening year of Magic Kingdom.

The **Hard Times Café** sign on the left side after you exit the Ventilation Room advertises apple dumplings as the specialty of the house, but in reality it is a tribute to the 1975 Disney movie *The Apple Dumpling Gang*. In the movie, there is also a mention of the Hard Times Café.

At the end of your ride, or if you're a non-rider, check out the **geysers along Nugget Way**. The one on the far right is an "old faithful" of sorts. It goes off with predictable regularity.

Big Thunder Mining Company is clearly budget-conscious. They've made **lampposts** out of rusty pipes, broken wagon wheels, and a discarded pickaxe, and the **signpost for Nugget Way** is made from a shovel.

As you retrace your steps to the train station on your way into Adventureland, you have symbolically reached the West Coast, completing your cross-country trek. But lands beyond America are calling for those brave enough to face the dangers of the jungle, pirates on the high seas, and a room full of loud, singing birds.

Adventureland

With the comforts of Hometown America, the mellow charm of Europe, and the thrill of discovering the New World behind you, the next step is to head off on a grand adventure exploring Mexico, the Caribbean Islands, Polynesia, and oddly enough, the Middle East. In terms of the Show, it is the realm of *In Search of the Castaways*, *The Jungle Book*, *Swiss Family Robinson*, *Aladdin*, and the Pirates of the Caribbean movie series.

As you round the corner from Frontierland into Adventureland, the architecture is distinctly Spanish. Moving farther along, the details transition beautifully into the flavors of a Caribbean island, and then become a whole new world as you fly over the imaginary Middle Eastern realm of Agrabah before you land, somehow, in the South Seas.

Pirates of the Caribbean

Pirates of the Caribbean recalls the 1700s West Indies during the time the Spanish were finding gold in what would become the United States. Just before you enter Castillo del Morro, take a look at the large rock on the ground to your left. Most people pass by it never noticing it looks exactly like a **skull**.

As you walk through the outdoor covered queue, before you reach the drawbridge leading into the fort, you may be able to hear the **pirate radio station** coming through the speakers above you. What are the call letters for this broadcasting outlet? W-ARR, of course. Be sure to say it like a pirate: "W-Arrrrrrrrr!"

Once inside the castle, there are two separate queues that wind their way toward the boarding area. In keeping with the story, the Standby queue takes you through the **soldier's living quarters** while the FastPass+ queue takes you through the **castle's dungeon**.

The dungeon holds the hidden magic, and as you walk toward the boarding area, watch for a window with bars on it, on your right-hand side. If you look into the cell below, you'll see another Imagineer signature. Disney Legend Marc Davis has marked the attraction with his love of chess. The two **skeletons playing chess** are at a total impasse. In keeping with the Imagineer's obsession with accuracy, Davis researched past masters tournaments for a no-win outcome, and the chess pieces were correctly placed on the board between the skeletons so they would appear to ponder their next move for eternity.

Once you begin your water journey, you'll come upon one of the neatest bits of visual hidden magic in the Magic Kingdom. The rock formation on your left-hand side, just as the pirate beach comes into view, looks like an **evil skull with teeth**. But wait. Keep looking at it as you pass by. It appears to be a single rock from a distance, but when you reach it you can see that it's an illusion created by four separate rocks. Ragged teeth are first, then the nose, then the right eye, then the left eye and the top of the skull.

Although it is difficult to see in the dark, look for the crest as you pass by the last scene, above where Jack Sparrow is laughing over his loot. Wouldn't you know it, Imagineer Marc Davis came as close to a signature as possible when he added the faintly Spanish-sounding name **Marci Daviso** to the crest. Mr. Davis didn't miss another chance to express his love of chess. He placed **rooks** in the upper right and lower left corners of the crest.

The Jungle Cruise Celebrating Fifty Years!

This classic Disney attraction has evolved over the years and it now has a much stronger tie to other stories in Walt Disney World, including the Adventurers Club nightclub that used to make its home in now-defunct Pleasure Island. Look at the tags on the items in the wire cage at the start of the queue. Many of them reference **Adventurers Club members**. You'll discover more about them when we reach Jungle Navigation Co. LTD. Skipper Canteen.

You would have to be in the queue for forty-five minutes to hear the entire background music loop, which certainly isn't unusual during peak times, but if you're lucky you'll be making your way toward the boating area when Cole Porter's song "You're the Top" comes on. It was originally from the 1934 musical *Anything Goes*, starring Ethel Merman as Reno Sweeney and William Gaxton as Billy Crocker. In the back-and-forth vocals the singers wax poetic about how terrific each friend finds the other, and Reno pays the ultimate tribute to her pal Billy by stating, **"You're Mickey Mouse!"** Listen for a swingy version of that stanza here in the queue.

A **light blue book** under the bell on the office desk is titled *Paha Sapa: Land of the Gods*, and while it sounds like it could be a strange and wonderful story about Africa, it's really the tale of a man and his grandson traveling in a camper truck from Texas to South Dakota's Black Hills, or *paha sapa*, sacred to the Sioux. Still, it fits the theme, to a point. Although it's a story of adventure, the Jungle Cruise is set in the 1930s and the book wasn't published until 1967.

The back wall of the office holds an even more modern secret, circa 2019. Look for the framed photos of the **Skippers of the Year**. Although the plaque states they were awarded the honor in 1938, in reality the event took place in 2019, marking the first time front-line Cast Members were incorporated into an attraction. You'll find the same framed tribute in the Mess Hall at Skipper Canteen.

While you're waiting in line for the Jungle Cruise, look across the river. See that **small hut** that looks like it has a straw roof? With the heat, rain, and humidity in Florida, that roof wouldn't last long if it were real straw. Instead, it's made of metal strips. The ability to create a lasting thatched roof was only implemented once Disney's Animal Kingdom was under construction. Authentic thatching grass and Zulu craftsmen were brought in from KwaZulu-Natal in South Africa to create the thatched roofs you see in the Africa section of Animal Kingdom.

Jungle Navigation Co. LTD. Skipper Canteen

Disney restaurants often have interesting decor that supports their theme, but Jungle Navigation Co. LTD. Skipper Canteen, better known as simply Skipper Canteen, goes the extra mile and then some. Detouring into a restaurant when you're not dining there isn't usually recommended, but make an exception in this case, ideally during off-peak hours and remembering not to block servers' and diners' way. If they're not busy, Cast Members will sometimes give you a guided tour.

The rather stoic gentleman in the portrait you see in Skipper Canteen's indoor waiting area is none other than **Dr. Albert Falls**, founder of the Jungle Navigation Company, now known as the Jungle Cruise. The stylized painting next to him is his granddaughter, **Alberta Falls**, current owner of the Jungle Navigation Company and its dining outlet, Skipper Canteen.

The restaurant is divided into three distinct sections: The main dining room is the Jungle Cruise Crew's Mess Hall, the smaller room off the back of the Mess Hall is the Falls Family Parlor, and the room behind the bookcases is the S.E.A. Room, former secret meeting place for the Society of Explorers and Adventurers. We'll visit them in that order.

The crew's notice board on the wall to the left of the kitchen door is chock-full of funny notes between crew members and allusions to other Adventureland attractions, most notably, of course, the Jungle Cruise. Case in point is the **Schweitzer Follies Callback List**. Schweitzer Follies is a take on Jungle Cruise's Schweitzer Falls, but the cast being called back are actually designers and Imagineers for Skipper Canteen.

Imagine That!

Alex Grayman, art director, Walt Disney Imagineering, was one of the primary directors for Skipper Canteen, and he shared how the concept came together: "With the [Pixie Hollow] fairies moving to Main Street, U.S.A., [we had] a facility that could be turned back into a restaurant. If we were going to introduce a character presence, what fit in Adventureland? Is it Tarzan? Aladdin? Pirates? Someone threw out the idea of jungle skippers, an iconic character. To any Disney fan, Jungle Cruise skippers are the pinnacle of a Disney Cast Member. Everyone knows and loves the skippers, and everyone wants to be a skipper. A perfect tie-in. So we thought, what if this building is the headquarters of the Jungle Navigation Company? Skippers clock in, they bunk here, they have their meals here...and the story kept evolving. It practically wrote itself."

See that **parrot talisman** hanging from a thin leather strap in the left half of the crew's notice board? The letter behind it is addressed to **Rosita** from the Enchanted Tiki Room attraction in Adventureland. It's a cute, but expected, feature. The less-expected detail is the **United States postage stamp** on the letter. It's a Susan B. Anthony three-cent stamp issued in 1936, commemorating the nineteenth amendment to the US Constitution, which granted women the right to vote. While Jungle Cruise was designed as a nod to the 1930s, it's a fun coincidence that, with a little bit of mental gymnastics, we can transpose the "36" in 1936 to get 1963, the year Enchanted Tiki Room opened in Disneyland.

In a move that harkens back to Dopey and the gem vault in Fantasyland, some smart aleck (or dim bulb) has left a note reading, "I'm putting the **spare key** for the notice board cabinet here for safekeeping." Sure enough, there it is, locked inside the cabinet. Let's hope no one loses the original key.

As you're browsing the notices, pay attention to the **sounds coming from the kitchen** off to your right. Some of them are real, but many are recorded. You may even hear dishes breaking.

The **voice** you hear coming from behind the office door on the second floor, across from the kitchen, is Alberta Falls. She has a slight Indian accent, a hint that she's traveled around the world.

The **names on the office doors** along the balcony are: Skipper Marc, Animal Biological Studies (Marc Davis, who was responsible, among other things, for adding the famous elephant pool and the "rhino stranding a lost safari" scenes to Jungle Cruise); Skipper Harper, Cartography (Harper Goff, one of the main designers of Jungle Cruise); and Skipper Bill, Plant Studies (Bill Evans, horticulturist for Jungle Cruise). The exception is the office of Albert Falls, original owner of the Jungle Navigation Co. LTD. Skipper Canteen. Notice the dramatic **letter A, in gold**, which has been added to the name? It's an indication that his granddaughter, Alberta Falls, is the new owner.

Midway through the mess hall you'll see the **Lost and Unfound shelf** hanging on the wall, with several stacked-up items, including a green box marked "J. Lindsey" with a bright yellow sticker that reads, "Warning: May Contain Live Snake." This is a reference to Indiana Jones's pilot friend Jock Lindsey, whose snake, Reggie, terrified Indy in the movie *Raiders of the Lost Ark*, and a tie to Jock Lindsey's Hangar Bar in Disney Springs.

Walk to the far-left corner of the Mess Hall and you'll find a small barrel marked **Backside of Water**. This is a reference to what is arguably the most famous line in the Jungle Cruise spiel. Notice the word is "backside," not "back side." Given that it's a noun rather than a location indicator, you're not looking at the back side of water on the Jungle Cruise, you're looking at the water's backside (aka its derriere).

Step back so you have a view of the wall above the barrel and you'll see two shelves holding **Christmas decorations**. They are a reference to the seasonal overlay, Jingle Cruise, which puts a festive spin on the regular Jungle Cruise attraction in November and December. You'll also see an **advertisement for Jingle Cruise** on the crew's bulletin board.

The balcony to the right of the Christmas decorations pays homage to the much-missed Adventurers Club in Disney's former Pleasure Island. Several items on the balcony and around the restaurant came from the popular nightclub, including the **horned mask** on the far-right wall and the **large birdcage** in the center of the balcony.

Imagine That!

WDI Art Director Alex Grayman broke down the backstory of Skipper Canteen, saying, "Dr. Falls was a proper Englishman who came to Africa as part of British colonialism in the late 1700s and brought with him things from home, such as the family china [in the parlor] that would make him feel comfortable. In the S.E.A. Room it's all about discoveries that were made by the Society of Explorers and Adventurers. In the Mess Hall it's things the skippers discovered in the jungle and brought back to decorate their space. One of our props designers was English, so we asked him to go to antique shops and buy a whole lot of stuff and ship it over. It's authentic."

There are numerous references to other attractions in the Falls Family Parlor, with the most obvious being the **parrot light fixtures** and their tie-up to the Enchanted Tiki Room attraction.

Also notice the **decorative wood carvings**, which are based on animals and scenes in the Jungle Cruise.

The pretty **peacock stained glass windows** are an homage to Pamela Perkins from the Adventurers Club. Pamela wore various outfits during her tenure as club president and one of them included an extravagant hat with a peacock on it.

Every fireplace needs a distinctive **mantel decoration**, and the mantel in the parlor certainly has one. It's a model of a Jungle Cruise–style riverboat, *Molopo Marie*, beautifully juxtaposed against the landscape painting behind it for a sepia throwback to Jungle Cruise's 1930s vibe.

The **painting above the fireplace** in the S.E.A. Room is obviously a fanciful version of the Jungle Cruise attraction. But wait. What's going on with that boat? You can tell you're looking at the front of the boat by the netting you see on the bow, but if you know the Magic Kingdom attraction well, you know it reaches the temple *after* it sails behind Schweitzer Falls. Is it an "oops"? Nope. In an early Disneyland version of the ride the boats went through the Cambodian temple before reaching Schweitzer Falls, and just beyond the falls were the Kilimanjaro Rapids, an element that is no longer there. The painting refers to that long-ago setup.

The **bookshelves** that line the hallway and hide the door to the S.E.A. Room are filled with unexpected references. Kevin Lively, story editor, Walt Disney Imagineering, and former Jungle Cruise skipper, wrote four hundred titles with hidden meanings and turned them into the books on these shelves. Let's take a look at a few.

The Jungle Book by Rudyard Kipling is a first edition obtained by Disney's props department, but that's only half the reason it's so special. It's pulled out to indicate it's the

book that activates the bookcase's hinges, revealing the door to the secret meeting room.

Many of the books refer to **extinct attractions**. Look for the brown book by B.L. titled *A Flight Through Dreams* and the green book next to it, *If You Had Wings You Could Fly*. Delta Dreamflight and If You Had Wings were attractions that used to occupy the space where Buzz Lightyear's Space Ranger Spin now lives. With that in mind, it's easy to figure out who B.L. is, isn't it?

The books also act as little **time capsules** capturing snippets of Disney history, from television to movies, attractions, and homages to Imagineers, plus silly puns. Find *True Life Adventures* by W.E.D., referencing Walter Elias Disney's documentary films from 1948 to 1960; *The Wildest Ride* by J. T. Toad, remembering the Mr. Toad's Wild Ride attraction in Magic Kingdom and its star, J. Thaddeus Toad; and *Meeting Royalty* by Sklar. Over the course of fifty-four years and through many roles with Walt Disney Imagineering, Marty Sklar became true Disney royalty.

Naturally, the fezzes on the bookshelves hold meaning too. While Chef Tandaji and Luana Teixeira only exist as part of Skipper Canteen lore, and Albert Falls is the founder of Jungle Navigation Co. LTD., Captain **Mary Oceaneer** has also earned the right to have her fez displayed, as a member of the S.E.A. and an adventurer who had a hand in Miss Adventure Falls at Disney's Typhoon Lagoon Water Park, the Oceaneer Club on Disney's Magic and Wonder cruise ships, Disney's private island Castaway Cay, and even far-flung destination Mystic Manor in Hong Kong Disneyland.

What about the fezzes for **Albert the Monkey and Sango Sio**? Lord Henry Mystic, owner of Mystic Manor (Hong

Kong Disneyland's version of the Haunted Mansion) had a monkey named Albert. And Sango Sio? Well, he or she is a mystery, though it's interesting to note Sango Dishes made Disney character dinnerwear at one time. Any connection? Not really. The likely connection is much more subtle. *Sangoshō*, roughly pronounced "sangosio," means "coral reef" in Japanese, an entirely appropriate reference to the S.E.A.

Tomorrowland

After exploring the world, the next frontier to conquer is the future, specifically as it relates to space. The Show theme of Tomorrowland is firmly of the science-fiction variety, with all things metal and machinery, most of it in motion. Even the pavement puts you in mind of the planets and what's out there just beyond our reach. Things buzz around you and above you, with progress as the theme du jour.

Tomorrowland was intended to be a **working city** and the headquarters for the League of Planets, though the land is due for a major overhaul. For now, notice all the community's needs are catered for: transportation, dining, shopping, and communication. Whether you're a human citizen, an alien, or a robot, everything you need is right here!

Walt Disney's Carousel of Progress

Serious Disney geeks know that Carousel of Progress is a groundbreaking attraction that helped set the wheels in motion for advancements in Audio-Animatronics, and indeed for the creation of the Magic Kingdom itself. Gentle and unassuming, it is often overlooked in favor of big-thrill attractions, but it's chock-full of wonderful hidden magic.

For the best chance at seeing these gems, sit in the center of the theater, or just to the right of center.

You may notice a few incongruent elements in the story, including the **unnamed girl** in the wash-day scene, cranking the handle of the washing machine while Sarah does the ironing; a **paint mixer** being used in the Rumpus Room scene, though Sarah is wallpapering, not painting; and Grandma's comment, **"Give him a left, ya big lug!"** during a wrestling match rather than a boxing match.

When you reach the 1920s scene celebrating Independence Day, look through the window on the left-hand side. There is a Chinese restaurant across the street from John's house, but the real gem is the small sign advertising **Herb Ryman, Attorney at Law**. It's hard to read, but it's a tribute to Imagineer Herbert Ryman, concept artist who sketched the interior of the G.E. Carousel of Progress attraction for the 1964 New York World's Fair.

Fascinating Fact

The original version of the Carousel of Progress created for the 1964 New York World's Fair featured four eras: 1890, 1920, 1940, and the "modern day" of the 1960s. It was the first time Imagineers created Audio-Animatronic cats and dogs, and the first time Audio-Animatronic humans were used on a large scale. The characters' heads for the show were designed by sculptor Blaine Gibson, who used the face of Imagineer Dick Irvine's daughter as the model for the show's young daughter.

The final scene is due for updating, but for now, watch for these gems.

Christmas wouldn't be complete without a little something from Walt Disney World, and one lucky family member has a **large plush Mickey Mouse** waiting under the tree, to the left of Grandpa's rocking chair. Look carefully and you'll see the top of Mickey's head poking up from behind some wrapped gifts.

Mickey also appears as a **nutcracker on the mantel** at the far-left side of the room, in an **abstract painting of sorcerer Mickey** behind the television set Grandma and Jimmy are using to play a video game, and as **salt and pepper grinders** on the kitchen counter. If you are sitting far enough to the right, you'll also see a Mickey cutout pasted to the gift next to Grandpa.

The notices on the corkboard behind Sarah's computer in the final scene are difficult to read, but they're also incredibly interesting. Look for the white paper with lettering in black marker, partially obscured by a school photo of a boy against a blue backdrop, which reads, **MARTY CALLED WANTS CHANGES**. It is a reference to Marty Sklar, former vice chairman and principal creative executive at Walt Disney Imagineering. Until his death on July 27, 2017, Marty was a true ambassador for the Disney philosophy.

Space Mountain

While you're in the queue, look for interplanetary route maps on the left-hand side. There are a few Disney references here, for **Disney's Hyperion Resort** and for the characters **Pluto** and **Ariel** who, not so coincidentally, are also a dwarf planet and a moon, respectively. Disney's Hyperion Resort is a reference to one of Walt Disney's studios and is also the name of one of Saturn's moons.

Just after you enter Space Mountain, take a look at the sign that lists various Earth Stations. **Tomorrowland Station MK-1** is the station here in Tomorrowland. MK refers to

Orlando's Magic Kingdom and the numeral "1" indicates it was the first Space Mountain built in a Disney park. **TL Space Station 77** honors Disneyland's ride, which was built in 1977. **Discovery Landing Station—Paris** is Disneyland Paris's ride. There is no Tomorrowland in Paris, so the ride is located in Paris's Discoveryland. **Ashita Base—Tokyo** comes next, a reference to Tokyo Disneyland; *ashita* is Japanese for "tomorrow." And finally, **HK Spaceport E—TKT** is the spaceport in Hong Kong Disneyland. What does "E—TKT" stand for? Space Mountain was an E-ticket attraction when it opened at Magic Kingdom, meaning your admission booklet (which had ticket designations A through E) allowed you the choice of one of eight "major" attractions per E-ticket. The term is now synonymous with "thrilling ride."

Once you're on the ride, pay attention (if you can!) as you make your way up the lift hill. The front of the spaceship suspended above you has the markings **H-NCH 1975**, a reference to Disney Legend John Hench, designer of the original Space Mountain, and to the year the attraction opened.

Although you won't see much during your journey into space because, well, it's dark and you're whizzing along at what feels like 100 miles per hour (although it's really only 28 mph), there is more magic when you return to the spaceport. As you walk along the themed corridor toward the attraction's exit, pay attention to the **stickers on the luggage** on the left-hand side. "Mesa Verde," on the purple container, is one of the destinations riders could choose to visit during their journey on the long-gone Horizons attraction at EPCOT. The larger of the two silver suitcases behind it sports a Space Station X-1 sticker, remembering the Disneyland attraction of the same name, which opened in Anaheim's Tomorrowland in 1955. It was an A-ticket attraction, which tells you something about how (non-) thrilling it was, and it closed five years later, which tells you something about how (un-)popular it had been.

Next, take note of the panels being attended to by a robot. The top panel to the extreme left is labeled "Collision Prevention Control" and it includes a list of **Traffic Codes**. If you know your major Floridian roads you can work out which location each code refers to using the hints about their current status, listed after each code.

Spoiler alert! Stop reading for a moment if you want to figure them out yourself.

In order, the Traffic Codes are:

5-A1A-Coast Clear (State Road A1A runs along Florida's eastern coast, from Fernandina Beach to Miami Beach).

6-I4-Heavy Construction (Interstate 4, the constant-construction bane of Central Florida).

7-192-Alert-Tour Zone (Highway 192, one of Orlando's busiest tourist centers).

8-C50-Alert-Collision (County Road 50, north of Walt Disney World, a place where tourists rarely collide with locals, but also a long road with nearly two hundred auto repair shops and car dealerships).

9-INTL7-Visibility Low (International Drive, a major tourist hub notorious for visitors who dart into the street unexpectedly).

10-VSTA-Visibility High (Buena Vista Drive transects Walt Disney World, a highly visible place everyone knows; *Buena Vista*, translated from Spanish, means "good view").

Below the Collision Prevention Control panel you'll see a second panel labeled **Space Tug Dispatch**, an homage to a selection of Magic Kingdom attractions that have closed or been added. See if you can figure them out from their land's initials and the attraction's initials. You'll find the answer in Appendix: Solutions to Hints, Solution 3.

Open Sectors (opened attractions) are:

FL-MAWP

AL-AFC

FL-MPM

FRL-SM

TL-BLSRS

TL-MILFaFt

Below the Open Sectors you'll see the following **Closed Sectors** (closed attractions). Their identities are also in Solution 3.

FL-20K

FL-MTWR

TL-SK2FL

MSU-SB

FL-MMR

TL-M2M

The **Space Tug Duty Roster** to the right of the Open and Closed Sector graphics displays five tugs, and while their names are letters or letter-and-number combinations, they really just refer to each tug's color, such as PRP-1 (purple) and AQ-MR (aquamarine). Now that you know, you can easily figure out the rest. There is a lot of fun wordplay on the panels, so take a quick look before you rush to the next ride.

You're almost at the end of the exit corridor, but watch for a moment when you reach the tableaus on the right-hand side. The monitor the space dog is looking at scrolls through several scenes, one of which is **20,000 Light Years Under the Sea**, a reference to Fantasyland's long-gone attraction 20,000 Leagues Under the Sea.

Although Magic Kingdom was not Walt Disney's primary intent for his great Florida project (that honor goes to the next park we'll explore), in terms of the historical time line it had to come first. Profits from the park were necessary to raise the funding needed for Walt's true pet project, EPCOT Center. But from the perspective of the Show, Magic Kingdom comes in second to none. Open your eyes wide as you tour and imagine your own happy stories in this most magical of places!

Magic Kingdom Time Line

In 1958, the Walt Disney Company hired a private consultancy, Economics Research Associates, to begin a quest to find the ideal location where Walt could build his second theme park. The study indicated the obscure sites of Ocala and Orlando in Florida were most suited to the project. By 1963, Roy O. Disney and attorney Robert Foster proposed the purchase of 5,000 to 10,000 acres of land, prompting Walt to pay a visit to the area and make a final decision. After viewing the options, he settled on Orlando as the location for what would eventually become Walt Disney World.

Acting under the name Robert Price, Foster purchased 12,400 acres at a mere $107–$145 per acre, later adding another 9,750 acres at a relatively low cost. The total land purchase would span nearly 30,000 acres at a final cost of a little more than $5 million.

The *Orlando Sentinel* originally agreed not to reveal Disney's involvement in the land purchases, but, by the end of May 1965, the cat was nearly out of the bag. In June 1965, the *Orlando Evening Star* ran a feature referencing forty-seven transactions by Florida Ranch Lands, Inc., a boutique brokerage firm that was eventually revealed as working on behalf of Walt Disney in securing central Florida property. On October 25, Florida governor Haydon Burns confirmed Disney's purchase of the land and, on November 15, in the Cherry Plaza Hotel in Orlando, Walt, Roy, and Governor Burns formally announced plans to build the fledgling Disney resort.

Sadly, Walt never saw a single brick laid at the Florida location. He died of lung cancer on December 15, 1966. Roy O. Disney changed the name of the project from Disney World to Walt Disney World in honor of his brother, one of the great creative visionaries of the modern era. On May 30, 1967, ground broke for Magic Kingdom, "The Most Magical Place on Earth."

Opening Day 1971

The Magic Kingdom's grand opening took place on October 1, 1971, to a crowd of ten thousand visitors and at a cost of $400 million. Attractions open that day were **Cinderella's Golden Carrousel**, **Country Bear Jamboree**, **Diamond Horseshoe Revue**, **Dumbo the Flying Elephant**, **Frontierland Shootin' Arcade**, **Hall of Presidents**, **Haunted Mansion**, **it's a small world**, **Jungle Cruise**, **Mad Tea Party**, **Mickey Mouse Revue**, **Audio-Animatronics**, **Mike Fink Keel Boats**, **Mr. Toad's Wild Ride**, **Skyway to Tomorrowland** and **Skyway to Fantasyland**, **Snow White's Adventures**, **Swiss Family Treehouse**, **Tropical Serenade**, **Grand Prix Raceway**, and **Walt Disney World Railroad**. In addition, there were a full array of shops, dining options, a **Penny Arcade**, **House of Magic**, **Main Street Cinema**, various novelty vehicles, horse-drawn streetcars, and horseless carriages.

Admiral Joe Fowler **riverboat** opened on October 2, with **Peter Pan's Flight** debuting the next day. On October

14, **20,000 Leagues Under the Sea** made its inaugural dive, and on Christmas Eve, the first guests blasted into outer space compliments of **Flight to the Moon**.

1971–1972: The Early Days

Admission into the park in 1971 was $3.50 for adults, $2.50 ages twelve to seventeen, and $1 ages three to eleven. Unlike today, guests then had a choice of two attraction tickets: an Adult 7-Attractions booklet ran $4.75. For an additional $1, adults could get an 11-Attractions booklet. Coupons allowed for one ride per coupon, from A-rides (such as Main Street Vehicles and Cinderella's Golden Carrousel) to E-rides (state-of-the-art attractions such as Haunted Mansion, Country Bear Jamboree, Jungle Cruise, and it's a small world).

Roy O. Disney presided over Magic Kingdom's dedication ceremony on October 23, 1971. In November, the **Electrical Water Pageant** parade made its first journey along Bay Lake while the Circle-Vision 360° film *America the Beautiful* debuted in Tomorrowland. December 1 saw the addition of a fourth locomotive, the *Roy O. Disney*.

Tragically, on December 20, Roy died of a cerebral hemorrhage. Control of Walt Disney World passed to Donn Tatum, acting as chairman, with Esmond Cardon "Card" Walker serving as president.

Eastern Airlines, the official airline of Walt Disney World, sponsored the **If You Had Wings** attraction in Tomorrowland, which opened on June 5, 1972, featuring a cutting-edge Omnimover ride system. By October 1, Walt Disney World's first anniversary, 10.7 million guests had passed through its gates.

1973–1974: Something New

The year 1973 saw a barrage of new attractions, including **The Walt Disney Story** in April, **Tom Sawyer Island**, **Tom Sawyer Island Rafts**, **Plaza Swan Boats**, and the **Richard F. Irvine riverboat** in May. But the most notable attraction debuted on December 15 when **Pirates of the Caribbean** opened in Adventureland. It would become a true Disney classic and go on to inspire a classic adventure movie series thirty years later.

America the Beautiful closed on March 15, 1974, reopening a day later with a new film, **Magic Carpet 'Round the World**, which lasted all of a year before being replaced by *America the Beautiful* again. **Star Jets**, the area's new centerpiece attraction, followed in November, providing a dizzying rocket-ride high above Tomorrowland.

By the end of 1974, Walt Disney World's popularity had grown to astonishing proportions. On December 29, a record 74,597 day-guests passed through the gates, causing the park to close due to capacity for the first time in its history.

1975: Liftoff for Tomorrowland

Long-awaited thrill ride **Space Mountain** launched on January 15, 1975, adding a much-needed boost of adrenaline to an otherwise gentle park experience. Space travel remained very much in the public consciousness, though travel to the moon had lost some of its mystique. In response, Flight to the Moon became **Mission to Mars** on June 7, giving the attraction a new name and destination, although it remained essentially the same ride.

On June 6, **America on Parade** began running twice daily along Main Street's parade route in honor of the upcoming American Bicentennial.

A "great big beautiful tomorrow" arrived when the classic **Carousel of Progress** was moved from Disneyland in

California to Magic Kingdom's Tomorrowland in 1975, with a new theme song, "The Best Time of Your Life." The original theme song would return in 1994, when the attraction was refurbished and renamed **Walt Disney's Carousel of Progress**.

1976–1981: Main Street Milestones

Although 1976 was quiet in terms of new attractions, the Magic Kingdom hit a milestone when day-guest Susan Brummer passed through the gates, achieving the distinction of being the park's fifty millionth visitor.

Destined to be a Disney classic, **Main Street Electrical Parade** premiered on June 11, 1977. It would grace Magic Kingdom three times, first for a fourteen-year run (1977–1991), then for two years (1999–2001), and finally, for six years (2010–2016).

The period from 1978 through mid-1980 was quiet at the Magic Kingdom as a second gate—EPCOT Center—broke ground in preparation for an October 1, 1982, opening. Mickey Mouse Revue closed at Magic Kingdom on September 14, 1980, followed by the retirement of the *Admiral Joe Fowler* riverboat. But big news came on November 8, with the opening of the park's second coaster, **Big Thunder Mountain Railroad**.

The Dream Called EPCOT film began showing at the EPCOT Preview Center in Magic Kingdom, generating excitement for the new park scheduled to open eleven years to the day after Magic Kingdom welcomed its first guests.

But 1981 also focused on Magic Kingdom's ten-year anniversary, with the stage show *Disney World Is Your World* and the **Tencennial Parade** running from October 1, 1981, through September 30, 1982, highlighting a celebration dubbed "a year long and a smile wide"—and smile wide, they did! Walt Disney World welcomed its 126 millionth guest during its Tencennial festivities.

1982–1983: The Quiet Year

Most of Walt Disney World's energy was focused on Epcot during this time; hence, the Magic Kingdom endured a quiet year. The Plaza Swan Boats no longer swam the park's inland waters as of August 1983, victims of ongoing maintenance problems. However, their main docking area, a green-roofed platform next to the rose garden between the castle and Tomorrowland, could still be enjoyed as a shady rest area until 2014.

1984: A New Boss

A change in power occurred at Walt Disney World in 1984. Michael Eisner became the new chairman and chief executive officer following a major boardroom upheaval, with the company in the doldrums and losing money on both their theme park and film divisions. But the Magic Kingdom was not initially a primary focus for investment in new attractions.

A weak effort arrived in the form of the **Show Biz Is** show, which opened on July 12, 1984, only to close two months later. *America the Beautiful* was replaced by Circle-Vision 360° film **American Journeys**, while the new **Frontierland Shootin' Arcade** offered little buckaroos the opportunity to spend a bit more of Mom and Dad's hard-earned cash on the chance to knock over a few prairie-themed targets. It was not a banner year.

1985–1987: More Development—but Not at Magic Kingdom

After the upheaval of 1984, it would take another four years before any new development occurred in Magic Kingdom. Time and money were focused on a rather quick decision to move forward with a third gate at Walt Disney World, the $300 million "Hollywood that never was and always will be" of Disney-MGM Studios.

In the meantime, **Merlin's Magic Shop** closed in Magic Kingdom in May 1986 and the Diamond Horseshoe Revue was renamed the **Diamond Horseshoe Jamboree**. Eastern Airlines was dropped as the If You Had Wings sponsor in January 1986. The name was changed to **If You Could Fly** on June 6. Capping off a rather uninspired year, *Magic Journeys*, the first in-park 3D effort by Walt Disney Imagineering, debuted at the Fantasyland Theater on December 15. The park would remain quiet throughout 1987, with no new attractions.

1988–1990: Junior Jamboree

The year 1988 would make up for the lack of investment in the park in the mid-1980s, especially for families with young children. **Mickey's Birthdayland** opened on June 18, originally intended to be a temporary land for the duration of Mickey's birthday celebration.

The area consisted of **Mickey's House**, **Grandma Duck's Petting Farm**, **Mickey's Playground**, and three circus-style tents with character meet-and-greets and two live shows, including highlight show *Minnie's Surprise Birthday Party*. One of the prime attractions was a cow living at Grandma Duck's farm named Minnie Moo, born with the classic tri-circle Mickey head on her side.

Ending an ongoing struggle to find its identity, If You Could Fly closed for the last time on January 3, 1989. Debuting in its place, **Delta Dreamflight** opened on June 26 and became a guest favorite for its pop-up-book style and the illusion of entering a jet engine.

Due to its enormous popularity with families, the decision was made to keep Mickey's Birthdayland. It closed on April 22, 1990, reopening on May 26 under the name **Mickey's Starland**, with *Minnie's Surprise Birthday Party* replaced by the **Mickey's Magical TV World** show. Cheap cutout storefronts were replaced by more substantial façades.

1991–1993: Parades—and a Big Splash

September 14, 1991, saw the last running of the popular nighttime Main Street Electrical Parade. It was replaced on October 1 by the visually magnificent **SpectroMagic**. The **Surprise Celebration Parade** ran each afternoon, beginning September 22.

It had been twelve years, though, since Magic Kingdom had brought in a major attraction. Finally, in 1992, on July 17 (with a dedication ceremony on October 2), **Splash Mountain** generated screams of delight, with its gentle log flume ride through vignettes based on the 1946 film *Song of the South* culminating in a final 52-foot plunge with Br'er Rabbit, straight into the briar patch!

The Walt Disney Story closed on October 5, 1992, followed by Mission to Mars on October 4, 1993. The Hall of Presidents underwent a refurbishment, adding President Bill Clinton to the lineup on November 18, 1993, with new narration by poet Maya Angelou, who recited her poem "On the Pulse of Morning" at President Clinton's January 20 inauguration.

On December 1, *Magic Journeys* at the Fantasyland Theater was presented for the last time. A month later, *American Journeys* closed, followed by Surprise Celebration Parade and Star Jets.

1994–1995: City of the Future

By 1994, Tomorrowland needed, and got, a major overhaul. It had begun to look dated, so in an effort to avoid that happening in the future, the Imagineers gave it a more general design, creating a "city of the future," with all the services of a major interplanetary metropolis.

In the process, the WEDWay PeopleMover adopted the name **Tomorrowland Transit Authority** in June of 1994, creating instant confusion for new visitors looking for the TTC (Transportation and Ticket Center). Despite the name change, many purists persisted in calling it the WEDWay.

On July 8, 1994, *The Legend of the Lion King* show debuted in the former Mickey Mouse Revue theater, with a unique blend of animation from *The Lion King* movie, human-animal puppet performances, and some wonderful lighting effects. On September 5, the classic attraction 20,000 Leagues Under the Sea closed, another victim of difficult maintenance, and on November 21, 1994, **the Timekeeper** attraction with Circle-Vision 360° film *From Time to Time* opened in Tomorrowland's Transportarium, with voices by comic duo Robin Williams as the Timekeeper and Rhea Perlman as time-traveling camera droid 9-Eye. And finally, Carousel of Progress was renamed **Walt Disney's Carousel of Progress**, and reclaimed its original theme song, "There's a Great Big Beautiful Tomorrow."

The wonderfully hometown Penny Arcade and the House of Magic closed on March 19, 1995, and on April 7, the Diamond Horseshoe Jamboree returned to its original name, the Diamond Horseshoe Revue. On the heels of the major refurbishment of Tomorrowland, Star Jets was reborn as **Astro Orbiter**, with the central rocket tower being replaced by a futuristic orbiting-planets theme.

Flying in circles around Tomorrowland wasn't enough to hold teenagers' attention, so on June 20, 1995, the **ExtraTERRORestrial Alien Encounter** began scaring the daylights out of little Mouseketeers (and big ones). Incredibly innovative, Alien Encounter was the theme park equivalent of a psychological thriller and ultimately proved too un-Disney-like, especially as a Magic Kingdom attraction.

1996–1997: Goofy for More

Mickey's Starland, now called **Mickey's Toontown Fair**, enjoyed an expansion in June 1996, adding kiddie coaster the **Barnstormer at Goofy's Wiseacre Farm** (which replaced Grandma Duck's Petting Farm) and **Toontown Hall of Fame**. The Grand Prix Raceway's track was shortened to make room for the added attractions in Toontown, reopening on September 28 as **Tomorrowland Speedway**. On the other side of the park, the *Richard F. Irvine* riverboat was rechristened the **Liberty Belle**.

One of Disney's Nine Old Men, animator and railroad enthusiast **Ward Kimball**, received the honor of a namesake fifth locomotive, which made its debut at Magic Kingdom on March 1, 1997. That April, popular King Stefan's Banquet Hall restaurant was renamed **Cinderella's Royal Table**.

1998–1999: Silver Anniversary Stunner

After a May 17, 1997, accident dumped a boatload of guests into the Rivers of America at Disneyland California, the Mike Fink Keel Boats attraction there and in Orlando closed for good. Some Disney purists believed a more startling catastrophe occurred when Cinderella Castle was transformed into the **Cinderella Castle Cake** during Walt Disney World's 25th Anniversary Celebration in late 1996, and they were delighted to see the balloon-like covering removed in January 1998.

On the strength of three enormously popular movies, *Aladdin*, *The Lion King*, and *Toy Story*, the Tiki Room reopened as **the Enchanted Tiki Room—Under New Management**, with Jafar's (from *Aladdin*) screeching parrot, Iago, acting as joint host with *The Lion King*'s Zazu, while the brand-new **Buzz Lightyear's Space Ranger Spin** became an instant E-ticket hit. Sadly, September 7 saw the closing of a Disney classic, Mr. Toad's Wild Ride. Toady handed over the deed to his former home on June 5, 1999, when **The Many Adventures of Winnie the Pooh** arrived.

2000–2002: New Millennium, New Shows

The year 2001 added new entertainment to the park, hot on the heels of a major promotion for Walt Disney World's Millennium Celebration in 2000. These included *Cinderella's Surprise Celebration* stage show, the daily parade **Share a Dream Come True**, and the return of the nighttime parade **SpectroMagic**, which replaced Main Street Electrical Parade on April 2. Geared toward the Dumbo the Flying Elephant crowd, **the Magic Carpets of Aladdin** provided a much-needed kiddie ride in Adventureland. On October 1, Disney's 100 Years of Magic celebration began, honoring the anniversary of Walt Disney's birth.

2003–2004: More Mickey and Friends

The 3D multisensory treat *Mickey's PhilharMagic* took over the former *Legend of the Lion King* theater in 2003, a year after *Lion King* closed. Nearby, the Diamond Horseshoe Revue closed, replaced by the ill-conceived **Goofy's Country Dancin' Jamboree**, a preschool free-for-all with Cowboy Goofy and Friends.

The poignantly beautiful **Wishes: A Magical Gathering of Disney Dreams** fireworks show lit up the sky for the first time on October 8, 2003, and four days later, the ExtraTERRORestrial Alien Encounter closed, a victim, perhaps, of its own success. The attraction set out to be terrifying—and did so in grand style.

Its replacement arrived on November 16, 2004, when the mischievous alien from the megahit movie *Lilo and Stitch* teleported to Magic Kingdom with his own show, **Stitch's Great Escape**. Preschoolers were frightened by it, elementary-age kids loved it, and many parents dubbed it "just plain gross."

2005–2007: Movie Makeovers

New attractions were not high on the list for 2005–2006, but Disney could not ignore a generational problem caused by the wild success of 2003's blockbuster movie *Pirates of the Caribbean: The Curse of the Black Pearl*. Youngsters clamored for the movie's star, played by the iconic Johnny Depp, prompting Audio-Animatronics of the inimitable Captain Jack Sparrow to be added to the Adventureland attraction.

In keeping with the trend of creating movie-inspired attractions, **the Laugh Floor Comedy Club** soft-opened briefly in December 2006, with one-eyed comedian Mike Wazowski of *Monsters, Inc.* movie fame acting as the show's Monster of Ceremonies. In December 2006 it was renamed **Monsters, Inc. Laugh Floor Comedy Club**, and finally **Monsters, Inc. Laugh Floor** in March 2007. The attraction did not generate the screams of laughter expected, though many guests found the show's acronym to be hilarious, as it was, unfortunately, also an obscene pop-culture cinematic reference.

Urban legend came full circle during a Haunted Mansion overhaul in 2007, formally introducing the ghostly bride story line, which was not intended in the original design. Purists railed at the idea that this classic attraction would be tampered with, but just as the Imagineers did a beautiful job in making Pirates of the Caribbean a more contemporary story without losing any of its original charm, so, too, did the Haunted Mansion's remake find favor. Some would argue it was better than ever!

2008–2014: Expanding the Fantasy

The years 2008 and 2009 were quiet, with rumors floating around about the next big thing coming to Magic Kingdom. By mid-2009 blueprints were leaked that showed a major Fantasyland expansion in the area occupied by a Winnie the Pooh playground, the former 20,000 Leagues Under the Sea attraction, and Toontown. While most of the plan's attractions came into being, some, including Pixie Hollow, fell by the wayside.

With an estimated five-year span before the expansion would be realized, very little happened to breathe new life into the park. The long-running parade **SpectroMagic** ended June 5, 2010, and was replaced by **Main Street Electrical Parade** the next day. Seven months later a small fire occurred at **the Enchanted Tiki Room—Under New Management!** on January 12, 2011, closing the attraction. On August 15, 2011, the original version returned, effectively doing what millions of visitors wished they could do: bump off that annoying bird, Iago.

The Haunted Mansion's queue was extended, giving guests the option of a detour through an interactive graveyard, which opened in March 2011. The augmented Hitchhiking Ghosts scene at the end of the attraction began on April 4, 2011, and after the successful addition of Captain Jack Sparrow and other characters from the hit movie series, mermaids from *Pirates of the Caribbean: On Stranger Tides* were added to the Adventureland attraction in October 2012.

Mickey's Toontown Fair closed permanently on February 11, 2011, as part of the Fantasyland expansion plans, and on March 12, 2012, the Barnstormer at Goofy's Wiseacre Farm reopened as the Barnstormer featuring Goofy as the Great Goofini. Dumbo the Flying Elephant was relocated from Fantasyland to Storybook Circus (formerly Toontown), reopening on March 12, 2012. A second Dumbo opened next to it, in July 2012. The remainder of Storybook Circus, including Casey Jr. Splash 'n' Soak Station, opened in July 2012.

Enchanted Tales with Belle and **Under the Sea: Journey of the Little Mermaid** opened December 6, 2012, as a debut of the addition to Fantasyland, nicknamed Fantasyland Forest.

Princess Fairytale Hall meet-and-greet began receiving visitors on September 18, 2013, and the final element of the Fantasyland expansion, **Seven Dwarfs Mine Train**, opened May 28, 2014, adding a sense of kinetic excitement to the most magical land in the park.

Celebrate a Dream Come True Parade, the third version of Share a Dream Come True Parade, ended on January 4, 2014, and was replaced by the spectacular **Festival of Fantasy Parade**, which debuted on March 9, 2014.

With little change to the experience itself, Move It! Shake It! Celebrate It! Street Party morphed into Move It! Shake It! Dance and Play It! Street Party on October 4, 2014, and again as the **Move It! Shake It! MousekeDance It! Street Party** on January 18, 2019, continuing the serious "earworm" nature of its theme song, impossible to get out of your head.

2015–2020: It's All about the Shows

Jungle Navigation Co. LTD. Skipper Canteen restaurant opened in Adventureland on December 16, 2015, introducing a story concept that tied to the Jungle Cruise attraction across the walkway and to a beloved former nighttime venue, the Adventurers Club, in the former Pleasure Island area of Downtown Disney, now reimagined as Disney Springs.

On June 17, 2016, *Mickey's Royal Friendship Faire* replaced *Dream Along with Mickey* on the Castle Forecourt Stage, with a focus on the joys derived from lasting friendships.

Longtime friends Kermit the Frog, Fozzie Bear, Miss Piggy, the Great Gonzo, and Sam Eagle mangled well-known moments in America's story in *The Muppets Present...Great Moments in American History*, which made its debut performance in Liberty Square on October 2, 2016, then closed on October 5, 2019.

Celebrate the Magic projection mapping show on Cinderella Castle ended November 3, 2016, replaced the next day by **Once upon a Time**, with its slew of Disney characters in a bedtime story told by Mrs. Potts to her son Chip, from the movie *Beauty and the Beast*.

Just like tacos and Tuesdays, Disney dared to pair two complementary things in the hopes of a happy outcome when they replaced the long-running Wishes, A Magical Gathering of Disney Dreams fireworks display with the projection mapping show **Once upon a Time** and a new fireworks show, **Happily Ever After**. The duo made their debut over—and on—Cinderella Castle on May 12, 2017.

Festival of Fantasy Parade began a hiatus on May 11, 2018, after the Maleficent dragon proved too realistic and caught its own head on fire, but it began prowling the streets again as the parade's icon on January 26, 2019.

1. **Mission: SPACE:** The pretty constellation on the gift shop ceiling isn't just any old constellation. It's **Mickey Nebula**, which is appropriate given that it's the shape of Mickey's profile.

2. **Test Track:** Watch for the round sign on a pole to your right, immediately after you crash through the doors and find yourself outside. The number 82 on the sign pays homage to 1982, the year EPCOT opened.

3. **Soarin' Around the World:** Immediately after you pass over the Matterhorn's summit and begin your downward swoop, look to the right at the mountain below. You'll see a cartoony version of a yeti's face, shoulders, and arms drawn in the snow, spanning the entire mountainside.

4. **Mexico:** Why is it always twilight inside Mexico's Plaza de los Amigos, which is based on the town of Taxco? Because twilight is the time friends and family gather in the plaza for socializing.

5. **Norway:** Check out the shelves and look up to the rafters as you make your way through Oaken's Tokens. You'll see authentic carvings of trolls, including the fan-favorite three-headed troll that harkens back to the attraction's original incarnation as Maelstrom.

6. **Germany:** The golden rooster that makes a periodic appearance above the Biergarten Restaurant mimics the golden rooster above the Rathaus-Glockenspiel in Munich, Germany.

7. **Italy:** The drinking fountain at the far-right side of the Italy pavilion features a pretty tile-work slogan. What does *Alla Salute* mean? "To your health!"

8. **Japan:** The pond next to Katsura Grill represents the journey of life, through quick-moving water that tumbles into chaos and the quiet tranquility that comes with age and experience.

9. **Morocco:** The pavilion's minaret, the tall tower to the right of the central courtyard, is based on Marrakesh's Koutoubia Mosque minaret and is accurate right down (or up!) to the gleaming copper globes on top.

10. **France:** The petal-shaped glass covering over the arcade to the left of Plume et Pallete is a re-creation of the Porte Dauphine station entryway of the Paris Métro.

11. **United Kingdom:** One of the books in The Toy Soldier shop is the *Society of Explorers & Adventurers Handbook*, referring to the Adventurers Club in the former Pleasure Island.

12. **Canada:** Artist David Boxley's The Tale of the Whale totem pole is an origin story of the potlatch ceremony, a feast celebrating major life milestones.

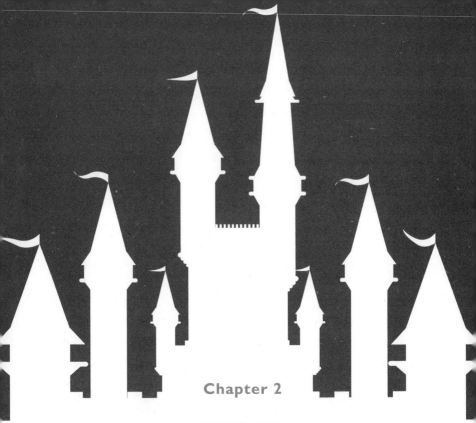

Chapter 2

EPCOT

After the world journey of Magic Kingdom, Walt Disney World's second park comes as a complete change, and "change" was certainly the watch-word as 2019 saw the beginning of a major transition at Epcot, including an early 2020 name change to EPCOT. Throughout 2020 and 2021, this transformation will be ongoing, with some attractions seeing minor tweaks and some areas undergoing a huge reimagining.

Walt Disney did not live to see even the beginning of the creation of EPCOT Center, the **Experimental Prototype Community of Tomorrow**, which opened on October 1, 1982. But his vision detailed a self-contained community with all peoples working in harmony toward the common goal of a better world. After Walt's death in 1966, the plans for EPCOT Center divided it into two separate, distinct parks, one showcasing the latest technology and the second a tribute to world cultures. In the end, they became the "theme park of discovery," through Future World and World Showcase.

In 2020, the park divided into four "neighborhoods" of World Celebration, World Discovery, World Nature, and World Showcase.

As you walk toward the front of the park from the bus depot, tram stop, or monorail on the right, or the parking lots to the extreme left, notice the **EPCOT logo** and the **logo for Spaceship Earth** embedded in the perforated fences.

Pause for a moment before you rush headlong into the park. Just outside the turnstiles, at the base of the flagpole, you'll find **EPCOT's dedication plaque** with CEO E. Card Walker's comments on the official park opening day of October 24, 1982, though the park actually opened on October 1.

World Celebration

As EPCOT transitions toward its new identity, the theme in Spaceship Earth will turn toward the bonds humans feel through the use of storytelling, with the addition of a magical "story-light" narration and enhancements or changes to some scenes. Until the new version is unveiled there is still plenty of EPCOT hidden magic to uncover.

Imagine That!

Gene Columbus, former manager of Magic Kingdom Entertainment, was instrumental in organizing the grand opening ceremony at EPCOT, and recalls some of the challenges prior to the park's debut. He says, "I was assigned to work on the grand opening of EPCOT Center with my primary duty to be the dedication. Leading up to this event there were a number of walk-throughs of the construction site. Trucks and earthmovers were everywhere, so the site had planks of wood laid down for us to get from place to place. This is Florida and a swamp, with the ground mainly of wet muck! As we planned the events, we needed to take folks out to see the space, and it was my job to take them on tours. Keep in mind that this was a time in which we wore ties and often jackets, but hardhats were also required. I would tell the group where things were and what was going on in each location, and at times I would walk backward to ensure they could hear me as well as making sure we were all looking at what we needed to see. The challenge was that if you stepped off the plank in the muck, it was not pretty. I did, and the muck sucked my shoe off my foot! I finished the tour promising myself never to let that happen again. A couple of weeks later I was doing a tour, and near the location of my first encounter it happened again. In both cases it was my left shoe. Over the years I've thought it would be interesting that thousands of years from now when someone digs in this area they will find these two shoes and conclude that people of this period in human development had two left feet, and to tell the difference they wore shoes of different colors."

World Discovery

EPCOT's former nod to left-brain thinking lives on through technology-focused attractions in World Discovery.

Mission: SPACE

Mission: SPACE holds the secret to space travel, providing an experience the average person could not have any other way. When the attraction originally opened, it was too much like the real thing. Although it was toned down, it remains the only attraction in Orlando equipped with motion discomfort bags.

Mission: SPACE is loosely based on the 1955 movie **Man in Space**, written, directed, and produced by Disney Legend Ward Kimball.

The **gold spheres** scattered across the mockup of the moon in the Planetary Plaza represent each of the twenty-nine moon-landing missions sent up by the United States and the Soviet Union between 1959 and 1976.

While you're in the courtyard, look for a **plaque** embedded in an oval of red dirt. Within the context of the story, they were made by the Mars exploration rovers, *Spirit* and *Opportunity*. *Spirit* landed on Mars on January 4, 2004, and *Opportunity* landed on January 25, 2004. **Sean O'Keefe** was the NASA administrator who implemented the MER mission.

Fascinating Fact

On April 6, 2004, Sean O'Keefe and a group of NASA scientists and mission managers attended a ceremony at EPCOT, accompanied by a Mars exploration rover, which made a ceremonial pass over the red dirt (which is really cement) now embedded in the courtyard at Mission: SPACE. This little plot of Red Planet celebrates the accomplishments of the rovers *Spirit* and *Opportunity*, including the discovery of evidence that indicates the surface of Mars once held water.

See that **Horizons logo** in the center of the rotating gravity wheel in the queue? Horizons was the name of the attraction located on the site that now houses Mission: SPACE. It centered on possible future habitat options in the harsh environments of the desert, the ocean, and space.

How did Disney decide what the Red Planet would look like during the landing portion of the ride? They contacted NASA's Jet Propulsion Lab for **satellite imagery of Mars' surface**. But that's not all they consulted with NASA about. The design of the **X-2 trainer** stems from scientific projections for future space travel; the **Ready Room** at Mission: SPACE is based on Kennedy Space Center's "White Room," where NASA astronauts waited before boarding their spacecraft; and the Mars landscape in the computer game **Expedition: Mars** in the post-show area's Advanced Training Lab contains imagery based on information provided by NASA.

After your successful training expedition, turn your hand to the interactive post-show elements. Take a peek in the cabinet on the left side of the alcove. The little yellow book titled *Expedition: Mars Noctis Labyrinthus* refers to the Noctis Labyrinthus, or "labyrinth of the night," which is a complex of winding valleys on Mars.

Imagine That!

Developing attraction concepts isn't as simple as coming up with a terrific idea, especially when it requires new technology and financial backing. Mission: SPACE was one such attraction. Imagineer Eddie Sotto, senior vice president of concept design with Walt Disney Imagineering from 1986 to 1999, describes the process when he says the Imagineers wanted to "give the most accurate ride experience that would simulate a rocket launch, as that was what most guests were fascinated with when it came to space. The funny thing about Mission: SPACE is that we really wanted management to know the ride experience was going to be unique. In order to get the funding to convince them, I had to lie on my back suspended between two chairs, facing the ceiling, making all manner of 'communications chatter' and engine noises, contorting my face to simulate the sustained g-forces on my body, all in a business suit. Think Cirque du Soleil meets *Apollo 13*. Marty Sklar, WDI's president, enthusiastically decided to fund the development of the show, but thankfully never asked me to demonstrate the effect again!"

Every ride ends with a gift shop, and this one has, of course, a space theme. The pretty constellation on the ceiling isn't just any old constellation, though. Look closer and you'll see it's labeled **Mickey Nebula**, which is appropriate given that it's the shape of Mickey's profile.

Before you leave the shop, take a quick look at the **power boxes** immediately to the left of the exit door. You'll find another Mickey profile and a classic tri-circle Mickey head there.

Test Track

Test Track is themed as a **Chevrolet Design Center** where guests can create and test their own cars inside a computer-driven environment. While all the whimsical hidden magic of the previous ride was removed in 2012, there are still a few little gems to look for as you make your way through the digital world of this virtual testing ground.

World of Motion, the former attraction in what is now the Test Track pavilion, may have closed in 1996, but as a much-missed fan favorite, a few nods in its direction are appropriate. Watch for the **World of Motion logo**—a small sphere semi-enclosed by what look like three backward, elongated letters "C," all of which are enclosed in concentric circles—in various places throughout the attraction. The first one you encounter is the watermark above the Chevrolet logo on the left-hand side of the large blue structure that forms a gigantic letter "T" at the front of the attraction. You'll also see it at the top of the Standby line sign, and on the sides of the pavilion's trash bins.

Enter the queue and you're in a Chevrolet Design Center complete with concept cars, then it's on to the studio where riders can design their own cars based on Capability, Responsiveness, Efficiency, and Power. But the real fun begins when you board a test car and take "your" design for a spin on the Sim Track. And this is where a bit of hidden magic can be found.

Although the Imagineers didn't originally intend it to be a tribute to World of Motion, the **cityscape model** on your left once you round the corner after the lightning strike in the Extreme Weather portion of the testing sequence has become an accepted nod toward the CenterCore city of the future in World of Motion's final scene.

Like many "hidden" details, this one will require eagle eyes, but if you look carefully at the wheels on the wall graphic as your vehicle is scanned during the Drive System Analysis section of the ride, right after the aerodynamics scan, you should be able to make out the words **WED Performance**, honoring Walt Disney (whose middle name, you'll recall, was Elias) and WED Enterprises, which would later become Walt Disney Imagineering.

As you reach the first bend after the glowing pine trees, look to your right. You'll see what looks like a School Crossing sign with **two people crossing a road holding an artist's palette**. They are based on the profiles of two engineers who worked on the attraction.

Just after your OnStar guide says, "Okay, the Responsiveness data is now being synchronized," watch for a **three-tiered road sign** on the left-hand side of the track that points to Motion Lane, General Motorway, and Bowtie Boulevard, all nods to the experience and the attraction's sponsors.

Shortly after your OnStar guide says, "Automated driving technology verified and active," watch for a sign on the right-hand side of the track with a character that looks like a squirrel but is actually a **beaver**. It is a reference to Big Beaver Road in Troy, Michigan, a General Motors branch location and the workplace of many of the employees who helped design the attraction.

Immediately after the beaver sign, look to your left. You'll see a sign in the shape of Superman's logo, with a convoluted arrow and text that reads, **Turn Right To Go Left**. It isn't an instruction sign for the ride you're currently on, it's a cute nod to the movie *Cars*, when Lightning McQueen learns a hard lesson about turning right to go left, a technique known by thrill-seeking race car enthusiasts as "drifting."

If you can keep your wits about you, watch for the round sign on a pole to your right, immediately after you crash through the doors and find yourself outside. The **number 82** on the sign pays homage to 1982, the year EPCOT opened.

Remember the **CenterCore city** you saw inside? You'll also see its image on the second sign you whiz past, on your left, once your car hits the outdoor section of track.

And finally, the third sign, also on your left, reads, **FN2BFRE**. Try to work out what it means, then check to see if you're correct in the Appendix: Solutions to Hints, Solution 4.

Imagine That!

Disney Legend Ron Logan was a member of the team that created EPCOT. He recalls hosting a media preview while the park was under construction, taking journalists through what was then mostly scrubland: "We got a big flatbed truck and put a band on it, which we called the Hardhat Orchestra, who played as we took the media to the place where Spaceship Earth was going to go. All the pavilions were marked with balloons. When my driver arrived to pick me up I noticed he had all these flea collars around his ankles. When I asked him what they were for he just said, 'You'll find out.' The whole area was covered in mud, with mosquitoes and snakes everywhere. We had to carry machetes when we worked in there. It was like a jungle!"

World Nature

World Nature celebrates the balance between human interaction and the preservation of nature's diversity. It's the "right-brain" counterpart to World Discovery's technological focus.

The Land

The Land pavilion draws guests in with sweeping mosaics along both sides of the walkway. The artist designed the mosaics as representations of the **layers of the earth**, exposed after a volcanic eruption.

The mural running along each side of the walkway to the entry represents **sixty different natural materials**, including gold, granite, and pumice.

Also notice the walkway as you make your way up to the pavilion's door. The pigmented pavement is an extension of the theme—in this case, of the creation of land—and is meant to represent **lava** flowing from a volcano. The red pavement is hot lava; the black is cooled lava.

Not only does the building's design represent a volcano, the **upward pitch of the walkway** leading to the front doors makes it feel like you're mountain climbing, especially after a long, hot day when your legs are tired. It's a noticeable challenge!

Inside, the theme you see ahead of you is whimsical, with **hot air balloons representing the four seasons**, and although it is huge, another reference to the seasons generally goes unnoticed. As you're standing on the second floor, look over the balcony and notice how Sunshine Seasons food court's dining rooms have been sectioned into four separate areas (one of them is off to your extreme right). Now head down to the first floor and look at the **tabletops** in each section. They're themed to winter (snowflakes), spring (flowers), summer (suns), and fall (autumn leaves).

Living with the Land

In keeping with Walt's vision for his city of tomorrow, **quotations** adorning the wall along the queue for the Living with the Land ride offer eloquent insights into humankind's relationship with the environment. As profound as they are, each quotation comes from the unique perspective of the children who wrote them. These quotations come from children around the world, some as young as five years old!

During your boat ride, note the **house number** on the mailbox as you pass through the farmhouse scene on the ride. It's number 82, a subtle nod to 1982, the year EPCOT opened.

Fascinating Fact

Plants in the Living with the Land greenhouses are grown using a soil-free technique called hydroponics (*hydro* meaning "water" and *ponic* meaning "labor"). It seems like a high-tech method, but it has been around for centuries. Ancient hieroglyphs show the Egyptians grew plants in water; the Aztecs and fourth-century Chinese created floating gardens; the Hanging Gardens of Babylon used hydroponics; World War II troops stationed in the Pacific without usable soil were fed partially through hydroponic systems; and later, even NASA got in on the act.

If you dine at Sunshine Seasons food court, choose one of the single-serving side dishes that rest on a lettuce leaf and you're guaranteed to be dining on lettuce grown in the Living with the Land attraction.

Soarin' Around the World

The pavilion's other big attraction, Soarin' Around the World, was originally built as Soarin' over California at Disney's California Adventure park in Anaheim in 2001, then opened at Epcot on May 5, 2005. It underwent a major renovation and reopened as Soarin' Around the World on June 17, 2016, taking riders to far-flung icons across the globe.

Pay attention to the **metal walls** as you walk through the queue. The screen for Soarin' is made of the same material.

Although your entire flight path has changed from soaring over California to soaring over the world, some things remain the same. Well, mostly the same, anyway. The safety narration is exactly as it was, but the background your chief flight attendant, Patrick, stands in front of before and after he enters the flight room used to have the **Soarin' logo** on it. Now it's gone.

When Patrick tells you to store cameras, purses, and hats during the safety spiel, notice the two guests sitting at the end of the row, to the right of the man wearing "these little beauties" (to your left as you view the scene). They're dressed as **old-time aviators**.

The smaller aviator, whose seat belt goes through the center strap, is dressed for the part too. His shirt has a **graphic of Grumpy** on it, and there is a **Mickey graphic** on his shorts. In the original version of the safety spiel, his shirt also featured the words "Disneyland" and "Grumpy." They are now obscured with a black stripe.

Where you sit when riding Soarin' Around the World does matter. Some elements are best seen from the bottom row, some from the middle, and some from the top, and there are differences depending on whether you're on the right, in the center, or on the left vehicle. If you find yourself on the far end of the row on the left-hand or right-hand vehicles, you're in for a treat. Sort of. Taller images, such as the Matterhorn and the Eiffel Tower, will bend dramatically toward the center of the screen. Oops!

Fascinating Fact

Your flight path in the preshow starts in Greenland and ends in Brazil, progressing by way of France, Switzerland, Germany, Egypt, India, China, Utah, Florida, Tanzania, Australia, and Fiji, but that isn't the route you take in the film. Instead, your journey proceeds from the Matterhorn in Switzerland, then on to the Ice Fjords in Greenland, Australia's Sydney Harbour, Neuschwanstein in Germany, Tanzania's Mount Kilimanjaro, the Great Wall of China, Egypt's Great Pyramids, the Taj Mahal in India, Utah's Monument Valley, the Lau Islands of Fiji, Iguazu Falls in Brazil, France's Eiffel Tower, and, finally, EPCOT in Florida. Why are the flight paths different? The preshow path is linear, even though you would have to circle the globe twice. The film's path is a whirlwind of random backtracking. Geeky detail? You would travel 44,619 miles in total, progressing easterly, taking the preshow route, and 72,529 miles taking the route in the film, as you hop all over the map.

Some of the locations you'll visit while hang gliding over the world were chosen not only because they're icons but also for their connection to Walt Disney World or Disneyland. Florida's EPCOT scene obviously honors the theme park, while France and China are both pavilions in the park. But there is a special significance to the **Great Wall of China scene** too. The non-CGI section of the wall was shot along China's northern border, in the same place as the Great Wall scene in the China pavilion's original show, *Wonders of China Circle-Vision 360°*.

Although they were not chosen specifically for their connection to Disney movies, **honorable mentions** go to India's Taj Mahal and the Disney film *Aladdin*; *Finding Nemo*'s adventures in Australia's Great Barrier Reef and Sydney Harbour; and Egypt's Great Pyramid connection to the Steven Spielberg movie *Raiders of the Lost Ark* and the Hollywood Studios attraction *Indiana Jones Epic Stunt Spectacular!*

Switzerland's majestic Matterhorn is a well-known geographic location, but Soarin' Around the World's scene also refers to the Matterhorn Bobsleds attraction in Disneyland. And, just like that attraction, the mountains here have their own **abominable snowman**. Immediately after you pass over the Matterhorn's summit and begin your downward swoop, look to the right at the mountain below. You'll see a cartoony version of a yeti's face, shoulders, and arms drawn in the snow, spanning the entire mountainside. Look quickly, before the fog rolls in! You'll see this best from the center middle or top rows.

The palace you soar over in Germany is the world-famous **Neuschwanstein Castle** in Bavaria, built in 1869. It served as Walt Disney's inspiration for Sleeping Beauty Castle, which opened at Disneyland in 1955. Fifty years later it earned its place in Soarin' Around the World because of that connection.

Fascinating Fact

Elephants may not be the first animal you think of when you hear the words "Mount Kilimanjaro," but nearly one-third of Tanzania is protected land, giving rise to national parks and game reserves that are home to large mammals, including lions, wildebeests, hippos, zebras, and elephants. Conflicts with humans create a tenuous situation, but scenes like the one in Soarin' are still possible, helped greatly by Tanzania's ever-growing eco-tourism industry.

Considering you're touring the savannah above a herd of elephants, with Mount Kilimanjaro in the background, it would be difficult not to notice you're taking a **Kilimanjaro safari** of sorts, as you do in Disney's Animal Kingdom.

When you pass over the Great Wall of China's beacon tower with a small building on it, notice the tiny statuettes at the end of each corner of the building's roof. That's evil **King Min**, being held captive by helpful animals. You'll see them better when you visit EPCOT's China pavilion and learn more about them in that section of this chapter.

As you soar over the sand dunes heading for Egypt's pyramids, watch for **three riders on horseback** thundering along a trail at the bottom of the screen. They recall the Anza-Borrego Desert State Park scene in Soarin' over California. The riders are best seen from the bottom rows.

The stunning vistas of **Monument Valley, Utah**, must have been daunting to early pioneers who crossed the plateau, but if you've ridden Big Thunder Mountain Railroad in Magic Kingdom, you've traveled in relative comfort as your train whizzed through landscape inspired by this natural wonder of the American west.

The second **rainbow-colored hot air balloon** you see in the Monument Valley sequence briefly intersects with two hot air balloons behind it to form the well-known outline of Mickey Mouse's head, as do two enormous fireworks behind Spaceship Earth in the EPCOT finale.

Fascinating Fact

How was Soarin' Around the World's magnificent footage shot? High-tech drones would be the obvious answer, but it was really shot using technology whose concepts were sketched out by Leonardo da Vinci in 1483. An ultra-high-resolution digital camera was strapped to a landing skid or dangled below the cockpit by a cable, giving Soarin's visuals the illusion of flight thanks to the humble helicopter.

The Seas with Nemo & Friends

As you walk through the queue toward your "clamobile," notice the **beach signs** on the tall white signpost. If you look carefully at the advertisement for Daily Diving Departures, you will notice they are provided by Nautical Exploration and Marine Observation, or NEMO.

The **Tanks a Lot Dive Shop** is the place to rent diving equipment while you're visiting Coral Caves Beach, and its street address holds a special meaning. It is a reference to Walt Disney Imagineering's address, 1401 Flower Street in Glendale, California.

A subtle tribute to the pavilion's original incarnation as the Living Seas can be found on the wall to the right as you head toward the exit doors in the gift shop. A small brass **Civil Engineering Achievement of Merit plaque**, given to the pavilion by the American Society of Civil Engineers, remembers the work that went into creating the pavilion, including advances such as the use of special cement that was resistant to chlorides in seawater; the aquarium's ability to contain 5.7 million gallons of water; and the techniques engineers used to minimize settlement. It was awarded in 1987, after the Living Seas' opening in 1986.

Imagination!

As you make your way toward World Showcase, you'll find the last of the World Nature pavilions, Imagination! This pavilion is all about whimsy and the strange and wonderful places our imagination can take us with "just one spark."

Never satisfied with the obvious when a bit of ingenuity could be employed, the Imagineers have taken a twist on the waterfall concept. Look at the **water feature** as you walk toward the pavilion. The water isn't flowing downward; it's shooting upward, a mental nudge to viewers to allow their creativity to run wild.

Journey Into Imagination with Figment

Check out the names on the doors as you walk through the Imagination Institute. **Dean Finder** is a reference to Dreamfinder, the original host of the Imagination pavilion. **Professor Wayne Szalinski** is from the movie *Honey, I Shrunk the Kids*, which had a spin-off attraction, Honey, I Shrunk the Audience, at the Imagination pavilion from 1994 to 2010. **Professor Philip Brainard** is from the movies *The Absent-Minded Professor* and its retelling, *Flubber*. Here it refers specifically to *Flubber*, as evidenced by the picture of Robin Williams as Professor Brainard, located in the institute's lobby. **Dean Higgins** is from the series of movies that were set in Medfield College, as is **Dr. Nigel Channing**, played by the actor Eric Idle of *Monty Python's Flying Circus* fame.

Stop for a moment or two when you reach Dr. Channing's office. His **harried secretary** is struggling to keep up with Dr. Channing's phone calls, with hilarious results!

You'll hear several **humorous announcements** over the intercom as you make your way to the attraction's boarding area. Listen for the comment, "Attention, Dexter Riley. Please bring your tennis shoes to the Smell Lab." Dexter Riley is from the 1969 Walt Disney Company movie *The Computer Wore Tennis Shoes*. It seems Dexter heard the announcement. When you reach the Smell Lab you'll see his **tennis shoes** sitting outside the door.

You'll also see Dexter's **Medfield College letterman jacket** in the Smell Lab. It is a reference to several Walt Disney Company movies in which Medfield College features, including *The Computer Wore Tennis Shoes*, *The Absent-Minded Professor*, and *Flubber*.

Notice the artwork in Figment's house. Two portraits are the dragon versions of the famous **Blue Boy** and **Pink Girl** paintings.

The **cartoon-style images** in the final reveal at the end of the ride are a nod to the pavilion's former attraction, Journey into Imagination, with beloved characters Figment and Dreamfinder.

World Showcase

The layout of the international pavilions that make up this half of the park is well established. The original concept placed the U.S.A. pavilion at the front of World Showcase, with near-neighbors Mexico and Canada bordering on either side. Guests would walk through an archway into World Showcase, with the main attraction, the American Adventure, housed in a building situated above the archway. Ultimately it was decided America should "play host to the World," and the pavilion was centered at the back. Mexico and Canada remain in their original positions.

A curiosity as you walk toward Mexico from Showcase Plaza again highlights the attention to detail Disney Imagineers bring to their work. Once you pass the shop in Showcase Plaza, begin looking toward the Morocco pavilion. Does something look slightly out of place? What appears to be a Moroccan building far off in the distance is actually the top of the **Tower of Terror** at Disney's Hollywood Studios. When the Imagineers realized you could see the tower from EPCOT, they included stylized minarets on the roof to help the tower blend more harmoniously with the Moroccan theme.

Mexico

As authentic as it looks at first glance, the Mexico pavilion's pyramid actually represents three distinct cultures. The pyramid architecture is **Mayan**, with one temple built at the top rather than two, as would be seen on an Aztec pyramid. The decor is **Aztec**, with brightly colored murals and menacing heads guarding the entry. Many of the design elements throughout are representative of **Toltec** art. The pyramid itself is a representation of an **Aztec temple of Quetzalcoatl**. Each serpent head symbolizes Quetzalcoatl, son of the Creator God.

Why is it always **twilight inside Mexico's Plaza de los Amigos**, which is based on the town of Taxco? Because twilight is the time friends and family—relationships central to Mexican culture—gather in the plaza for socializing.

Once you enter the pavilion, you can't miss the enormous **round stone tablet** in the middle of the lobby area that leads to the Plaza de los Amigos, but what's so important about it that it deserves such a prominent placement? It's a replica of an **Aztec calendar**, the original of which can be found in the National Museum of Anthropology in Mexico City.

Gran Fiesta Tour Starring the Three Caballeros

Before you enter the queue for the attraction, pause for a few minutes and watch the volcano scene just across the River of Time. Every now and then **the volcano erupts**.

That **googly-eyed head** you pass when you enter the first scene after the tunnel is a replica of an actual stone carving in the National Museum of Anthropology in Mexico City.

Apparently, Donald has passed this way before. During the Day of the Dead celebration you'll see children whacking a **Donald-shaped piñata**.

Fascinating Fact

If you think the Three Caballeros get around quite a bit in the attraction, that's nothing compared to where these distinctive Audio-Animatronics have really been. They began their careers in 1969 as part of a set piece that previewed Walt Disney World to Orlando dignitaries, then moved on to star in Magic Kingdom's opening-day attraction Mickey Mouse Revue, before making their international debut with the rest of the Revue cast in Tokyo Disneyland's version of the show, this time in Japanese. The trio returned to Orlando and now play the central roles in Gran Fiesta Tour.

Norway

The Norway pavilion underwent a complete transformation in 2016, when its former attraction, Maelstrom, was removed to make way for movie-based Frozen Ever After, featuring characters from the animated film *Frozen*. While not strictly Norwegian, the fictional kingdom of Arendelle does have a lot of snow.

Disney has a penchant for hiding names around its parks, and a happy tie-up occurs here. While it is true that there is a municipality in Norway called Arendal, of which Arendelle in the movie *Frozen* is a variation, there is also an important name in Walt Disney's history that acts as a reference point for the fictional village. Walt's great-grandfather was none other than **Arundel Elias Disney**.

If you listen carefully in the Norway pavilion, you'll hear the cries of **birds in distress**. But don't worry, they're not real. It's a noninvasive means of avian control, and these recorded cries keep your caramel corn or soft pretzel safe from abduction.

If you think the Royal Sommerhus must surely be based on a real building, you'd be correct. It takes its inspiration from **Detlistua (Detli House)**, an 1817 farmhouse now located in the open-air Sverresborg Trøndelag Folk Museum in Trondheim, and that fair town in real life is so happy about it they even mention EPCOT's replica building on their tourism website.

Stand near the large boulders across the pathway from the entry into the Sommerhus queue for Anna and Elsa's meet-and-greet and turn to your right. The view you get of the **distant stone hill** juxtaposed against the Sommerhus replicates the view you would have standing in front of Detli House, with the ruins of Norway's King Sverre Sigurdsson's twelfth-century castle, Sverresborg, in the background. Notice how the mountain's lower rock seems as if it occurred naturally, while the stones piled on top of it appear to have been assembled by hand. The lower rock represents the hill while the rocks piled on top of it are the castle ruins.

Inside, the Royal Sommerhus features "artifacts" from Anna and Elsa's childhood, but you'll also find several **rune stones** in the courtyard with carvings that act as a nod toward those found in the former Maelstrom attraction.

The **paintings of Anna, Elsa, and Olaf**, located in the first room you reach when you enter the Sommerhus, set the time frame. You've arrived during the period when the girls' parents have passed and the summer residence now belongs to Anna and Elsa.

Fascinating Fact

What is the style of painting that gives the royal summer house such a unique look? It's called rosemåling, and it was a widespread decorative motif throughout Norway beginning in the mid-1700s. Careers as a rosemåler were originally the purview of the less affluent, and as such it was a folk art of sorts, often commissioned by wealthy homeowners and local churches. In time, the technique was brought to America by immigrants. It fell out of favor in the mid-1800s but was revived by Norwegian Americans in the mid-1900s and is still seen on bowls, plates, and linens today.

It is pretty clear Anna and Elsa summered in the Royal Sommerhus. Their **images as young girls** are literally carved into the woodwork and woven into a tapestry. Note the golden crocus, symbol of Arendelle, painted above each of the girls' carved likenesses as you walk from the first room into the second. That floral motif is used throughout the royal residence. You'll also see a snowflake painted above Elsa's carving and a sunflower painted above Anna's.

Also watch for Anna and Elsa in a **painting with their parents** and in **ragdoll form** at the turn in the stairway that leads to the second floor as you wind your way through the queue.

Imagine That!

Re-created lands, such as Africa and Asia at Disney's Animal Kingdom, often include details taken directly from their real-life counterparts, and that is also true of fictitious lands based on less specific, real-life locations, such as the "village" of Arendelle in the Norway pavilion. Imagineer Laura Neiderheiser explains: "You see the architecture that we saw on our trip to Trondheim reflected in the Royal Sommerhus, along with the merchandise shop to its right. The real-life Norwegian royal family has a summer cabin much like this one, so we were able to reflect that aspect of things with our home for Anna and Elsa."

Authenticity is key when creating a location or attraction that is based on real life, and that is certainly a feature here. **Wood-carvers** who worked on the original Maelstrom attraction returned to bring authenticity to the carvings in and around the Royal Sommerhus, and not all of the furnishings are replicas.

It is impossible to miss the wooden board painted with a mythical **three-headed troll and a rock with big eyes** as you make a turn in the queue, but unless you know who the popular characters were in the Norway pavilion's previous ride, Maelstrom, you may not know this is a charming homage to beloved scenes in which the trolls and the rock played starring roles.

Frozen Ever After

Arendelle is throwing a **Summer Snow Day Celebration** commemorating the day Anna risked her life to save her sister, Elsa, from execution by the evil Prince Hans, and you're invited to the festivities. That's the premise, presented beautifully through scenes *Frozen* fans already know, plus several that are new.

Waits can be long for this attraction, but at some point during your visit it's worth taking the time to walk through the Standby queue. The big benefit in doing so is that the Imagineers have created Oaken's Tokens, which is only experienced by those using Standby. In it you'll find lots of humorous details, the highlight of which is Oaken himself, inside his sauna. Watch the **steamed-up window** where he occasionally draws fun little pictures in the condensation.

Before you enter the indoor portion of the queue, or as you're wandering around outside taking in the scenery, look up at the **statue on a small shelf** on the front of the orange Bryggestredet Kjølelager "cold storage" building to the left of the queue. It sure does look like Kristoff, and the reindeer holding up the shelf with its antlers is a dignified version of Sven.

Once you reach the indoor portion of the queue, immediately watch for the sign overhead and to your left, which reads, **Ice Master & Deliverer of Arendelle**. It refers to the scene in *Frozen* in which Anna gifts Kristoff with a new sleigh, telling him Elsa has officially named him the Ice Master and Deliverer.

Also watch for **humorous advertisements** on the notice board, along with the *Southern Isles Gazette* newspaper clipping that relays the story of a freak weather phenomenon affecting only one person—Prince Hans Westergaard of the Southern Isles. It's a direct reference to the scene in the eight-minute Disney short film *Frozen Fever*, in which Elsa launches a massive long-distance snowball that lands directly on the prince, with rather smelly results compliments of the manure cart into which he topples.

While you're browsing the news clip, take note of the top right corner. It has been torn from volume XXI, number 1122, page 6 of the *Gazette*. The number 1122 is **November 22**, the 2019 release date for the Disney movie *Frozen II*.

Oaken is a true entrepreneur. The shop you walk through doesn't look like his store in the movie, and it's obviously not the cart he trades from in *Frozen Fever*. Instead, it's the **third business** in his burgeoning empire.

Check out the shelves and look up to the rafters as you make your way through Oaken's Tokens. You'll see authentic carvings of trolls, including the fan-favorite **three-headed**

troll that harkens back to the attraction's original incarnation as Maelstrom.

You'll even see a white **polar bear** on the rafter, standing on its hind legs, just as a full-sized version did in the former attraction.

Fascinating Fact

The red building you see as you walk through the queue is the Golden Crocus, and it's appropriate and expected here because the crocus is the symbol for Arendelle in the movie *Frozen*. But there is a deeper meaning too. Crocuses are one of the few flowers that bloom during the transition from winter to spring, and they're capable of surviving snowfalls as well as sunny days, making them wonderful metaphors for Anna and Elsa.

While you're waiting to board your Viking boat in the loading area, turn around and look for a wooden chalkboard with information about the current weather. While the barometric pressure and temperature are both doing what your boat is about to do (dropping!), the real gem here is the warning. Underneath the Weather Conditions and Tidal Status labels is a reference to the former attraction. Apparently there has been a **Maelstrom Sighting in the Southeast Bay of Arendelle**.

What is that lovely music you hear as you ascend the lift hill? If you're like many *Frozen* fans you'll know it right away. If *Frozen* isn't on your daily playlist, it's "**The Great Thaw (Vuelie Reprise)**" from the defining moment in the movie, when Elsa realizes her love for her sister can bring Anna and Arendelle back to life after they've been frozen by Elsa's icy powers. It's also a defining moment in the attraction, letting you know something momentous is about to happen, and it has to do with Elsa having fully accepted the gifts and challenges of her abilities.

If you time it right and take a photo (no flash, please!) just as you approach Olaf and right after he looks back at Sven in the first scene, you'll get the most adorable **photobomb** ever. (Miss it? It's Sven, looking directly at you in the dim distance, with his eyes as wide as saucers.)

The first time you meet Anna and Elsa in Frozen Ever After, they're wearing **clothes from the original movie**. When they say their final goodbye, they're dressed in the gowns they wore in *Frozen Fever*.

The music and the visuals follow you as Elsa uses her **ice magic** to gently push your boat backward, away from her balcony, emphasizing the message that the story you're experiencing isn't during the time frame of the movie *Frozen*, but post-movie, when Elsa has embraced her power in a positive way. The "Let It Go" verse chosen for this scene, with the line "I'm free," makes that clear.

That sentiment is further advanced as your boat travels backward into the wintery outdoors, where the fierce snowman **Marshmallow** and his adorable snowgie friends (the snow babies that appear each time Elsa sneezes in the *Frozen Fever* short) are waiting. Marshmallow has embraced his gentler side, and as a tiny glimmer of his monstrous nature takes over and he casts you over the falls, he shouts the happy reminder to "let it go," or announces his new mood by shouting, "I'm free!"

Wait…what's up with the **puffins**? Somehow three of them have migrated from the polar bear scene in Maelstrom to the castle scene you've just plunged into, immediately after your boat goes over the falls. Look for them on your right-hand side—if you can momentarily ignore the ice-crystal fireworks going off above the castle.

China

The China pavilion's Temple of Heaven, a true half-scale representation of the Beijing Temple, is filled with symbolism. The real Temple of Heaven in China is a complex, and the Hall of Prayer for Good Harvest is the central, circular building.

Built as a place of prayer for a successful harvest, each element has meaning, with a surprising secret in the heart of the temple.

It's easy to overlook the writing you see all around World Showcase when it's in a foreign language. But don't. Some interesting things are being expressed. Notice the writing on the Zhao Yang Men, **Gate of the Golden Sun**, at the entry to the pavilion. It's Mandarin for "Going toward the sun gate," but its meaning is more than simply moving toward the sun. It really means something akin to "moving into daylight and basking in the beauty of the sun."

Look at the floor as you walk through the temple's front doors. The **concentric circles** move inward in multiples of three (three symbolizing living or giving life, and also the trinity of heaven, earth, and man in Chinese numerology) until they reach the center circle. Stand with your feet directly over the circle and say something, anything. The building is acoustically perfect, causing your voice to vibrate directly back into your ears. Step outside the circle, even just one step, and speak again. Notice the difference? You can whisper as you stand over the circle and still have the effect of hearing your voice as it bounces back to you. Notice how it sounds slightly different from the way you hear it inside your head.

Looking progressively upward, the temple's **four columns** represent the four seasons, the **twelve pillars** are representative of the twelve months of the Chinese year, and the **twelve outer pillars** are the twelve-hour division of day and of night. Combine the two sets of pillars and you have a representation of **one solar term**.

As you stand under the domed roof look for key symbols in the elaborate design. **Pairings of nine** in Chinese cosmology represent the heart, heaven, and the eight directions plus the center. **Earth** is represented by squares, while **heaven** is represented by round elements. The building's **three stories** signify heaven, earth, and humans. **Blue** indicates heaven, **yellow** indicates earth, and **green** signifies mortality and the mortal world.

Two recurring themes are the **phoenix and the dragon**, representing the empress and the emperor, respectively. Notice some dragons have only four fingers. They represent masculinity in general; in a spiritual context, such as here in the temple, they are the generators of wind and rain, aptly placed in a temple of prayer for abundant crops. Only the five-fingered dragon represents the emperor.

Fascinating Fact

Dragons can be found in male and female form, though only male dragons are depicted in EPCOT's China pavilion. How are female dragons identified? They have fans on their tails instead of clubs, the spikes on their manes are rounded on the ends, their snouts are straight, and their horns are thicker at the base than at the tips. Next time you encounter a dragon you'll know whether you're facing a male or a female, but rest assured, unlike their Japanese cousins, Chinese dragons are benevolent…unless you anger them!

As you tour the pavilion you'll notice more writing on some of the columns outside the shops and homes. During festivals or other special occasions, shop and home owners in China adorn their columns with **quotes from poets** or with **wishes for health or prosperity**. When writing is seen on temple columns, it indicates a prayer. The owner of the first shop you reach on the right-hand side is covering all the bases. The writing on the column on the left is a request for greater income year by year and the writing on the column on the right is a wish for good luck.

At the end of each ornate upward-tilting roofline, you will see a small character on the back of a chicken (yes, it's a chicken!). That's evil **King Min of the state of Qi**, ruler of China, who was hung from his ancestral temple's rooftop in 284 B.C.E. at the command of the prime minister.

Superstition dictates that a representation of King Min sitting on the roof will protect that building from evil spirits. As added insurance, he is guarded by helpful animals that line up behind him keeping watch. The number of animals guarding King Min indicates the status of that particular building.

Germany

As you stroll from pavilion to pavilion, each one captures your imagination in a different way. Many visitors feel Germany in particular has something just a bit special about it. The theme here feels familiar and homey, perhaps due to all those Brothers Grimm fairy tales we heard as children, many of which have their roots in Germanic folk stories.

If you've ever visited Germany and recall that there are four **Habsburg princes** on the façade of the Kaufhaus in Freiburg (on which EPCOT's Das Kaufhaus is based), you'd be correct. Why are there only three here? Because there wasn't room to place all four of them on the ledge and still maintain the illusion of size through forced perspective, so only Philip I, Charles V, and Ferdinand I made the final cut. Maximilian I is the missing prince.

A cute bit of hidden magic here isn't hidden all the time. In fact, it pops out of the small doors just above the shelf over the clock face at the center of Biergarten Restaurant's façade. The **golden rooster** that makes a periodic appearance (on or near every half hour; it isn't always punctual) mimics the golden rooster above the Rathaus-Glockenspiel in Munich, Germany. The glockenspiel below the Biergarten's clock works too. Timing, once again, can be flexible.

Fascinating Fact

Munich's Rathaus-Glockenspiel in Marienplatz is world-famous, but it's also in keeping with the traditional role of a glockenspiel in any German town, acting as a storyteller to amuse and inspire the citizens. Munich's glockenspiel tells two stories. The first recounts the lavish 1568 wedding of Wilhelm V, duke of Bavaria, to the lovely Renate of Lorraine, in a two-week celebration that included a joust. That sporting event also plays out in the glockenspiel, with the Bavarian knight triumphing over the knight from Lorraine every time. When the story ends, visitors can make the five-minute walk to Munich's famous Hofbräuhaus, founded by Duke Wilhelm. The second story remembers the end of a plague in Munich, after which the town's coopers enticed citizens back outside with their boot-slapping *Schäfflertanz* (barrel maker's dance), which is still reenacted in Marienplatz once every seven years.

The painting on the wall opposite the Sommerfest quick-service dining location is designed to look like a tapestry featuring the famous **Rothenburg ob der Tauber**, considered one of Germany's most romantically styled villages. In reality, the painting covers what would have been the entry to a never-built Rhine River cruise attraction intended for the pavilion.

Italy

Much of the Italy pavilion is based on the timeless city of Venice, with a nearly exact replica of **Saint Mark's Square**, but in mirror image. Why is the square backward? Because the blueprints Disney was using were taken from a photograph that was transposed when it was developed.

Here you'll find a hidden gem that has the kind of creepy backstory I just love. Walk to the end of the pink Doge's Palace and turn left. See that **face on the wall** with its mouth wide open? It isn't just a decorative element. Faces like this one were akin to mail slots, through which the good townspeople were encouraged to slip notes reporting the transgressions of their neighbors. The catch was, you had to sign the paper so everyone knew who was doing the snitching. If you didn't sign it, your complaint was considered nothing but gossip.

The Doge's Palace is beautiful indeed, but the palace in Venice also has a darker side. Deep inside the palace was **a prison and torture chamber**, where enemies of the state endured interrogation. The famous lover Casanova was incarcerated there until his escape to Paris in 1756.

With that in mind, notice the bridge on the second story at the back of the Doge's Palace. It represents the infamous **Bridge of Sighs** that convicts would have crossed on their way to the palace's prison. Those who entered had little hope for survival, hence the bridge's sorrowful name.

The colorful donkey cart representing Sicily and Naples tends to move around, but when you see it you'll know it.

Less obvious are the small heads on the cart's wheels and panels. These are *teste di Moro*, or Moor's heads, a popular Sicilian decorative icon.

Fascinating Fact

Like all good folklore, the Moor's head story has more than one version. In the first telling, a Moor saw and fell in love with a young girl tending plants on her balcony, and the girl returned his affections. Secretly he was married with children, and when the time for him to return home arrived, the girl chopped off his head and used it as a planter for basil, which grew succulent with watering from her tears. Her envious neighbors then wanted pots just like hers in which to plant their own basil. In a second, more plausible story, a Sicilian nobleman's daughter and a young Moor fell in love, but their union was considered shameful and they were beheaded. That's the reason *teste di Moro* are generally found in pairs.

The drinking fountain at the far-right side of the Italy pavilion as you walk toward the American Adventure features a pretty tile-work slogan. What does *Alla Salute* mean? "To your health!"

The American Adventure

Welcome, one and all, to the United States of America! Situated as the central pavilion in World Showcase, the American Adventure plays host to all the countries surrounding her, spreading her architectural arms wide in a gesture of hospitality. The spaciousness afforded to the pavilion and inclusion of the America Gardens Theater serve to highlight Walt Disney's pride in his country and his desire to share her bounty with all nations.

The **American eagle** on top of the attraction's sign plays a key role in the nation's psyche. Here, he's looking to the left, toward the olive branch grasped in his claw, widely considered an indication that the nation is at peace. Before you enter the rotunda notice the direction the eagle above the door is facing. While he is still facing the olive branch, his head is now pointing to the right.

Fascinating Fact

The original left-facing eagle is "militarily incorrect." This head placement changed in 1945 under President Harry Truman's administration, inspired by President Roosevelt's petition to correct a discrepancy between the number of stars on the flag of the commander in chief and the number of stars generals or fleet admirals in World War II were given. When the military status of five-star was added, President Roosevelt felt the four stars on the commander in chief flag were inadequate. It was during this transition that heraldic expert Arthur E. DuBois noticed the eagle's incorrect head placement, and since 1949 the eagle faces right, a direction customarily indicating honor, regardless of the nation being at war or at peace.

While you're waiting in the rotunda for Voices of Liberty to sing, or to be escorted upstairs for the main show, browse the paintings that line the wall, particularly the **World War II B-17 Bomber**. There's a fascinating bit of magic hidden here. Stand parallel to the painting and walk its length, looking at the front of the bomber as you go. Notice how it seems to follow you? Walk back and forth a few times to give your eyes time to adjust to the perspective. No matter which side you start from, the bomber will turn, always pointing in your direction.

Mickey Mouse is hiding in the *Election Day* painting to the right of the *B-17 Bomber* painting, and while you'd think his famous tri-circle head would be formed by some of the men's boater hats, he's much more subtle than that. See the woman in the extreme foreground, at the bottom middle of the painting? Three of the four best-defined **red roses** in her hat form Mickey's well-known silhouette.

As you are watching the American Adventure show, take note of Mr. Brady, the photographer in the Americans Divided scene. He is meant to be **Mathew Brady**, famed Civil War photographer.

Fascinating Fact

As impassioned as Chief Joseph's speech is in the American Adventure, the real-life Chief Joseph's concession to General Nelson Miles as he surrendered on October 5, 1877, was far more graphic and heartrending. As the Nez Perce retreated in an attempt to reach Canada, the tribe fought for three long months against US troops who were taking over native lands and resources in a push through Oregon. During that time, Chief Joseph saw the deaths of many chiefs, warriors, elders, women, and children, and several tribe members fled into the mountains with their children to avoid being killed. Provisions were nearly non-existent. In the midst of that horrendous reality, he maintained his dignity and composure. Although EPCOT's version of his desperate pleas takes three of its seven lines from two separate speeches given by Chief Joseph, in reality he did famously surrender to General Miles by saying, "From where the sun now stands, I will fight no more, forever."

The **gas station scene** is beautifully evocative of the era, and for a good reason. It is based heavily on a photograph taken by renowned photographer Dorothea Lange in 1936.

Lange specialized in photographing migrant and homeless people during the Great Depression, and may be most famous for her portrait *Migrant Mother*.

Most of the voices you hear in Disney attractions are provided by professional actors and voice actors, but Imagineers occasionally step in to get the job done. Joe Rohde left a voice "signature" in the American Adventure using a Scottish accent that requires a bit of getting used to. He voices **Alexander Graham Bell**, and if you're familiar with Joe's natural voice you can certainly hear it when Bell reminds Mark Twain of the telephone's contribution to American progress.

Imagine That!

Other voices you hear during the American Adventure might have a vague ring of familiarity. Betty Jean Ward voices Rosie the Riveter, but she also voiced Sarah, the mother in Carousel of Progress; singing opossums and rabbits in Splash Mountain; and the safety and unloading spiels and other narration for several attractions, including Spaceship Earth, it's a small world, Peter Pan's Flight, and Tomorrowland Transit Authority PeopleMover. She even "voiced" a blaster in Buzz Lightyear's Space Ranger Spin.

Dal McKennon provides the voice for Benjamin Franklin, and he also voiced characters in the Disney movies *Bedknobs and Broomsticks*, *Lady and the Tramp*, *One Hundred and One Dalmatians*, *Sleeping Beauty*, and *Mary Poppins*. But you probably know him best as the voice-over in Big Thunder Mountain Railroad. During the boarding spiel Dal utters the immortal line, "This here's the wildest ride in the wilderness!" Finally, who is the most obvious person to voice Will Rogers, given that Will himself passed away in 1935? Why, his son, Will Rogers Jr., of course! And that's exactly who brought the character to life in the American Adventure.

Japan

Arriving in Japan, the main building sets a graceful tone. Warm wood and clean, flowing lines combine simplicity with timeless beauty, and as you would expect, there is a great deal of symbolism present.

The garden you see at the front of the pavilion is a **Japanese dry garden**, with its arrangement of elements in odd numbers. The most important arrangement of stones is that of the *sanson*, or **the three Buddha**. Look for the three rocks on the extreme right side of the small rock garden as you are facing Mitsukoshi. The large stone in the middle of this pairing represents the Buddha and the two accompanying stones represent bodhisattvas, individuals who have achieved enlightenment but delay their journey to nirvana so that they may assist others who are suffering or in need of compassion. Bodhisattvas also represent the past lives of the Buddha.

Further symbolism is found to the left of Katsura Grill, through the **pond and its waterfalls**. While only those of the aristocratic class would have such splendor in their gardens, the concept of *wabi-sabi* presented in the pond's gentle curves, natural design, and use of dynamic energy and peaceful flow is one that belongs to all people. The pond represents the journey of life, through quick-moving water that tumbles into chaos and the quiet tranquility that comes with age and experience.

The **golden fish** on the blue roof above the fortress at the back of the pavilion is one of Buddhism's eight auspicious symbols. It is a reminder to live in a state of fearlessness, moving freely through life. Just as fish do not fear drowning, humans should not fear drowning in their suffering.

Morocco

Morocco is one of EPCOT's most beautiful pavilions, full of vibrant colors and startling patterns. It was important to the sponsors that traditional artistic customs be honored; hence they used their own artists to create the thousands of tiles and carvings you see.

The pavilion's most outstanding structure is its minaret, the tall tower to the right of the central courtyard. It is based on Marrakesh's **Koutoubia Mosque minaret** and is accurate right down (or up!) to the gleaming copper globes on top. Missing from EPCOT's tower is the flagpole from which a green flag is traditionally flown on Fridays and religious holidays.

You'll know you've reached the **Fez House** when you enter the small courtyard decorated almost entirely in tiles. The upper story is the homeowner's living quarters. If you stop and listen, you'll hear the family inside (wait for it!). Apparently a guest has shown up unannounced and the family is bustling about to get refreshments. If you pay close attention, you may hear the tea service hit the floor when one of the children trips over another in his haste to set out a snack. Stand there long enough and you'll hear the English-speaking guest arrive.

Several attractions feature a semi-hidden Cast Member signature book or sign, and you'll find a lovely version of that sentimental memorial here in Morocco. On the wall just inside the second door to the right of the entry to the Tangier Traders shop, you'll see a **pretty wooden board** that looks like a work of art. Moroccan Cast Members doing their international internship program at EPCOT sign their names in Arabic, and this is just one of several boards that have been filled with signatures since the pavilion opened.

Stand near the Nejjarine Fountain for a few minutes and you may hear a **conversation from within the shop** behind you. The merchant and one of his patrons are discussing some of the shop's items.

On the opposite side of the courtyard you'll hear other sounds of everyday life. Particularly enchanting are the **singing children**, happily chiming out a song about their school life and lessons, just as they do in real-life Morocco.

Directly across from Restaurant Marrakesh you'll see a simple brown sign on the wall, which translates to "**House of the storyteller**" and hints at the meet-and-greet inside, featuring Jasmine from Disney's mega-hit animated movie *Aladdin*.

France

Imagineers strive to create realistic settings, remaining true to the experience you would have when traveling abroad. Usually the inspiration is taken from real life. That is certainly the case here in the France pavilion.

See that unusual **petal-shaped glass covering** over the arcade to the left of Plume et Pallete? It's a re-creation of the Porte Dauphine station entryway of the Paris Métro. The original archway was designed by Hector Guimard, widely considered to be France's most important art nouveau architect.

Les Halles (pronounced "ley-al"), at the back of the pavilion, features some of the most appealing quick-bite offerings in all of World Showcase. The counter service section is based on the **Parisian fresh-food market** of the same name, while the exterior, the seating area, and the gift shop are designed to look like a typical **French train station**.

This may not be hidden magic as much as an almost-hidden oops! As you are watching *Impressions de France*, look quickly to the extreme right-hand screen when the Vézelay Abbey scene ends and the church bells finish chiming. The movie's editors didn't notice the **reflection of the**

cameraman and the camera trolley in the shop window, but now that you know what to look for, you'll notice it!

While it makes for a convenient pathway from France to the United Kingdom pavilion, the bridge you cross is based on the real-life pedestrian bridge **Pont des Arts**, which links the Louvre and Institut de France, crossing the River Seine. Don't forget to look over each side of the bridge as you make your crossing.

United Kingdom

British visitors may feel they have returned home when they reach the United Kingdom pavilion. At least, they would if they lived at **Hampton Court**, the palace that inspired the building housing The Toy Soldier shop and the Sportsman's Shoppe, across from the Rose & Crown Pub.

A standout feature of the Crown and Crest shop is the **carved wooden door frame** depicting a knight on one side and a priest on the other. Carved door frames were a sign of wealth, and the number of elaborate rosettes, horns of plenty, and heavenly hosts indicate this homeowner was well-off indeed.

Take a look at the books behind the Kidcot Fun Stop in The Toy Soldier shop. Many are Disney-related references. Take special note of the book under the skull. It's the *Society of Explorers & Adventurers Handbook*, referring to the Adventurers Club in the former Pleasure Island. Other titles include *The Little Mermaid* and *Twenty Thousand Leagues Under the Sea*.

Pop into The Tea Caddy and stock up on England's favorite hot beverage, which pairs perfectly with crumpets for a midday snack. You'll find three **vintage toasting forks** to the left of the fireplace, which would have been used to toast crumpets next to the flames.

The Rose & Crown Pub and Yorkshire County Fish Shop each have an obvious purpose, but what is that little building in between? In reality, it's a Cast Member area. In the story, it's a lockkeeper's home. Walk down the path behind the house and the fish and chip shop, and look for a sign on the back of the building. It reads, **Grand Union Canal, Thomas Dudley, Lockkeeper.** England's Grand Union Canal spans 137 miles between Birmingham and London and features 166 locks. Walk down to the waterfront and you'll see the United Kingdom pavilion's version of the canal.

Canada

Arriving at the final pavilion on our clockwise tour, **two distinct styles** become obvious. Eastern Canada is represented by the brick structures, while wood was the building material of choice in western Canada. The history of Canada, from the early European trappers to the nineteenth-century Victorian influence, blends seamlessly, while the impressive Butchart-inspired sunken garden brings a grace and beauty to the otherwise rough terrain of the Canadian Rocky Mountains.

Canadian hotels Chateau Frontenac in Quebec City, Chateau Laurier in **Ottawa**, and Fairmont Banff Springs in Alberta were the inspiration for **Hotel du Canada**, but there is a tragic historical tie-up here too. Chateau Laurier was commissioned by American railroader Charles Melville Hays, who never saw the opening of the hotel. He perished just days prior to the opening while making the return trip to Ottawa from England onboard the RMS *Titanic*.

Imagine That!

Being in a position of authority comes with its challenges, especially when an issue is personal. Ron Rodriguez recalls, "When Disney brought in BeeBee La Crème, a French Canadian jazz accordion player for the Canada pavilion, he had a big beard. I was the one who had to tell him he had to shave it off to conform to Disney standards of the time. The next day he came in with a plastic container with his beard in it and gave it to me."

Alaskan artist David Boxley's **totem poles** depict a traditional **Raven story**, the story of **Eagle and the Young Chief**, and **The Tale of the Whale**, three of many legends told by the Tsimshian people. Here, Raven (the totem on the left) is forcing the Chief of the Skies to release the sun, the moon, and the stars; Eagle and the Young Chief (the totem on the right) tells of an eagle repaying the kindness of a boy who later became a chief; and The Tale of the Whale totem (at the back) is an origin story of the **potlatch ceremony**, a feast celebrating major life milestones.

The Northwest Mercantile is a rustic outpost that carries all the goods a logger or trapper might need. Surely those tins lining the ceiling are all Canadian-based items, right? Wrong. They're from places as varied as Cincinnati, Ohio, and Norwich, Great Britain. But one tin stands out for its adorably backwoodsy name: **Squirrel Confections**. Squirrel Confectionery was known for its Cherry Lips and Floral Gums, gummy-style candies of the 1930s. Folksy Canadian history? Nope. It was a British firm, but it helps set the mercantile's time frame as after Canada's self-governing independence from Britain in 1867.

EPCOT Time Line

Walt Disney first described plans for EPCOT, the Experimental Prototype Community of Tomorrow, in October 1966, envisioning a working city where technology and creativity would combine, showcasing American ingenuity and the concept of free enterprise. He never saw his dream realized, because Walt passed away on December 15, 1966.

The park opened on October 1, 1982. During the opening-day ceremonies, Card Walker greeted guests with what is now a quintessential Disney slogan: "To all who enter this place of Joy, Hope, and Friendship—Welcome."

1982: Opening Attractions

The park opened with a series of special dedication ceremonies for the various attractions. The ceremonies took place during the first few weeks of the park's existence and highlighted each of the main attractions in turn.

Spaceship Earth was dedicated on October 1, 1982, followed by the **China** pavilion on the third, **Universe of Energy** on the fourth, **World of Motion** on the fifth, **the Land** on the sixth, **the American Adventure** on the eleventh and twelfth, **Canada** on the thirteenth, **Italy** on the fourteenth, **Germany** on the fifteenth, **Communicore** on the eighteenth, **United Kingdom** on the nineteenth, and **France** and **Japan** on the twentieth.

The official **grand opening** took place October 22–24, 1982, with a dedication ceremony on the twenty-fourth. Representatives from around the world participated in a water-pouring ceremony, adding water from major rivers and seas around the world to the fountain in Innoventions Plaza. On October 23, Epcot's first nighttime fireworks show, **Carnival de Lumiere**, began.

On December 4, 1982, **Journey into Imagination** was dedicated, followed by **Mexico** on December 13.

1983–1988: A Period of IllumiNation

Horizons opened on October 1, 1983, with **New World Fantasy** replacing Carnival de Lumiere as the evening fireworks spectacle. On June 9, 1984, Epcot hosted World Fest, featuring its first lagoon-based fireworks show, **Laserphonic Fantasy**. **Morocco** followed on September 7, 1984, the tenth pavilion in World Showcase.

Daytime show **Skyleidoscope** air and water pageant debuted in 1985, along with China's **Nine Dragons Restaurant** and **Lotus Blossom Café**, but it would take until January 15, 1986, for another major attraction, **The Living Seas**, to open its doors, adding an eighth significant element to Future World.

The groundbreaking **Captain EO**, a blockbuster 3D film produced by George Lucas, directed by Francis Ford Coppola, and starring pop singer Michael Jackson, debuted on September 12, 1986, at the Magic Eye Theater, located in the same building as Journey into Imagination.

Two years later, on January 30, 1988, the breathtaking **IllumiNations** nighttime laser and fireworks show premiered, replacing Laserphonic Fantasy. Then, on May 6, 1988, World Showcase welcomed the **Norway** pavilion, with the pavilion's ride, **Maelstrom**, opening four days later.

1989–1994: Wonders, Surprises, and Innoventions

On October 19, 1989, the **Wonders of Life** pavilion opened in Future World, and Walt Disney World celebrated its twentieth anniversary a year later, an occasion honored at Epcot by the arrival of **Surprise in the Skies** daytime show over the World Showcase Lagoon.

Another three years would pass before any major changes occurred, including an alteration to the park's name, as EPCOT Center officially became **Epcot '94**. On March 26, **Food Rocks** replaced Kitchen Kabaret at the Land pavilion, while Communicore closed in January, returning as **Innoventions East and West** on July 1, and the very first **Flower and Garden Festival** was held—now one of the park's most successful annual events.

Next up was **Honey, I Shrunk the Audience**, a 3D experience based on the hit movie *Honey, I Shrunk the Kids*, which arrived at the Magic Eye Theater on November 21, replacing *Captain EO*.

1995–1998: New Years, New Names

With the New Year came (another) new name, **Epcot '95**. Also new, on January 21, 1995, *Circle of Life: An Environmental Fable* replaced *Symbiosis* at the Land pavilion. The show featured characters from the blockbuster motion picture *The Lion King*; Disney movies had begun to play a role in Epcot's attractions. That summer, the first **Food and Wine Festival** debuted, another popular annual event that has gone on to become a major money-spinner.

Again, as the year changed so did the park's name, this time simply shortened (thankfully) to **Epcot**. World of Motion pavilion closed on January 2, 1996, in preparation for a new attraction that would be so technologically advanced, its original projected opening date of summer 1997 was delayed for nearly two years as Imagineers worked out the bugs.

Ellen's Energy Adventure, starring popular television personalities Ellen DeGeneres and Bill Nye, replaced the original Universe of Energy show on September 15, 1996, adding a lighter touch to an attraction that was considered by some to be "too dry and factual."

1999–2000: Millennium Milestones

After a sixteen-year run, the Horizons pavilion closed on January 9, 1999, and finally, on March 7, **Test Track** made its long-awaited debut in the former World of Motion pavilion, racing its way into EPCOT history as the attraction with the worst track record for breakdowns. However, the ride also became wildly popular, in contrast to **Journey into Your Imagination**, which effectively killed off beloved characters Dreamfinder and Figment when it replaced Journey into Imagination on October 1, 1999.

Unveiled on September 29, 1999, the massive **Mickey Wand** towered alongside Spaceship Earth, with its glittering Epcot 2000 signage. It would remain there for seven years, minus the "2000" portion once the Millennium Celebration ended.

The year-long celebration also scored a huge hit with the **Tapestry of Nations** parade and the specially revamped **IllumiNations: Reflections of Earth** laser and fireworks show, which debuted along with Journey into Your Imagination. Tapestry of Nations would be renamed **Tapestry of Dreams** in 2000, before ending its run in March 2003.

2001–2004: Figment Returns!

With a nod toward the public outcry caused by the original attraction's closure, **Journey into Imagination with Figment** replaced the 1999 version on June 1, 2002, and, happily, resurrected the little purple dragon.

Reflections of China replaced Circle-Vision 360° *Wonders of China* on May 22, 2003, and another three months would pass before the state-of-the-art ride **Mission: SPACE** debuted on August 15, undergoing various adjustments over the course of the next few years as guests suffered motion sickness due to the realistic sensation of launching into space provided by the ride system's centrifuge.

Food Rocks at the Land pavilion closed in January 2004, making room for a new attraction due the following year. At the Living Seas, the hugely imaginative **Turtle Talk with Crush** debuted in November 2004, adding more entertainment geared toward the six-and-under crowd, bringing another megahit movie character (from *Finding Nemo*) to Epcot—and creating far bigger crowds than anyone imagined!

2005–2006: The Land Has Liftoff

On May 5, 2005, Disneyland import **Soarin'** opened at the Land pavilion, housed in a brand-new building branching off the main pavilion. A direct copy of Soarin' over California from Disney's California Adventure park, the attraction was an immediate success, with waiting time frequently topping 180 minutes.

Riding a tidal wave of popularity caused by Turtle Talk with Crush, the Living Seas underwent a much-needed refurbishment and emerged with a new name, **the Seas with Nemo & Friends**, in October 2006.

2007: Twenty-Five Years to Celebrate

El Rio del Tiempo in the Mexico pavilion went down for refurbishment and returned on April 6 as the **Gran Fiesta Tour Starring the Three Caballeros**. The park's icon, Spaceship Earth, also closed for a major overhaul shortly after its post-show area reopened—after several years of dormancy—as **Project Tomorrow: Inventing the Wonders of the Future**.

In another long-overdue move, the Circle-Vision 360° film *O Canada!* returned on September 1, redone with comedian Martin Short as its onscreen host.

October 1, 2007, marked Epcot's twenty-fifth anniversary. Though no celebrations had been announced by Disney, a dedicated fan base organized a grassroots acknowledgment of the milestone called **Celebration 25**. Epcot's vice president, Jim MacPhee, announced a rededication ceremony would take place, highlighted by a second water-pouring ceremony and "A Conversation with Marty Sklar," during which Disney Legend Sklar spoke about the creation of the park, the challenges the Imagineers faced, and the impact Walt Disney's grand vision, realized in part through EPCOT, has had upon the world.

2008–2014: A Time of Rediscovery

The years 2008 through 2014 were a time of shifting and changing rather than grand debuts. **Honey, I Shrunk the Audience** closed May 9, 2010, to make way for the reopening of *Captain EO* on July 2, 2010.

Test Track closed on April 15, 2012, reopening on December 6, 2012, with a new theme and with Chevrolet as its sponsor.

World Showcase Players had their last performance September 25, 2014, while hugely popular musical groups **Off Kilter**, **Spirit of America Fife and Drum Corps**, and **Mo'Rockin'** each had their final performances on September 27, 2014, to make way for new entertainment. The **Canadian Lumberjacks** show began performances on October 6, 2014, at the Mill Stage next to the Canada pavilion; flag-waving performers **Sbandieratori di Sansepolcro** began on October 19 in Italy; **the Paul McKenna Band** brought Celtic folk music to the United Kingdom on November 26; and folk music and dancers **B'net Al Houwariyate** began performing at Morocco on November 2.

Fan favorite **Maelstrom** closed October 6, 2014, and the Norway pavilion was rethemed to Disney's movie *Frozen*.

2015-2020: The Calm Before the Storm

After the avalanche of interest in **Frozen Ever After** and Norway's **Royal Sommerhus** meet-and-greet with Anna and Elsa, there were more closings than openings.

Captain EO ended on December 6, 2015; *Circle of Life: An Environmental Fable* ended February 3, 2018; and the **Innoventions pavilions** limped along until September 7, 2019, before closing to make way for a whole new concept that moved away from the theme of Future World.

Universe of Energy pavilion and **Ellen's Energy Adventure** closed on August 13, 2017, ending Epcot's era of "edu-tainment" and ushering in a new focus as the pavilion and surrounding area made way for the movie-based **Guardians of the Galaxy: Cosmic Rewind** roller coaster.

On October 1, 2019, temporary nighttime show **Epcot Forever** replaced **IllumiNations: Reflections of Earth**, which had been a huge fan favorite since its debut at the turn of the millennium. A permanent show, **Harmonious**, was destined to light up EPCOT's skies in 2020.

On January 17, 2020, *Canada Far and Wide* in the Canada pavilion and *Awesome Planet* in the Land pavilion each made their debut, replacing *O Canada!* and the long-gone *Circle of Life*, respectively.

The winds of change were blowing as 2019 wound down. 2020 and 2021 will see the most profound transformation of any Disney theme park, ever, as a seismic shift in focus splits the park into the four "neighborhoods" of **World Celebration**, **World Discovery**, **World Nature**, and **World Showcase**. On the way are reimagined shows, interactive entertainment, a restaurant with a view of outer space, and a spectacular nighttime extravaganza, plus a mouse with a taste for fine dining, adventurers who guard the galaxy, and one practically perfect nanny, Mary Poppins.

Disney's Hollywood Studios

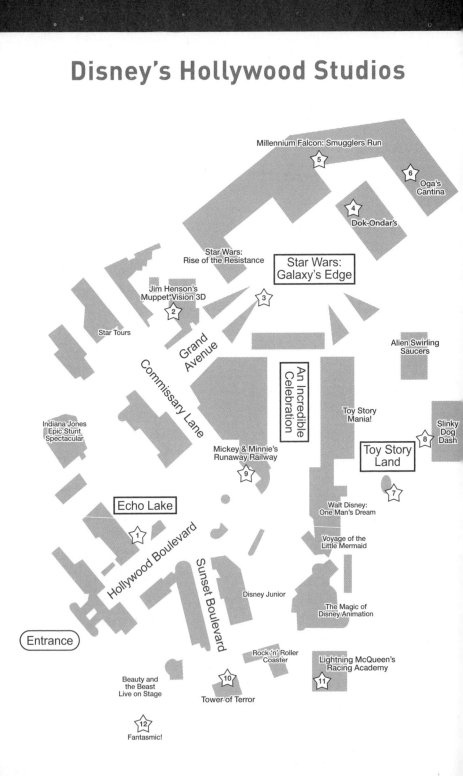

Millennium Falcon: Smugglers Run
5

6
Oga's
Cantina

4
Dok-Ondar's

Star Wars:
Rise of the Resistance

Star Wars:
Galaxy's Edge

Jim Henson's
Muppet Vision 3D
2

3

Star Tours

Grand
Avenue

Alien Swirling
Saucers

An Incredible
Celebration

Commissary Lane

Toy Story
Mania!

Slinky
Dog
Dash

Indiana Jones
Epic Stunt
Spectacular

Mickey & Minnie's
Runaway Railway
9

Toy Story
Land

8

7

Echo Lake

Walt Disney:
One Man's Dream

1

Hollywood Boulevard

Voyage of the
Little Mermaid

Sunset Boulevard

Disney Junior

The Magic of
Disney Animation

Entrance

Rock 'n' Roller
Coaster

Lightning McQueen's
Racing Academy
11

Beauty and
the Beast
Live on Stage

10

Tower of Terror

12
Fantasmic!

1. **Echo Lake:** Eddie Valliant, private investigator, advertises his service on the window above the Hollywood & Vine restaurant. Although Eddie insists on "No Toons," if you look closely you may notice Roger Rabbit isn't far away.

2. **Muppet*Vision 3D:** Watch for wooden boxes marked with items appropriate to the Muppet receiving them, including one sent by Gary and Mary to Walter, Whistler-in-Residence. They are characters in the 2011 movie *The Muppets*, and Walter was named to honor Walt Disney.

3. **Star Wars: Galaxy's Edge:** Aurebesh letters on the trash bins read, "Trash to Sector 3263827," which refers to the garbage compactor on the Death Star that nearly squashed Chewbacca, Luke Skywalker, Han Solo, and Princess Leia in *A New Hope*.

4. **Dok-Ondar's Den of Antiquities:** The giant foot near the door, stripped of its black paint and slightly resculpted, formerly belonged to one of the Anubis statues holding up the ceiling in The Great Movie Ride's Egyptian scene.

5. **Millennium Falcon: Smugglers Run:** A container behind the dejarik table holds a helmet with its blaster cover pulled down and a round training remote, used by Luke Skywalker during his early instruction in the ways of the Jedi.

6. **Oga's Cantina:** Oga's notice board includes an advertisement seeking a competent Chandrilan Class 1 starship mechanic, ideally fluent in Shyriiwook. Take the job and you'll be working with Wookiees on the *Halcyon*. This is a reference to Walt Disney World's *Halcyon* Starcruiser Hotel.

7. **Toy Story Land:** In the original Toy Story Midway Mania!, riders were "shrunk" to the size of an unspecified toy, but here in Toy Story Land you're the size of specific toys: the Green Army Patrol.

8. **Slinky Dog Dash:** After you pass under the Standby line sign, turn around and look at the back of the dog tag. You'll see Andy's dog Buster's name, and the address of Andy's home in *Toy Story 2*.

9. **Mickey & Minnie's Runaway Railway:** As you enter a short hallway to the loading area, look at the wood grain on the wall. You'll see large stylized letters that spell "Mickey" in the graining.

10. **Tower of Terror:** Why did Imagineers choose 8:05 p.m. as the time lightning hit the tower and all the clocks stopped? Add up the numbers 8 and 5, and the resulting unlucky number gives you the answer.

11. **Lightning McQueen's Racing Academy:** When the honeycomb pattern comes up on the screen, look for the Pizza Planet truck from Toy Story, which finds its way into all Pixar movies.

12. *Fantasmic!:* The riverboat ferrying the characters at the end of the show is a replica of the boat in *Steamboat Willie*. Notice who is up in the wheelhouse piloting the boat?

Chapter 3

Disney's Hollywood Studios

"Welcome to the Hollywood that never was and always will be," or so said Michael Eisner, chairman of Walt Disney Company when Disney-MGM Studios opened in 1989. Entering the original studios placed guests firmly amid the glamour of Hollywood during its golden age, surrounded by sights, sounds, and characters that would have been familiar to the likes of Clark Gable, Rita Hayworth, Marilyn Monroe, and Richard Burton—the brightest stars of the '30s, '40s, and '50s.

But, much like EPCOT's big transition throughout 2020 and 2021, Hollywood Studios saw a galactic reimagining in 2019 with the opening of two new lands, and only tenuously held on to the concept of purely entertainment-based attractions, as deeply immersive, experiential adventures that gave guests active roles took precedence.

While the original concept for the studios has been diluted over the years, the allure of being in that most glittering of towns and the pull you feel on your heartstrings when high drama is played out on stage and screen—with *you* firmly in the spotlight—is not the stuff of make-believe; it's alive, vibrant, and immensely convincing. To be a star or to see the stars; the choice is yours!

And now, the scene is set, you know your inspiration, and you have excellent direction. Ready? *Action!*

Hollywood Boulevard

One of the first elements greeting guests as they enter Disney's Hollywood Studios is the Crossroads of the World information kiosk, its spire rising high above Hollywood Boulevard. The crossroads is a replica of the original Crossroads of the World in Hollywood, California, with the addition of a **1930s version of Mickey Mouse** standing proudly on top. Not only does the kiosk serve the functional purpose of providing park maps and various necessities to guests, but it also serves a less obvious purpose. Mickey has one ear higher than the other and his right hand is outstretched. What is he doing up there? His copper ear is grounded and acts as a lightning rod.

Walk down Hollywood Boulevard or Sunset Boulevard and you're likely to run across **"streetmosphere" actors**: a starlet hoping to be discovered, a soon-to-be-famous director looking for extras for his blockbuster film, and public workers who just know their big break is right around the corner.

When you reach the junction of Hollywood Boulevard and Sunset Boulevard, stand in front of the Tip Board and look down at the half-oval plate in the pavement. It is marked **Est. 1928**, the year Mickey Mouse was first featured in the cartoon short *Steamboat Willie*.

You will see **1928** on various buildings all over Hollywood Studios, so keep an eye out for them. To get you started, Hollywood & Vine restaurant across from Echo Lake is another location marked with Mickey's debut date. See how many more you can find as you tour the park.

Each of the parks has a reference to its opening day, and you may be wondering where Disney-MGM Studios' (using the park's original name) opening day is commemorated. It's in the central courtyard, in the green space across the pavement from **Keystone Clothiers**. Look for the large bronze statue of a producer with a movie camera. The park's dedication plaque is next to the statue. Michael Eisner dedicated the park on May 1, 1989.

Echo Lake

When Disney-MGM Studios was being built, the crater that would become Echo Lake was the first thing to go in, and the park grew up around it. Located around a small lake, just as the tiny town of Echo Lake, California, is set around its namesake body of water, this charming area of Hollywood Studios has several opportunities for a snack or a meal, and some lovely hidden magic.

Turn left when you reach the end of Hollywood Boulevard, where the dubious business **Sights and Sounds Acting and Voice Lessons** has "Finished some of Hollywood's finest." It's hard to say if that's a good thing or not. Their suspect reputation is further enhanced by the people who work there. Say the name **Ewell M. Pressem** out loud and you'll know what I mean. **Singer B. Flatt** and the money-grubbing **Bill More**, account executive, don't inspire confidence, either.

Turn the corner to the left again and take a quick peek at the **Cosmetic Dentistry** building, across from the Dockside Diner. There is a directory on the right-hand wall next to the door that advertises for **C. Howie Pullum, DDS**; **Ruth Canal, DDS**; and **Les Payne, DDS**.

The building next to Cosmetic Dentistry has a **For Rent** sign in the upper window, which isn't particularly compelling on its own, but as with all things Imagineering, it was placed there for a reason. When Walt and Roy Disney were just starting out, their initial base was in an uncle's garage until they amassed enough money to rent their own studio space. They finally found a location they could afford, right above the Holly-Vermont Realty company, whose logo you will see on the door below the For Rent sign. A nice tribute to a humble start, don't you think?

Eddie Valliant, private investigator, advertises his service on the window above the Hollywood & Vine restaurant. Although Eddie insists on "No Toons," if you look closely you may notice **Roger Rabbit** isn't far away.

Indiana Jones Epic Stunt Spectacular!

High thrills are in store at *Indiana Jones Epic Stunt Spectacular!*, where the stunts are real and so is the danger. How does Indy avoid getting speared as he makes his way through the temple to retrieve the golden idol? He actually controls the release of the spears by stepping on **square keypads**, so he knows exactly when they will spring. But yes, they are real and he could get hurt.

There is no doubt about the villains Indiana Jones is dealing with in the movie *Indiana Jones and the Raiders of the Lost Ark*, but the *Indiana Jones Epic Stunt Spectacular!* has no direct references to the Nazis. The symbol you see on the tail of the German Flying Wing airplane isn't a swastika, though your eye is fooled into thinking it is, and when the attraction opened it was a swastika. It was changed to a combination of the background of the **Nazi flag** and the Luftwaffe insignia, the **Balkan Cross**. Clever, isn't it?

With everything going on above ground, it's easy to miss what's going on beneath your feet. As you pass by the entry to *Indiana Jones Epic Stunt Spectacular!*, to the left of the entry, down the path on the right-hand side, there is a well with a sign saying, **Do *Not* Pull the Rope**. Notice "Not" has been crossed out. You know what to do!

Star Tours: The Adventures Continue

Sign up for an intergalactic tour with Star Tours: The Adventures Continue and you'll embark on tours to some of the most popular planets in the Star Wars movies. With C-3PO and R2-D2 at the helm, what could go wrong?

There is so much happening on the **Information board** located shortly after you enter the queue that you could easily spend an hour taking it all in. The hidden gems you see will depend entirely on when you arrive and how quickly the queue moves.

While you are in the first half of the queue, pay attention to the intercom announcements and to the sales pitches for various intergalactic destinations. The sales pitches are presented by droid **Aly San San**, named for Allison Janney, the actress who voiced the character. Aly San San's look was based on the waitress droid **WA-7** from *Star Wars: Episode II—Attack of the Clones*.

One of the sales pitches is for a tour to Cloud City, which promises you'll see a special celebration, including **Fantasy in the Sky** fireworks. This refers to the fireworks show over Magic Kingdom's Cinderella Castle from 1971 until 2003.

Another important announcement may grab your attention, especially if you did not heed the advice to make a note of where you parked when you arrived today. Listen for an announcement asking the owner of a speeder whose license plate has the number **THX 1138**, if they would please remove it from the no-hover zone. *THX 1138* was the first feature-length movie made by George Lucas, in 1971, an adaptation of a short film he created while at the University of Southern California. *THX 1138* is also referenced as **Flight 1138 to Coruscant** on the Departures board.

While you're facing the Information board, look at the panel to your right. The letters above the top circle read **2R-OP3C**. Read them backward and you have the names of Star Wars's two most famous droids.

Just above the lower circle on the same panel, you'll see **NIC7C0I**. If you read every other letter, it spells out NCC-1701, the registry number of the starship *Enterprise* of *Star Trek* fame.

The next element you come across in the queue is the Starspeeder 1000. You will see the number **1401** in a few locations on the ship, a reference to 1401 Flower Street in Glendale, California, which is the street address for Walt Disney Imagineering. The ship you will be boarding is Flight 1401.

TK-421 refers to the Imperial Stormtrooper whose battle armor was stolen by Luke Skywalker in the first Star Wars movie, prompting the query, "TK-421, why aren't you at your post?" You may also hear his name in a comment made by G2-9T, the **luggage scanner droid**.

Fascinating Fact

If you would like to learn Aurebesh, there are plenty of websites that feature the alien language's characters. It's surprisingly easy to memorize, so take lots of pictures while you're in the queue at Star Tours and you can translate when you get home. Even better? Pull out your cell phone and translate them using the Play Disney Parks app.

Just after you enter the second portion of the queue, look immediately to your left. If you've ridden Star Tours before, you'll remember **Captain Rex**, the droid who should never have been a pilot. He now has a new job as DJ R-3X (better known as DJ Rex) at Oga's Cantina on the planet of Batuu, which he is somewhat more qualified for and seems to truly enjoy. Why is he still in Star Tours? The new story is, he's a prototype being sent back to the shop for repairs.

Star Tours: The Adventures Continue is not geographically linked to Star Wars: Galaxy's Edge because, well, they're in different planetary systems. But they are linked in another way. Although the outdoor queue that winds through the forest moon of Endor is rarely used, it's still there, so even though the spaceport you depart from isn't named, it stands to reason it's on the moon of Endor. One of the flights referenced in the queue's spiel is a flight to the planet of Endor, while *some* flights will end on Batuu, loosely tying the two areas together.

Grand Avenue

As part of Disney's Hollywood Studios' big redesign, Pixar Place was reimagined as An Incredible Celebration, and Streets of America became the short walkway that is now called Grand Avenue.

Muppet*Vision 3D

Muppet*Vision's preshow holding area is filled with jokes, some of them obvious, some less so. But don't rush down the hallway yet. Instead, pause and read the **Directory and The Rest of the Directory** on the left-hand wall immediately after you enter the building. It's filled with Muppet-style comedy.

Along the wall to the right after you enter the preshow area is the top of a shipping crate, referencing the painting *The Sleepy Zootsy*. Zoot is the saxophone-playing Muppet and the picture in question appeared in Miss Piggy's Art Masterpiece Calendar. *The Sleepy Zootsy* is a takeoff on the famous artist Henri Rousseau's *The Sleeping Gypsy*.

Imagine That!

Just as the Imagineers inspire kids of today, so, too, did other creative minds inspire today's Imagineers. Imagineering's prop fabricator and set dresser Eric Baker was influenced by one of the best. "My hero is Jim Henson; he's kind of my role model. Of course, I never got to work with Jim. I worked with the Muppets quite a bit, but Jim had passed away by then. But even years after he passed, everyone would talk about how kind he was. I just try to be kind to everybody. It makes your world a lot easier. It doesn't always work out originally, but it always comes back around."

Vogue has sent a special delivery to Miss Piggy, although the address on the big pink box at the front, left-hand side of the preshow area is that of an accounting and tax firm in Paris, France. Miss Piggy played the role of a *Vogue* editor in the 2011 movie *The Muppets*, and from the contents designation on the package (**Miss Piggy's Visage Mirage**), it appears to contain one of her favorite things: an extra-large mirror.

Along the front, left-hand wall of the preshow area you'll see a poster of a Muppet that looks oddly familiar. It is a fitting memorial to the Muppets' creator, **Jim Henson**, Muppetized, and with a movie camera lens around his neck.

Watch for wooden boxes marked with items appropriate to the Muppet receiving them, including one sent by Gary and Mary to **Walter, Whistler-in-Residence**. They are characters in the movie *The Muppets*, and Walter was named to honor Walt Disney.

See that round metal object hanging from the ceiling near the doors leading into the theater? It's a **spaceship-style pig**, referencing *The Muppet Show*'s recurring sketch, "Pigs in Space."

There are several jokes on the clapperboard hanging on the right-hand wall after you enter the Muppet*Vision preshow area. The Scene is **Happiness Hotel**, referring to the hotel in the movie *The Great Muppet Caper*; the Take is **My Wife, Please!** which was comedian Henny Youngman's signature line, variations of which have been used in many Muppet productions; the camera is a **Kodiak Brownie**, a takeoff on the Kodak Brownie camera popular in the early 1900s, but this time with a bear-inspired twist; and the Star is **Ursula Major**, a feminization of Ursa Major, a constellation also known as the Great Bear. It is worth noting the director of this particular film is none other than Fozzie Bear.

Imagine That!

Jim Henson didn't just inspire Eric Baker, he also modeled creative solutions to the working world's challenges. Eric says, "You have to laugh and have fun. One of the things Jim Henson would do when he opened a shop was, he'd put up a sign that read, 'Bang Head Here.' I've [put up that sign] a few times, and people love it. Sometimes you have to bang your head, but then you just smile and go on."

Star Wars: Galaxy's Edge

There are two entries into Galaxy's Edge. One is through Toy Story Land, while the main tunnel entry is via the walkway off of Grand Avenue, just past Muppet*Vision 3D. Plan your touring so that you enter through the tunnel and we'll begin our journey in Resistance Forest.

You'll notice straightaway that very little is done for you on Batuu. The pathways meander, so you can choose where you'll go rather than being guided toward a specific direction. You determine how you'll respond when Stormtroopers confront you. You get to decide if you're wary and afraid while you're in the First Order's territory, or if it feels more like home. And that's part of Galaxy's Edge's genius. If you landed on Batuu as a stranger, those are the decisions you would have to make as you navigated your way through Black Spire Outpost, haven for rogues, rebels, and the Resistance.

There is a reason everyday items in Black Spire Outpost look old and low-tech. Because *A New Hope* came out in 1977, props procurers tried to include only those items that were available **pre-1980**, such as the wiring, switchboards, and dusty metal scrap pieces in places like the *Millennium Falcon*, Ohnaka Transport Solutions repair shop, and Droid Depot. Some of the parts were stripped out of old Xerox machines.

Recycling doesn't stop with switches and wires, though. Some of the props in the Star Wars: Rise of the Resistance and Millennium Falcon: Smugglers Run queues were salvaged from a decrepit **Boeing 747** found in a cow pasture in England.

As you make your way into Resistance Forest you'll hear music in the background, droid chatter, and the occasional hum of electrical current, as well as strange animal sounds and birdlike calls. But you'll begin to hear something else too. Resistance fighters have made camp here, and they're actively looking for recruits (that means you). Listen when you reach the **red RZ-2 A-wing** and **blue T-70 X-wing starfighters** and you'll hear them doing repairs.

Every planet has to deal with trash, and Batuu is no exception. See those Aurebesh letters on the trash bins, with numbers below them? They read, **Trash to Sector 3263827**, which means it's headed straight to the garbage compactor on the Death Star that nearly squashed Chewbacca, Luke Skywalker, Han Solo, and Princess Leia into pancakes in *A New Hope*.

Pay attention to the ground and you'll see **tracks** left by animals, Gungans, and GNK power droids (aka Gonk droids), the latter of which are currently hanging out at the base of the communications tower near the X-wing.

You'll also find prints from a special hero droid. The **tracks left by R2-D2** were made using wheels that were created from rubbings taken from the movie series' R2-D2 and rolled onto the walkways.

Imagine That!

Guests often wonder which Star Wars movie Batuu is based on. The answer is, none of them and all of them. How is that possible? During a media preview for the land, Scott Mallwitz, executive creative director, Walt Disney Imagineering, explained: "This is not Luke's story or Leia's story, Han's story, or Chewbacca's story. This is a place for *you* to come to, and for *you* to explore. This is a very packed, vibrant, exciting outpost on the edge of the galaxy. Just the place you want to be. It's always been here, it's just the first time *you* got here."

Star Wars: Rise of the Resistance

Oga Garra doesn't just own Oga's Cantina, she also controls all of Black Spire Outpost, and if she hears about any spacecraft in Batuu's airspace that she doesn't like, she orders gunners to rotate the **heavy artillery turret** and fire at them. You can see tracks on the ground where the turret makes an arching turn.

The defense setup is quite sophisticated, right down to the **transparent tactical screen** to the left of the turret. The First Order and the Resistance used these screens in the movies to plot the movements and positions of spacecrafts.

Nearly everything in the queue for Rise of the Resistance is tinged with a Star Wars reference, including the **waterfall** outside the cave system. If you've read Delilah S. Dawson's book *Star Wars: Galaxy's Edge: Black Spire*, you'll recall the waterfall and its pool filled with venomous, translucent anemones, in which Vi Moradi discovers a corpse the first time she visits the sacred ruins. Best not to reach into this one!

Ancient carvings, urns, and pottery are abundant throughout the queue, along with equipment hidden by the current-day Resistance. Watch for pilot jumpsuits, helmets, and the see-through **flexpoly bacta suit** that helped Finn recover from his injuries in *The Last Jedi*.

Imagine That!

As impressive as Rey's hologram mission briefing is, an even more impressive bit of technology occurs when you board the transport shuttle. The door you entered will also be the door you exit, but the setting outside will be entirely different. While you're still on the Intersystem Transport Ship watching the battle unfold around you, notice the direction the action is moving and the subtle sensation of movement you experience underfoot. Perfect coordination between the two is what makes this scene change possible.

Pay special attention to what's going on outside as your transport leaves Batuu, and to the moments when you're caught in the tractor beam. The entire experience is perfectly coordinated. For example, **Poe, your wingman,** is in one of the X-wings behind you, but when you hear him say he'll check out an unusual signal his X-wing passes over your transport and shows up in the front window.

No one wants to end up in a First Order interrogation cell, but once you're there watch the bars and the ceiling above you when General Hux and Kylo Ren walk back and forth. You'll see **shadows mimicking their movements**. A clever detail that adds to the realism.

Imagine That!

Most people know the story behind the *Millennium Falcon*, but Rise of the Resistance is a tale that has never before been told. Scott Mallwitz, executive creative director, Walt Disney Imagineering, breaks it down: "Rise of the Resistance is the most technically advanced ride Walt Disney Imagineering has ever created. It is amazing storytelling, putting you in the midst of a battle between the First Order and the Resistance. Magnificent and menacing is exactly what you want from a Star Destroyer; it's exactly what you want out of [the first] scene. You've been drawn into the Star Destroyer, right through the space window, and you're about to be taken to interrogation. That's why the Stormtroopers are there. That's why you walk under the TIE fighter. The bad news is, you're going to come face-to-face with Kylo Ren soon. After that, it's up to you to escape the Star Destroyer, and Poe sends what's left of the Resistance to get you out."

There is no mistaking the method used to rescue you from the interrogation cell, but after you've settled into your astromech-driven transport take a look at the back of the newly created doorway. You'll see its **soldered outline**.

While it's true the troop transport you board moves along a somewhat random path, pay attention to which direction the **R5 astromech's three glowing "eyes"** are looking. R5 has been reprogrammed by Finn, and as he searches for a way out his eyes point in the direction you're going next.

The two troop transports you started with will split up when you reach the AT-ATs, and after a quick ascent, one transport faces the **AT-AT** head-on and the other has a side view. From head-on, you're shot at directly, with spectacular results. If your first ride features the side view, get back in line and ride again!

Also watch for **Finn hiding in the AT-AT room**. As seen from one transport, he's crouching behind cargo boxes. From the other, he's standing in a doorway to your left.

Remember the detailed coordination between the screens in your shuttle transport and the experience you had inside? This visual coordination also occurs while you're passing the turbo laser cannons during your final encounter with Kylo Ren (watch for an exploding **TIE fighter** on your right, just before it slams into your Star Destroyer), and in the escape pods.

If you survive your plummet from the Star Destroyer, turn around and look at the **Aurebesh writing** over the tunnel behind you when your transport docks and you exit the vehicle. It reads, "Savi and Son Salvage," and it's the location where Savi stores the items he scavenges. You passed his **smelting equipment** as you rounded the corner in the darkened tunnel after your escape from the Star Destroyer.

Street Market

Batuu's ambiance takes a turn toward the exotic when you reach the market. As you're taking in the first scene, notice the **apartments** above you. They're one of several forms of housing in which citizens of Black Spire Outpost live.

Pause for a moment and listen to the sounds in this area. Along with everyday conversations, you'll hear a radio station playing in the background. Not only is it a cool detail, it's also a hidden tribute. Radio station DJ **Palob Godalhi** is voiced by the name's anagram, Pablo Hidalgo, creative executive at Lucasfilm.

If you've seen *A New Hope* you probably remember the trash compactor inhabited by a creepy **dianoga**, with its single giant eyeball on a long, multi-tentacle stalk. Take a drink from the hydrator (drinking fountain) on your left as soon as you enter the market from Resistance Forest, and you might see this slimy creature lurking in the bubbling receptacle on the right-hand side. Don't feel like taking a drink with a monster so close by? You can activate this bit of hidden magic on your Data Pad (cell phone) using the Play Disney Parks app, under Hacks, then Fluid Container.

All of the refreshers (restrooms) in the Outpost are just as old and semi-decrepit as you'd imagine, with missing tiles on the floor, rusty plumbing, and mirrors in need of resilvering. But the **refreshers in the market** are even creepier. That dianoga you saw above the hydrator lives in the pipes, and you might just hear it sloshing around.

A wood-carver has set up a business in a small corner of the market, across from the refreshers. Visitors to Batuu will recognize some of the characters he carves, but take a look at his **kiln**. It's made from the body of an old astromech droid.

The child-sized red landspeeder, green speeder bike, and blue landspeeder to the left of Toydarian Toymaker were obviously cobbled together from recycled bits and pieces, but they're also a nod to an attraction that was removed to make way for Galaxy's Edge. See the Aurebesh lettering on the side of the **green speeder bike**? It reads, "LMA." The metal parts used to assemble it were taken from Hollywood Studios' former *Lights, Motors, Action! Extreme Stunt Show*.

The Creature Stall

Bina, owner of the Creature Stall, carries tempting foods in the **mysterious bags** you see tucked between the shop's shelves. If you're going to capture a baby rancor, you want to bring along treats that aren't your hands—or your head!

Loth-cats aren't known for having a cuddly nature, but the one in the cage does like to snuggle with its **porg toy**. That is, until it rips it to shreds. Happily, there is a limitless supply across the street at Toydarian Toymaker.

Most of the creatures up for "adoption" are the kind you don't have to feed or clean up after (because they're toys), but there are a few that show the lengths to which Bina will go in order to supply exotic animals for her clients. On the left-hand side of the shop is an aquarium holding a **dokma**, the blue-eyed snail-like creature from Atollon, and on the right side is a **worrt** from Tatooine, which stores venom in its teeth so powerful it can drop a bantha. Don't adopt him.

See those **glowing lights** shining from within the boxy cloth cage hanging from the ceiling? While most of the cages contain unidentifiable creatures, these are Felucian fireflies.

While you're standing near the Creature Stall you may hear an almighty racket coming from above. What's happening up there? **Kowakian monkey-lizards** have escaped from their cages and have opened a cage containing a Loth-cat. When they set it free, it, in turn, gets hold of a porg, and gruesome mayhem ensues.

Toydarian Toymaker

Restaurant and shop signs in Black Spire Outpost aren't always obvious, but with a little thought and the ability to translate Aurebesh, you can figure them out. If you're a Toydarian (like Watto in *The Phantom Menace*), perhaps it's a natural progression that you'd open a toy store, and Zabaka has done just that. Notice the sign to the left, before you enter her shop. The creature is a Toydarian and the word below it is "toys."

Before you enter Zabaka's shop, take a look at the **stone-and-tile floor**. It transitions from modern, rectangular stones to much larger hand-chiseled stones, and then to Moroccan-style tile. It's a hint that the market has been through many incarnations.

Zabaka handcrafts all of her toys from local woods and fabrics, referencing characters she knows from encounters and from legends. That's her **silhouette** you see behind the frosted window at the back of her shop, and like many shopkeepers, she lives in her store. Her round, **hammock-style bed** is hanging next to the window.

Earth children have rocking horses and Batuu children have **rocking fathiers** like the one at the top of the stairs, to the right of the frosted window. These gentle, if smelly, creatures helped Finn and Rose Tico escape from their imprisonment in a Canto Bight racetrack stall on Cantonica in *The Last Jedi*.

That **green light fixture** to the left of the red office door sure looks a lot like Greedo, Jabba the Hutt's bounty hunter. In the cantina on Mos Eisley, Greedo tried to swindle Han Solo out of the money Han owed Jabba. He was unsuccessful, of course, and he's dead now.

Imagine That!

Look closely at Jabba's sail barge in Toydarian Toymaker and you'll notice two things are out of place when it comes to the original Star Wars stories, with the addition of a miniature of Dok-Ondar (on the upper deck, left-hand side), and one of Han Solo trapped in carbonite (on the small desert skiff, tucked behind the other characters). Although neither was on Jabba's barge in the movies, Imagineers purposely blended separate Jabba and Han legends, as often happens by accident in real life, while also hinting at the possibility that Dok-Ondar was added by Zabaka as an appeasement. Perhaps she owed him money!

When you live in a small town you know everyone's business, and that's true for Zabaka, who has clearly heard all the legends. Hanging from the shop's ceiling is her **re-creation of the fight** between the *Millennium Falcon*, an Imperial Star Destroyer, and those pesky TIE fighters.

During that battle in *The Empire Strikes Back*, Han Solo was unable to make the jump to light speed and ended up hiding the *Falcon* in an asteroid field.

Remember the scene in *A New Hope* when Obi-Wan Kenobi sacrificed his life at the hands of Darth Vader in a dramatic clash of lightsabers? The legend of that famous duel is also re-created in the shop, through **two marionettes** Zabaka has carved and hung from the ceiling.

Jewels of Bith

The sign for Jewels of Bith describes what's inside, but you have to work hard for it. If you stand back a bit and really look, you'll see the sign's design forms a well-known face, with trinkets hanging from the place a mouth would normally be. Once you've tuned into the face, the shop's name makes more sense. It's the **head of a Bith**, the bald-headed, big-eyed aliens in *A New Hope*'s Mos Eisley cantina band, Figrin Da'n and the Modal Nodes.

Jewels of Bith suggests it's all about jewelry, but while you'll find evidence in a small **cove at the back of the shop** that indicates the owner dabbles in creating various trinkets, there are clearly greater profits to be made from off-world tourists looking for a souvenir to take home from Batuu.

Ronto Roasters

Why isn't the name "Ronto Roasters" in the possessive form, Ronto's? Because "Ronto" doesn't refer to the owner of this quick-service outlet, it refers to the meat itself. Within the story, you're dining on meat from the **humble ronto**, creature of Tatooine and cargo carrier domesticated by the Jawas. You're also feasting on Nuna, aka Naboo swamp turkeys. In reality, the meat is pork and Earth-based turkey.

Fascinating Fact

When creating the ronto pack animal for Industrial Light & Magic, TyRuben Ellingson based his concept designs on dinosaur, elephant, and rhinoceros bodies, eventually landing on a mash-up of elephant, rhino, and brachiosaur. His working model was given the nickname "Bronto," in spite of the fact it wasn't based on a brontosaurus. Pop culture insists Star Wars creator George Lucas shortened it to "ronto," and a new character was born.

Rogues and rebels aren't picky when it comes to fine dining, and Ronto Roasters has taken advantage of that fact. No high-tech smokers or top-notch Weber grills for them! Instead, the roaster you see in front of Ronto Roasters is actually an old **pod-racing engine**. Periodically, you'll see "smoke" come out when it fires up, and because it's so old it wobbles during exertion.

Hang around for a while and watch the **8D-J8 smelter droid** in his new job as spit-turner. If you listen closely you'll hear unhappy comments about his current state of employment. Among the funniest is his drone of "turn, turn, turn, turn…" and the obligatory, "How am I expected to work under these conditions?" As you're watching, you may recall a cousin of this droid roasting meat on a spit behind Jabba the Hutt during the scene in Jabba's palace in *Return of the Jedi*.

This little droid doesn't just complain, though. You may also hear **self-encouragement** that keeps him going in the heat of a Batuu day.

Not only does the droid have to deal with the blast of fire from the pod-racer engine, he also lives on a planet with three suns. Consequently he's a bit sweaty, and since he's made of metal his head is **sweating oil** instead of water.

It quickly becomes obvious that the Nuna roasting on the spit still have their faces and their claws, but in an inspired, if slightly gruesome, bit of Imagineering, you'll also see a **greasy build-up** of their juices on the metal base under the ronto haunch.

To the right of the pod-racing engine is the gory **butchering cove** where shop owner Bakkar introduces edible creatures to their final destiny. Among them are **gorgs**, the green amphibian Jar Jar Binks tried to steal from a market on Tatooine and the snack food favored by Jabba the Hutt.

Dok-Ondar's Den of Antiquities

If you've been wondering where the outpost's namesake **black spire** is located, you've found it. It's the ancient-looking spire to the right of the Den of Antiquities's front door. Why is there a tree growing out of it? It's a nod to the connected nature of past and present.

See the large stone to the right of the doorway? It's carved with an image of an Ithorian, the species to which Dok-Ondar, Den of Antiquities owner, belongs. The image, along with the items to the right of the stone, create a visual that reads, "Dok-Ondar antiquities." Even more interesting? This particular relic is an **Ithorian gravestone**.

That gorgeous **weathered bronze statue** is a small near-replica of a statue that once stood in the atrium of the Jedi Temple (aka Palace of the Jedi) on Coruscant. It is seen briefly in *Revenge of the Sith* as Obi-Wan Kenobi and Yoda walk through the temple and discover the results of Anakin's turn to the Dark Side. The Jedi Temple was built around a sacred spire, so this statue surely feels at home at the base of Batuu's black spire.

One of the shop's antiquities goes straight back to ancient Egypt. At least, ancient Egypt from 1989 to 2017.

The **giant foot** near the door, stripped of its black paint and slightly resculpted, formerly belonged to one of the Anubis statues holding up the ceiling in The Great Movie Ride's Egyptian scene.

You can't miss the **bas-relief panels** on the wall directly in front of you as you enter the shop. In their original form the four sections depicting the Great Hyperspace War, a battle between the Galactic Republic and the Sith, were one long piece hanging in the hallway in Chancellor Palpatine's office, and it was in front of this symbolic battle between good and evil that Palpatine began Anakin's transition to the Dark Side.

Once inside you may quickly feel overwhelmed by how much there is to explore, from ancient lightsabers to an elusive Y-wing pilot's helmet. Although we'll only explore a few, nearly everything on the second floor is tinged with movie, Star Wars, or Disney attraction history. Walk to the right as you pass the entry wall and start your tour from there.

The red tank just ahead of you contains one of the most terrifying creatures in the galaxy, but luckily, the **sarlacc** here is a baby. Adult versions of this Great Pit of Carkoon–dwelling mouth with tentacles are the creature of choice when Jabba the Hutt wants to dispose of his enemies quickly and without a trace.

Dok-Ondar is not only fascinating to look at, he's interesting to listen to as well. For now, notice the **seven wooden panels** behind him. They're an Aurebesh list of the items he sells, and they read: folk art, furnishings, minerals, utensils, weapons, and technology.

The scary **skull with curved horns and oversized teeth** hanging high on the wall is a nod to the TV series *The Mandalorian*. It's a skull of the now-extinct mythosaur, a gigantic dragon-like lizard and symbol of the Mand'alor, ruler of the Mandalorians. You'll also see its image on bounty hunter Boba Fett's armored shoulder plates.

The **metal helmet** and **dual-pronged Amban phase-pulse blaster** below and to the left of the skull are also from *The Mandalorian*. They are symbolic of an expanded story line in Galaxy's Edge, when the Evil Empire has fallen, the First Order has not yet arisen, and in the midst of the chaos the Mandalorian stepped in.

Next, look for the urn in the recessed cove below the Mandalorian helmet. There's no mistaking whose head is perched on top, and it hints at what's inside. The urn contains the **ashes of Zutton**, better known as Snaggletooth (for obvious reasons). Zutton was standing on the left when the Mos Eisley cantina bartender objected to the arrival of C-3PO and R2-D2 in *A New Hope*. Even better? The urn was repurposed from The Great Movie Ride's Egypt scene.

Directly above the glowing terrarium filled with Felucian fireflies is an elaborate **chalice**, with the red Galactic Republic symbol decorating the base on which it is standing. This style of chalice was used as an incense burner during Sith rituals. Chancellor Palpatine (aka Darth Sidious) even had one in his suite.

Look immediately to the left of the chalice and you'll see two elegant statues on small shelves. They are Braata (on the bottom) and Sistros (on the top), two of the **Four Sages of Dwartii**, whose ideology helped shape the evil Galactic Republic's constitution. Chancellor Palpatine had the full-sized versions of these statues in his suite.

Above and to the far left of the two sages is a **Medal of Yavin**. Princess Leia presented Luke and Han with the Yavin medal during a grand ceremony at the end of *A New Hope*.

It appears the Bright Tree Ewok tribe's shaman, Logray, had to sell his **headdress**, because there it is, on a staff at the top of the stairs, with his **ceremonial staff** to the left of the headdress. War isn't always profitable, even when your soldiers are stealthy teddy-bear bundles of annihilation rage, so perhaps Logray sold them to Dok-Ondar to help rebuild after the Battle of Endor.

Like a family tree you can hold in your hand, the wooden T-shaped item (to the left of the golden Gungan head), with large beads hanging down each side, is a **Kalikori**, which the Twi'lek from Ryloth pass down from one generation to the next, adding artwork with each transition. The beautiful alien Oola, who danced for Jabba the Hutt in *Return of the Jedi* was a Twi'lek. She was ultimately dropped through Jabba's throne room floor and eaten by a rancor, so no Kalikori for her.

At the top of the recessed section to the left of the Kalikori are two **gaderffii sticks** (aka gaffi sticks), weapon of choice for Tatooine's nomadic Tusken Raiders, better known as the Sand People. A gaderffii stick was used to pummel Luke Skywalker into unconsciousness in *A New Hope*.

Two of the four **shrunken heads** on that staff to the right of the IG-series droid may have met their end at a watering hole far, far away. The Advozse—with its big eyes, bald head, cranial horn, and perpetually perturbed face—and the faintly blue-green Duros—whose red eyes glow within their bulbous heads (when they're alive)—were aliens seen in the Mos Eisley cantina.

Look to the right of the shrunken head staff, down toward the balcony's floor. See the bust that looks like Yoda? That isn't him. Instead, it's a **bust of Yaddle**, a female Jedi Master who sat on the Jedi Council in *The Phantom Menace*.

If you look closely, you'll see she has a softer face than Yoda's, and she has hair.

In a move that proves he doesn't cater only to those of virtuous intent, Dok-Ondar has stashed an **IG-series droid** on the balcony. This isn't the villainous IG-88, bounty hunter and ruthless assassin hired by Darth Vader to discover the whereabouts of the *Millennium Falcon* in *The Empire Strikes Back*, though. Instead, he was once a security guard watching over the antiquarium's merchandise, until he met an untimely demise.

With that grim thought in mind, let's finish your tour back on the first floor. Remember the **dianoga** whose eye you saw above the market's drinking fountain? There's another one here, and it's a youngster floating in green water in a container at the far left of the counter.

A third creature, an **Ollopom** from the swamps of Naboo, lives in a big tank nearby, and he came to Batuu's spaceport as a stowaway in a cargo container. He was discovered by Hondo Ohnaka and given to Dok-Ondar as a gift. Aren't friendships wonderful?

Docking Bay 7 Food and Cargo

With the lure of the *Millennium Falcon* nearby it may be hard to concentrate, but cast your eyes upward before you walk to Docking Bay 7 and you'll see a beat-up **Sienar-Chall Utilipede Transport** on the roof. Chef Strono "Cookie" Tuggs has opened a restaurant in Black Spire Outpost, but his intergalactic cuisine is far too popular for one dining outlet to hold, so he uses that transport as a mobile kitchen and as a means of collecting ingredients from galaxies far, far away.

The transport on the roof is unloading its **shipping crates** through the docking bay's ceiling, and if you backtrack toward the market, keeping your eye on the transport, you'll see two shipping crates behind it, marked with the number 77 on the left crate and 83 on the right crate. The middle crate, which has already been lowered through the ceiling, features the number 80. You'll see it hanging above the dining room when you go inside. The numbers refer to the dates the first three Star Wars movies debuted in theaters (*A New Hope* in 1977, *The Empire Strikes Back* in 1980, and *Return of the Jedi* in 1983). You'll get a much better view of all three crates when you pass the windows looking out over the spaceport as you walk through the upper queue to board the *Millennium Falcon*.

Chef Tuggs isn't exactly refined when it comes to the decor of his makeshift dining outlet. In fact, Docking Bay 7 is more like eating in a warehouse than a restaurant, mostly because that's what it is. The tables and chairs are **items the chef has collected** from around the spaceport, including old cargo containers, used buckets, stripped-down starship seats, and even a dismantled wing from an X-wing starfighter.

See that smoke billowing around the top of the cream-colored shipping container? It's coming from a **portable carbon-freeze chamber** Cookie uses to keep items fresh when he ships them to his diner from around the galaxy. You'll also see **four creatures preserved in carbonite**, propped up next to the smoking chamber. Lunch, anyone?

Imagine That!

How do scene-enhancing details like the portable carbon-freeze chamber come about? Eric Baker, props fabricator and set dresser for Galaxy's Edge, remembers the process: "Chris Beatty and I were throwing ideas back and forth and I said, 'Wouldn't it be cool if we had a home carbon-freezing unit and stuck it on top of one of the pods, as if your food arrives carbon-frozen and they defrost it and cook it?' Chris loved it, so I picked up the phone and I called Lead Prop Fabricator Dave Hyde in Florida and said, 'We need a portable carbon-freezing unit that's going on one of the pods.' I was in Glendale for three or four more days, and by the time I flew back to Florida they already had the basic thing roughed out. In two weeks it went from us talking about it to being a finished piece that was ready to be installed in the park. That was pretty amazing!"

Millennium Falcon: Smugglers Run

You may tear up a bit when you reach the spaceport and first set eyes on the *Millennium Falcon*, but don't worry; you're among friends and we understand. Docked in the spaceport that backs up to the Bakkar Spire range (the rock outcropping in which Ohnaka Transport Solutions is located), the *Falcon* has some hidden magic of its own. Walk up to the cockpit and look for the spot where a dark ring of vents is located, then look directly under the center of the ring and above the two pipes. You'll get an obstructed glimpse of a small "parasite" that has attached itself to the *Falcon*. Keep your eyes on it as you move backward, until you have an unobstructed view, and you'll see that it's a **miniature version of the** *Millennium Falcon*. Clever!

Now look behind and to the right of the mini *Falcon* and you'll see Aurebesh letters. The first is "B," the second is "A," and the third is "NG," which adds up to **BANG**! Seems appropriate, given the sooty remains of an explosion all over the metal next to it.

Not only does the *Falcon* have a parasite, it also has a **porg infestation**. Watch for porg nests made of old wire and other scavenged materials as you walk through Ohnaka

Transport Solutions docking bay (the queue), and also once you reach the *Falcon*'s crew room.

Hondo Ohnaka's docking bay includes a working repair shop. Listen as you walk through it and you'll hear **mechanics chatting and arguing** as they go about their day. If you're eavesdropping at the right time you may also hear them reveal some of Hondo's secrets.

Lando Calrissian lost the *Millennium Falcon* to Han Solo during a **game of sabacc**, and judging by the overturned chair and game pieces on the ground next to the makeshift table on your left as soon as you enter the repair shop, it appears this game didn't end well, either.

The repair shop is chock-full of Star Wars references, from weaponry favored by the First Order and the Resistance to outright contraband, including flametrooper helmets used by the First Order. Of particular interest is a **blaster like the one Jyn Erso used** in *Rogue One*. You'll find it on the green crate to the right of the sabacc table.

Hondo isn't picky about who he hires, as long as they get the job done. Notice the two **orange jumpsuits** hanging at the back of the shop. One is small enough to be child-sized and the owner of the other one has four arms!

Sometimes droids get no respect. An outdated **R2 unit** had its head removed and has been pressed into service as a trash can. You'll see it, filled with various pipes, standing next to the second hydraulic lift.

The Battle of Endor didn't end as the Galactic Empire had hoped and an Imperial scout's helmet is now being used as an **oil-drip pan**. It's the upside-down, white helmet you see just before you make the first left-hand turn toward the second floor.

Imagine That!

During Star Wars Celebration 2019, Asa Kalama, executive creative director, *Millennium Falcon*, shared his thoughts on the quintessential Star Wars experience, saying, "As soon as we started developing Star Wars: Galaxy's Edge, we knew we had to give guests the opportunity to step aboard the *Millennium Falcon*, but we knew that wasn't enough. We wanted to give you the opportunity to *control* the *Millennium Falcon*. Everyone has an important role to play, and it's truly up to you and your flight crew to determine the fate of the ship....One of the amazing things about this experience is, even when it's over, the story continues. So as you make your way out of the cockpit at the end of your amazing smuggling adventure, that iconic hallway is going to look different depending on how you fly. If you had a beautiful, clean run, that hallway is going to be in pristine condition. If you've banged into every possible thing, and taken volleys of laser blast, lights are going to be broken, we're going to have sparks flying, and you're going to hear com chatter about the incredible damage you've managed to cause the ship. It's important that you do what you can to bring the ship back in good working order. Hondo Ohnaka is a phenomenal boss, but he doesn't take too kindly to those bringing his ship back in rough shape."

The focal point once you reach the building's next level is a gigantic **sublight engine** in the middle of the room. Mechanics are making repairs, and each time they try to fire up the engine the outcome is loud, dramatic, and (for the repairmen) disappointing.

When you reach the hallway with large windows to your left and orange girders above you, look up at the power box just above the door ahead of you. You'll find a **porg nest** on top of the box, wedged underneath a series of tubes and wires.

Don't forget to look out the windows at the **shipping crates** on Docking Bay 7's roof!

The queue will transition from Ohnaka Transport to the gangway leading into the *Millennium Falcon*'s main hold, and you'll know you've reached that point when the **floor starts to feel springy**, just like the gangway onto an airplane.

Stepping into the main hold (crew room) is almost surreal, and unlike in most Disney preshow rooms, you get to wander around and interact with the environment. Sit at the **dejarik table**, because every Star Wars fan has to, taking note of the container behind you. It holds a **helmet with its blaster cover pulled down** and a round **training remote** used by Luke Skywalker during his early instruction in the ways of the Jedi.

A pair of **electrobinoculars** in the style of those used during the Battle of Hoth are on top of the box, turned as if you're looking through them.

What's that lima bean–shaped area to the left of the dejarik table? It's the **medical bay** where Finn tried to dress Chewbacca's blaster wounds in *The Force Awakens*.

Below the medical bay you'll see what looks like a slender panel with two horizontal rectangles on it. That's the drawer where the **Jedi texts** were stored when Rey brought them onto the *Falcon* in *The Last Jedi*.

As you leave the main hold and head toward the cockpit, look at the panels on the hallways' right-hand wall. You're standing in the spot where Han Solo and Princess Leia had their first kiss. How will you know you're in the right place? Look for the **X and the O** in white lights on one of the panels, the traditional symbols for a kiss and a hug.

The *Falcon* is big, and there are interesting hallways besides the one you're waiting in immediately before entering the cockpit. If you peek into the short hallway to the left of the loading area hallway (or to the right, depending on which loading area you're in), you'll see a **ladder** leading to the upper and lower AG-2G quad laser cannons Luke and Han used in the TIE fighter battle in *A New Hope*.

You'll be too busy performing your role as pilot, gunner, or engineer to notice small details during your flight, but at the end of your coaxium-gathering escapade you'll discover Hondo has kept his promise to cut you in on the profits, at least to some degree. Look at the **data screen** next to you and you'll see how many (more likely, how few) credits you've acquired.

If you avoided too much damage during your smuggling run you won't notice a difference when you leave the *Falcon*'s cockpit. If you've done a fair bit of damage—as most will!— Hondo will let you know in no uncertain terms it's time for you to get out. Don't forget to look for **mangled areas in the hallways** that will crackle and spark.

You're probably still exhilarated from your wild ride through space, but as you turn the corner in the queue that leads directly outside, look at the wall to your right and you'll see a **gigantic, toothy rathtar**, frozen in carbonite.

Oga's Cantina

Things take a turn toward the precarious once you reach Smuggler's Alley, with Oga's Cantina acting as a geographical link between the two opposing factions on Batuu. The sign over the door obviously reads "Cantina," but in keeping with the style in Black Spire Outpost, there is a second sign that represents the name rather than spelling it out. Look at the wall to the left of the door and you'll see a **painted-on martini glass** with a citrus wheel draped over the rim, and the word "Oga's" under it in Aurebesh.

As you're passing by or waiting to enter the cantina, listen carefully and you'll hear **music coming through the walls**. In reality, it's piped in, but it sets an anticipatory mood.

On your way toward the smaller door into the cantina look to your right. That boxy thing on the wall, with the giant plus sign in the middle, is a **droid detector**, just like the one at the cantina in Mos Eisley's spaceport. Unlike that droid detector, this one isn't working, so go ahead and bring your droid with you. If you do, you won't hear the iconic line from the cantina scene in *A New Hope* when the bartender tells Luke they "don't serve their kind here."

Just before you enter the cantina, get out your data pad (cell phone) and translate the **sign to the right of the door**. Oga has some rules about who can—and who can't—come into her cantina, and how they should act when they do. Among other things, Wookiees are restricted to a two-drink maximum, Kowakian monkey-lizards aren't allowed at all, and if you planned on ripping someone's limbs off, don't.

Oga isn't above salvaging old parts if they suit her purposes, and she's requisitioned the hilt of a lightsaber, a primitive spear tip used during Ewok yub nubs (celebrations), a droid arm, and the carved end of an elaborate walking stick for use as **beverage tap pulls**. Walk along the bar and you'll see several other pulls made from repurposed items.

What are all those black spheres at the bottom of the worrt's aquarium? They're **worrt eggs**, and they provide Oga with a reliable source for the garnish in her Jabba Juice drinks as they travel down the clear tube at the left of the tank and into a holding cylinder. At least, that's the theory. Naturally, these aren't the eggs you'll get when you order the drink. Batuu expects you to be brave, but not *that* brave!

Imagine That!

Chef Brian Piasecki and his team had a blast creating drinks for the obligatory cantina, and one libation stands out as a serious nod to Star Wars geekery. "One of my favorites is a spin-off of a Bloody Mary, called a Bloody Rancor. In *Return of the Jedi* there's a scene where Luke Skywalker gets captured and he's in this pit, and they release a rancor to eat him. As he's fighting the beast he sees all these dead animals' bones. He grabs a bone, throws it in the rancor's mouth, its jaw gets stuck, and Luke is saved. So we made a meringue bone and used it as a garnish for the Bloody Rancor. You have this spicy drink and then you take a bite of this crunchy, dry meringue bone with Szechuan pepper in it, and it gives you a little tingle on your tongue and the back of your throat. Hardcore fans who understand some of these names and these unique plays on food are going to really be wowed!"

What's with the **hyperdrive** in Oga's Cantina? Like many things in the Outpost, it's been repurposed from its original use and isn't necessarily in great shape. The iconic moment during any visit to this watering hole occurs when the hyperdrive starts to fail, the electricity fades, and one of the bartenders has to whack the offending machine with a hammer.

Take a look at Oga's **notice board** on the wall to the right of the bar. Each note has its backstory in Star Wars canon, including one from a certain Hondo Ohnaka, who is recruiting crew members for his new business venture. Although he promises fair pay and a great experience, bear in mind he *is* a pirate and his version of fair pay may simply mean you'll probably come back alive. Plan accordingly.

You'll also see an advertisement seeking a competent Chandrilan Class 1 starship mechanic, ideally fluent in Shyriiwook (the language of Kashyyyk, Chewbacca's home planet). Take the job and you'll be working on the *Halcyon*. This is a reference to Walt Disney World's upcoming *Halcyon* Starcruiser Hotel, which will offer a seamless, fully-immersive, two-day "space cruise," including a port excursion to Batuu.

As you stumble out of the cantina, lighter in the wallet and possibly in the head, notice the **blaster holes and the broken section** at the top of the bridge that connects Oga's Cantina to the residences across the street. Rumor has it they're the result of Oga's revenge against the faithless Wookiee Dhoran, who she used to date. She leaves the damage there as a reminder to future suitors that they'd better remain loyal to her!

Savi's Workshop

Each location in Black Spire Outpost is relatively welcoming to off-worlders, at least from the outside, but Savi makes visitors work a bit harder, and with good reason: There is a secret ceremony going on inside. But first you have to find the workshop. Look for a salvage yard with a gated courtyard and a blue banner to the right of the front door. The **raised sword on the banner**, reminiscent of the lightsaber Luke Skywalker held upright in the 1977 promotional poster for *A New Hope*, is the clue you've found the place.

You won't have much time, but pause for a moment as you enter the small office immediately after you pass through the front door. Notice how many of Savi's tools are repurposed from **old lightsabers**.

Imagine That!

Along with great fun comes great responsibility, as Eric Baker attests to with his props fabrication and set dressing work on Galaxy's Edge. "Star Wars is one of the biggest franchises in the world, and we get to add to that lore. That's such an honor for us to be trusted to do that, because it's so dear to people's hearts. You don't want to mess it up. You've got to get it right."

In the same room, take a quick peek at Savi's welding apron. It has a chest plate that was repurposed from a **biker scout Stormtrooper's armor**.

His desk holds a secret too. It was made from the **hull of a B-wing fighter**, complete with a faded orange sun icon.

The experience of building your own lightsaber is powerful, perhaps more so when you realize you're performing a **timeless ritual** similar to the one younglings experienced during season 5, episode 8 of the Star Wars animated television series *The Clone Wars*.

Droid Depot

If you've dreamed of **creating a droid** ever since you watched Anakin Skywalker tinkering with C-3PO, the protocol droid he rebuilt, now is your chance. Droid Depot takes its inspiration, in part, from that scene in *The Phantom Menace*, from Chewbacca reassembling C-3PO in *The Empire Strikes Back*, and from the ill-fated droid factory scene in *The Phantom Menace*.

You could look for the blue droid painted on the wall to the right of Droid Depot's door, which acts as the depot's signage, but it's much easier to spot the five real droids hanging out to the left of the door. At least two of them should look familiar. The boxy droid is an **EG-series power droid**, as seen in many of the Star Wars films, and the large yellow droid with arms and something approximating a face is **B-U4D**, aka **Buford**. He was the heavy loader droid in *The Force Awakens* who helped the Resistance keep their Starfighters in working order.

Since droids are incredibly useful, you'd think they'd get more respect. Instead, several are in an embarrassing state in the **alley behind Droid Depot**. A U9-C4 astromech is soaking in a tub of oil, one of the droids in the metal cage is missing part of its face, a broken Arakyd Viper probe droid has been strung up in nets, and an upside-down GNK droid is being used as a generator to keep the outpost's power flowing.

First Order

The First Order has recently landed in Black Spire Outpost as they search the galaxy for Resistance hideouts, but the only indications they're hanging around are the First Order Cargo supply shop in Docking Bay 9, the prominent **TIE Echelon** docked near the Milk Stand, and a slew of Stormtroopers occasionally led by Kylo Ren. You won't find much hidden magic near their ship because, well, they're not really supposed to be here, are they?

Imagine That!

How do you bring something as iconic as blue milk to life for a fan base that has wondered about it for forty-plus years? Chef Brian Piasecki and his team went straight to the source. "The development process of blue milk and green milk has literally taken years to get to a really good spot. We know that blue bantha milk is not like anything on our planet, and let's be honest, nobody wants to drink blue-colored milk when it's ninety-five degrees outside. A lot of recipe ideation went into the flavor components. What did the bantha eat? Where did it come from? We asked Lucasfilm if it really was from a bantha what do we think the milk would taste like? Would it be sweet? Would it have melon undertones? Would it be thick in viscosity? Would it be thinner? Those conversations were so intense and so interesting because we're talking about a story that, at the end of the day, is all made up."

You've discovered a lot of hidden magic already, but there is far more to uncover. Much of the story you learn about Black Spire Outpost and beyond will come from getting into the good graces of—or, conversely, upsetting—the citizens who live and work here. You never know what information they might pass on that will help you in your role as a supporter of the Resistance or the First Order. The local gossip is pretty good too!

Toy Story Land

Enter Andy's backyard, where you get to play like the toys play! Everything you see in Toy Story Land sprang from Andy's imagination and was built using **typical items kids interact with** in the course of their day. You're meant to forget the hands of the Imagineers and see only the world of childhood creativity.

In the original Toy Story Midway Mania!, riders were "shrunk" to the size of an unspecified toy, but here in Toy Story Land you're the size of specific toys: the **Green Army Patrol**.

Andy's footprints in the dirt (really the pathway) indicate how huge a young boy would seem from the perspective of a toy.

Many locations in the land include hidden references through the use of classic ABC and 123 blocks, such as the **W blocks at the water fountains**. Hereafter, let's refer to them as alphabet blocks, even though they also feature numbers and simple designs.

It's true kids can get the coolest toy imaginable and still want to play with its box. Watch for **Lenny the Binoculars** and **Chuckles the Clown boxes**, both in the Toy Story Mania! queue. We'll discover more boxes as you tour.

As you explore, keep an eye out for **benches made from dominos, Brio train tracks, and Popsicle sticks**. You'll recognize the Popsicle sticks by the colored stains on one end, which most people remember from childhood summers.

Also watch for combinations of **the letter A and number 113**, a reference to the California Institute of the Arts (CalArts) classroom where first-year students, including many Disney Imagineers, studied graphic design and animation. You'll see it several times in Toy Story Land. Watch for it on the two alphabet blocks just past the big Pixar ball, to the left of the walkway leading to Woody's Lunch Box (look for the upturned red letter "A"); on the dominos behind the two A113 blocks; in the queue for Alien Swirling Saucers; on Buzz Lightyear's box (look for "Airlock Alpha" for the "A," and combine it with Bays 1 and 13); and in other locations. How does it tie to Andy's backyard? In the movie, the license plate on Andy's mom's car, presumably parked nearby, read "A113."

Toy Story Mania!

The **cartoony bear** Woody is holding on the Midway Games box at the first right-hand turn in the queue is one of several animal characters first seen in *Toy Story 2*, as Woody, Jessie, Bullseye, and Stinky Pete watched an episode of *Woody's Roundup*. During that scene, the animals helped save Stinky Pete and Jessie by alerting Sheriff Woody they were trapped in a mine with a lit stick of dynamite. You'll see more of them in the queue, and as animal crackers at Woody's Lunch Box.

A bear like the one you saw Woody holding is still on the **Critter Pop Outs card** across from Bullseye, but the vulture, bunny, bobcat, beaver, and buck are missing. You'll find the popped-out buck on the ground next to the Woody Red #9 playing card from the *Woody's Roundup* game, along the far-right wall as you look at the pop-out card. The beaver and vulture are just below the blue "O" block and the Etch A Sketch.

A delightful bit of Imagineering whimsy comes in the form of a balsa wood airplane along the right-hand side of the queue. While most people are familiar with the inexpensive childhood toy, this one has a rather special name. It's a **Blue Sky** flyer in reference to Imagineering's Blue Sky Studios and the process of brainstorming—called the blue sky phase—used by Imagineers when creating new concepts for shows and attractions.

Imagine That!

When designing new attractions, the Imagineers take their inspiration from many places. Chrissie Allen, senior show producer, recalls the initial process for Toy Story Mania! "We were really inspired by the Buzz Lightyear ride. How can we make it more competitive and more repeatable? You may notice every time you stop at a game, the vehicle records your score along with your percentage. That's the kind of technology we love nowadays. It's an invisible technology; guests have no idea how we're doing it, and that's what we like to achieve."

Once you reach the boarding area you have **symbolically entered Andy's room** and you're interacting with his toys, who have discovered a new Midway game under the bed.

Just before you enter the game itself you will see the Toy Story Midway Games Play Set on the right-hand wall, with a bar code on the bottom left side. There are several numbers around the bar code, as you would expect, but the number on the bottom left of the bar code is **121506**. It refers to the date Toy Story Midway Mania! was officially announced as Hollywood Studios' newest attraction in the making.

Your focus will be firmly on the game after you board your ride vehicle and set off for some Midway mania, but once you have launched your final dart at Woody's Rootin' Tootin' Shootin' Gallery and Buzz Lightyear tallies up your score, notice the split-fingered **hand gesture** he makes as he says goodbye. It's the Vulcan "live long and prosper" sign used by Spock in the television series Star Trek.

Buzz Lightyear is multilingual, as evidenced by him **speaking Spanish** when you reach the prize booth at the end of the ride. It's a reference to the movie *Toy Story 3*, when Buzz had some serious language issues.

Imagine That!

Trusting the creativity of your fellow Imagineers starts even before ground is broken on a new land or attraction, as J. Daniel Jenkins, former senior project design manager, recalls. "One thing Walt Disney Imagineering is known for are epic quantities of project team meetings. Many of them are crucial due to the immense amount of operational, financial, construction, and design decisions that are required to bring new projects, lands, and theme parks to fruition. As an Imagineer, there are always a few meetings that stand out amongst the thousands you will attend throughout your time with Imagineering.

"One of the meetings that stands out in my mind was one of the first project team meetings I attended for the proposed Disney's Hollywood Studios (DHS) expansion. I was transitioning off several years of new, large projects at the Magic Kingdom (as part of the Fantasyland Expansion and the MK Hub Renovation and Main Street bypass teams) to the new DHS expansion projects. In this meeting I was getting my first closed-door debrief of the plethora of proposed projects that would eventually reimagine and transform the Disney Hollywood Studios—projects that would later include the Toy Story Midway Mania! third track addition, Toy Story Land, and Star Wars: Galaxy's Edge.

"In this first DHS expansion team meeting I attended, the proposed scope and Master Planning and operational requirements were being discussed. The sheer scale of the complex effort to transform DHS, the smallest of Walt Disney World's theme parks, was nothing short of incredible. I remember early in the meeting thinking to myself, 'How in the world are we going to pull this off while keeping this theme park operational every day?'

"As the meeting progressed, I remember casually gazing around the table at the attendees and recognizing the incredibly talented Imagineers attending this meeting—many of whom I had worked with during the MK Expansion—individuals who were seasoned subject matter experts within their own disciplines and areas of theme park design. As the meeting wrapped up, I was not only exhilarated about working on this new, massive design effort, I was also confident that if any company could successfully pull off a group of projects of this magnitude it could a) only be Walt Disney Imagineering and b) more importantly would be under the direction of the incredibly talented Imagineers that I had the great fortune to work with during my time transforming Disney's Hollywood Studios."

One of the cutest features along the exit path is the **string of monkeys** from the game Barrel of Monkeys, hanging out over the walkway immediately after you leave the building. They, along with the blue barrel they came out of, used to live in Pixar Place, which once occupied the area to the left of the main entry into Toy Story Land.

Across the pathway from the blue barrel is a big **spool of kite string** leaning against an open K'NEX box. It also used to call Pixar Place home, when it stood near the former entry into Toy Story Midway Mania! It was being used by the Green Army Men in an unspecified, but probably very daring, mission.

Every school kid in the United States has used the iconic yellow **No. 2 pencils** like the ones Andy stuck in the ground to hold up half of his Little Bo Peep Lost Her Sheep game (to your right at the end of the exit path), and to hold up Christmas lights across the path from the entry to Toy Story Mania! What's so magical about that? Not much, unless you know they're made by the Dixon Ticonderoga Company, whose headquarters are in Lake Mary, Florida, just 34 miles north of Walt Disney World.

Farther along the path, watch for the **Popsicle Stick wall** on the left-hand side. It has become an Instagram star, so you know what to do. Snap that selfie!

Woody's Lunch Box

Pay attention to the number of dots on the long set of dominos standing upright on the left-hand side of the path near Woody's Lunch Box. In succession, the dots number two, three, one, nine, eight, and six. As a calendar date, they translate to **February 3, 1986**, the date Steve Jobs invested in Lucasfilm's Computer Division's technology rights, which led to the establishment of Pixar as an independent entity.

Look for the **word-circling game** acting as an umbrella above one of the tables in the courtyard. Andy has done the same thing with a Babybel wrapper and with part of a Buzz Lightyear Star Command Cookies box at the tables with Babybel chairs.

Like many parents sending their children off to school, Andy's mom included a **handwritten note** in his lunch box, which he turned into the top of the Babybel-themed table with the Buzz Lightyear cookie box umbrella.

It's obvious Andy has propped up the lid of his lunch box with a thermos and a straw to create a snack outlet for his toys, but there are less-obvious architectural decisions going on here too. Apparently he didn't eat all of his lunch the day he set up his backyard playland. It's understandable that he may not have eaten his celery and carrot sticks, and he has used them to hold up the **Tupperware windows** inside his lunch box, but who doesn't eat their **Oreo cookies**? They're stacked up under the Tupperware too.

A menu sign is a necessary element at a quick-service dining location, and Andy has used the side of his **juice box** to display the items his restaurant sells.

In the original *Toy Story* movie, the Green Army Men went on a reconnaissance mission during Andy's birthday party, to discover which gifts he received. The first present Andy opened was the lunch box he has set up as a restaurant for his toys, but also in that scene the Green Army Men warn Woody and the other toys that Andy is coming upstairs. The **soldiers on top of the K'NEX tower** in front of Woody's Lunch Box are performing the same function. Andy has left the backyard and they've climbed up the tower to keep watch for his return.

Remember the **animal Critter Pop Outs** you saw in the queue for Toy Story Mania!? You'll see them again here, in cookie form.

Kids like to play with their food, and the **Cootie bug** to the left of the giant Tinkertoy canister, on the right-hand side of Woody's Lunch Box, proves the point. Andy has attached a Cootie head and legs to an open Babybel cheese wheel.

Uh-oh! There are **Cooties all around the restrooms** too! Is their placement by accident or design? You decide!

Scrabble blocks spell out "Restrooms," and alphabet blocks let you know which restroom is for boys and which is for girls.

In an adorable act of creative genius, Imagineers turned ordinary gift kiosks into a **Fisher-Price Play Family Camper** and a **toy dump truck**.

Alien Swirling Saucers

One of the cutest things about the aliens is their collective exclamation, "Oooooooooh!" As you walk along the pathway leading to the queue, note some of the **lime-green railing joints**. They spell out a shortened version formed by the letters "O" and "H."

The two **armored guards** standing watch at the entry to the queue are the theme park cousins to the guards at the doorway into Pizza Planet.

What do you do when you have similarly themed attractions in two different parks? You tie them together! That **giant blaster** as you walk through the queue is based on the infrared laser cannons you shoot in Buzz Lightyear's Space Ranger Spin in Tomorrowland at Magic Kingdom.

In a nod to their former home, the spaceships the aliens are pulling feature the **rocket logo of Pizza Planet**, with the rocket's body designed as a slice of pepperoni pizza.

As you're whirling around the galaxy notice one of the fixtures you whiz past is a literal "**pizza planet**," complete with sliced mushrooms and onions, plus blobs of cheese and pizza sauce.

There are ten different **musical tracks** that play during your spin around the universe, each of them a peppier, somewhat chaotic extrapolation of music from the Toy Story movie series.

Slinky Dog Dash

Those cute **height indicators** at the entry to the attraction and in the boarding area are modified versions of the original tokens in the classic Candy Land board game.

Andy has pressed an old wristwatch face and his dog's ID tag into service to indicate the wait times for the FastPass+ and Standby queues. Turn around and look at the **back of the dog tag** after you pass under the sign. You'll see Buster's name and the address of the home Andy's family moved to in *Toy Story.*

Shortly after you make the first left-hand turn in the queue, look up at the giant Slinky Dog Pull Toy box in front of you. See that small writing under the word "Slinky," which reads, **James Industries**? It refers to Richard Thompson James, accidental inventor of the Slinky. You'll also see James Industries farther along, before you walk through a blue Slinky Dog box; on the book *Slinky Dog in Slinky-Land*; and in other locations. But here's the question: Does it really refer to Richard's wife, Betty? Read on and decide for yourself!

Fascinating Fact

Mechanical engineer Richard James hadn't intended to create a plaything when he wound 80 feet of lightweight steel into a springy coil. Instead, he was working on a solution to the problem of stabilizing sensitive shipboard instruments during rough seas, as part of the United States' war effort in 1943. Just like Lillian Disney's recommendation that led to Mickey Mouse instead of Mortimer Mouse, it was Richard's wife, Betty, who suggested the name "Slinky." Richard applied for a patent under the name James Industries, fame and fortune followed, and today more than 360 million Slinky toys have delighted children all over the world—primarily due to Betty taking complete control of the company when Richard abandoned the family and moved to Bolivia. It was her wit and intelligence that made Slinky a classic. Was the coil a wartime failure? Sort of. Slinkys weren't used during World War II but they did find use as makeshift radio antennas during the Vietnam War, when communications soldiers discovered they got better reception if they clipped one end of the coil to the radio and flung the other end over a tree branch.

Remember the dominos dots that translated to the date Pixar was established as an individual entity? That same date, **2-3-1986**, can be found on the blue Dash and Dodge box, about halfway through the queue.

What about the second number on that box? Break it down into a date again—**October 1, 1971**—and you've got the opening date of Magic Kingdom.

The big pink clipboard near the loading area is covered in stickers, and one of them holds a meaning steeped in Toy Story *and* Disney history. The triangular sticker with a bull's head in the center reads, **Triple R Ranch**. It's the name of the cowboy camp Andy went to in *Toy Story 2*, but it also has roots deep in Disney history. Disney's popular *Mickey Mouse Club* children's television show included a series of short segments called "The Adventures of Spin and Marty," featuring two boys with different backgrounds—and attitudes—who ultimately become friends at the Triple R Ranch. But wait. Keep digging. Scenes at Triple R Ranch were shot at Golden Oak Ranch, which Walt Disney leased at first and then purchased outright.

When Andy assembled his Slinky Dog roller coaster he followed the instructions in his **Dash and Dodge Mega**

Coaster play kit. You'll see the layout on the box above the attraction's loading area.

There is something peculiar about those clouds above the parachuting Green Army Men on Andy's drawing as you wait in the boarding area. In the triangular space between the three parachutes, where you see fluffy blue clouds, Andy has drawn the **three-circle outline of Mickey Mouse's head**.

You're finally on the ride! Immediately after you leave the loading area, look for the box Rex came in, on your left. The **yellow price sticker** on the front of the box indicates Rex was purchased for $19.95, and if you remove the decimal point you get 1995, the year the original *Toy Story* movie opened in theaters. But wait...the date at the top of the price tag, **11 22**, adds the day and year, creating the movie's full release date of November 22, 1995.

Remember the repurposed Barrel of Monkeys from Pixar Place? **Mr. Spell**, now sitting on top of a Rubik's Cube at the end of your ride, used to live there too. He was formerly suspended by a jump rope over the side of the Story Department building, where the gift shop used to be.

Look closely at the RC wireless remote control car box Wheezy is standing on and you'll see the model number is **TSL101118**. It isn't hard to figure out TSL refers to the land you're in, but the numbers are harder to interpret until you remember there are four versions of Toy Story Land. Toy Story Playland opened in Disneyland Paris in 2010, Toy Story Land Hong Kong opened in 2011, and the Toy Story Lands in Shanghai and Orlando opened in 2018. Hence, TSL 10, 11, and 18.

While "**You've Got a Friend in Me**" is an appropriate song at the end of a fun ride, it's also a nod to the scene at the end of *Toy Story 2*, when Wheezy sings it after getting a new squeaker.

The book balanced above Wheezy's head represents a 2009 Disney and Pixar collaboration, *Partly Cloudy*, a (fake) literary spin-off from the Pixar Animation Studios' short film of the same name. The story answers the question every kid asks: "Where do babies come from?" The answer, of course, is clouds.

You'll recall Pixar's establishment date as February 3, 1986, and you'll see **2-3-1986** as part of the bar code on the Dash & Dodge Mega Coaster Kit box at the end of your ride.

The book behind Wheezy is *Mr. Pricklepants Songs for Singing*. Mr. Pricklepants is a lederhosen-wearing hedgehog in *Toy Story 3* and *4*. You'll see the book on your right as you exit your ride vehicle and depart the loading area, with Mr. Pricklepants on the front cover and the list of singable songs on the back cover.

Animation Courtyard

Animation Courtyard originally debuted as the working heart of then-Disney-MGM Studios, a place where guests could watch Disney artists as they went about their craft, take a tram ride past a division of the wardrobe and construction departments, and get a sense of the true behind-the-scenes operations that bring movies to life. Now Disney's Hollywood Studios' central courtyard and its neighboring real estate are home to two shows and a wacky romp through the cartoon world of Mickey Mouse.

Mickey & Minnie's Runaway Railway

Mickey and Minnie are headed to Runnamuck Park for a picnic, but when train engineer Goofy passes by, all manner of chaos ensues! Bear in mind, what you see during your ride is partly affected by which ride vehicle you're in.

The magic starts even before you reach the Chinese Theatre. It's impossible to miss the marquee for Mickey & Minnie's Runaway Railway (especially at night), which acts as a dynamic anchor for the **neon styling** on several buildings along Hollywood Boulevard. The marquee's elaborate design was heavily inspired by the **CinemaScope marquee** at **Grauman's Chinese Theatre** in Hollywood, which advertised the latest movie features of the 1950s, including Marilyn Monroe's blockbuster hit *The Seven Year Itch*, with its iconic skirt-billowing scene as Marilyn stood over a subway grate.

As you walk through the queue, pay attention to the **posters on the walls**. Nine of them recall actual Mickey cartoon shorts, while the tenth advertises *Perfect Picnic*, the short you're about to experience.

There are countless hidden Mickeys in the attraction, from the patterns on the wallpaper in the queue to puffs of smoke in the preshow, bubbles when you're under the sea, and fireworks at the end of the ride. They're everywhere! Best ones? Look for the **very realistic Mickey heads** in the trim of the gold light fixtures on the ceiling in the final stretch of the queue. Hint: Mickey is looking to the left.

You'll find several references to The Great Movie Ride attraction, which made its home in the Chinese Theatre prior to Mickey and Minnie's arrival. The most hidden of these references sits above you in the preshow area. Look up at the ceiling light fixture. See those mushroom-shaped cutouts? They are a reference to the **Chinese mushrooms** that danced in the movie **Fantasia**, one of the films featured in The Great Movie Ride.

When Mickey and Minnie first set off on their ride to the countryside, notice how **their faces are dappled with light and shadow** as they pass under trees. It's a hint that you're about to enter a "real" world, albeit a cartoon one.

Imagine That!

The first-ever "sound" cartoon was *Steamboat Willie* in 1928, and that groundbreaking achievement is honored in the attraction through the use of the cartoon's tri-tone whistle, which gave voice to three whistles on the steamboat. Imagineers used the actual whistle for the sound of Goofy's locomotive. All of the sound effects you hear during your raucous romp were done by voice, hand, and foot, rather than through the use of digitally created audio tracks.

Immediately after you walk through the blown-out planks in the preshow and enter a short hallway just before the loading queue, look at the wood grain on the wall to your right. You'll see **large stylized letters that spell "Mickey"** in the graining.

Runnamuck Railroad's initials are two "R"s, but the insignia you see on the train features three "R"s. Another reference to Walt Disney's **Triple R Ranch**?

The directional sign to your right when you reach the first scene points to, among other locations, **Yensid Valley**. Yensid is, of course, "Disney" spelled backward. You'll see a similar sign near the end of your ride.

The adorable **orange bird** on the archway in the first scene is Chuuby (chew-bee), and you'll see him again at the end of your ride. His name came from a misspelling of Chubby, and it stuck.

The number on the archway is **1928**, and by now you know that's the year *Steamboat Willie* debuted.

If you're sitting in the **fourth train car**, notice what your car does when the train engine veers to the left and the three cars ahead of you go to the right. Your car saw what happened to the previous three, and it isn't sure it wants to go along!

The poster between Donald's hot dog stand and Horace Horsecollar's popcorn stand in the amusement park scene reads, **The Great Moving Ride**, another reference to The Great Movie Ride.

The amusement park's roller coaster is named Twister. Watch as one of the coaster's cars swoops down a big drop and turns **Twister's icon** into the real thing.

The poster for **Potato Land** to your left, next to Frontier Toss, recalls its namesake Mickey cartoon short.

It might feel like you're going to be sucked into the twister that whips around in the middle of the next scene, but while *you're* safe, there are several items (including Pluto!) that are caught up in its grip. Among them are a **trombone** harkening back to the one that captured Donald Duck by the neck during a concert in the Mickey short *The Band Concert*, just as it does when Donald is sucked into a vortex in *Mickey's PhilharMagic* at Magic Kingdom.

What about the **mailbox**? It refers to The Great Movie Ride, specifically the *Wizard of Oz* scene. How do we know? Because of the writing on the mailbox. It reads, "There's no place like home."

Fascinating Fact

Mickey Mouse and the real Grauman's Chinese Theatre go back a long way. The cartoon short *Mickey Steps Out* played there in 1931, and the theater debuted *Mickey's Gala Premier* in 1933, featuring animation that included the theater itself.

Yes, going over a waterfall may grab your attention, but don't forget to watch for **hidden Mickeys in the bubbles**!

Hmmmm. A **submarine and a giant squid** in the underwater scene? 20,000 Leagues Under the Sea, anyone?

As you're flushed into the sewer, look up at the archways. The number **1901** refers to the year Walt Disney was born. You'll see it again if you turn around when you enter the final picnic scene.

There is so much going on in the town you land in when you're flushed out of the drain, but watch for **1401 Flower Shop**, remembering the street address of Walt Disney Imagineering, and **Carter's Cameras** (taking note that Imagineer Charita Carter was senior producer/scenic illusionist for the attraction).

Be sure to turn around shortly after you enter the town. You'll see the sign for **Iwerks and Uwerks Water Works**, recognizing legendary animator Ub Iwerks.

The ice cream in the **ice cream cone sign** on your right when you enter the scene is a hidden Mickey.

Delux-O-Detergent's rooftop sign assures users it's Safe for Ink & Paint, a reference to **Disney's Ink & Paint department**.

There is a **Mickey Mouse T-shirt** hanging on the clothesline below the Grand Central Hotel sign.

Across from Carter's Cameras is a sign for **Maison de Souris**. It means "House of Mouse" in French.

Below Maison de Souris you'll see a lit-up sign reading **Retlaw**. It's Walter, written backward, an homage to Walt Disney.

The headline on the current edition of the *City News*, in a stand on the left immediately before you enter Daisy's dance studio, reads, **Oswald Wins!** It honors Oswald the Lucky Rabbit, Walt Disney and Ub Iwerks's animated character, pre–Mickey Mouse.

Conducting dancing lessons is thirsty work, but Daisy is a duck, so she's drinking a bottle of **Pond Water**.

When Daisy says, "Now, let's conga," a **disco ball** drops down from the ceiling.

If you're in one of the cars that dances next to the far-left wall, look for another reference to **1401 Flower Street** behind the cabinet's left-hand door.

The Brave Little Tailor sign to your left when you enter the back alley recalls the Mickey short of the same name, in which Mickey Mouse kills "seven [flies] with one blow," and is sent to vanquish a giant.

Don't forget to watch **Chuuby** up in the barn's loft at the end of your ride!

Sunset Boulevard

While you're walking as quickly as you can toward Sunset Boulevard's two thrill rides, take a gander at the street address for Legends of Hollywood, located over the red door to the left of the shop's main entry. It's number **Ninety-Four**, which, when added at the end of nineteen, makes 1994, the year Sunset Boulevard opened.

Take a peek at the letter holder in the box office in front of Legends of Hollywood theater. *The Great Gildersleeve*, referenced on the most prominent promotional blurb tucked into the letter holder on the right-hand side, was the first of four movie spin-offs from the radio show of the same name. The names **Fibber and Molly** refer to the main characters in the wildly popular 1935–1959 radio show *Fibber McGee and Molly*, which later transitioned to feature films and preceded *The Great Gildersleeve*. **Bergen** is ventriloquist Edgar Bergen, famous for his act with dummy Charlie McCarthy, both of whom are friends of Gildersleeve and the McGees. In keeping with the 1940s style, the movie was a triumph of mindless slapstick and chronic overacting.

If you think Carthay Circle Theatre gift shop, on the corner of Sunset Boulevard and Highland, just before the Theater of the Stars, must be a replica of something important, you would be right. It was inspired by the real **Carthay Circle Theatre**, where *Snow White and the Seven Dwarfs*, Walt Disney's first full-length animated film, debuted. Had it not been for the success of that movie, Walt Disney's financial future would have been seriously in doubt, as he invested nearly everything he had in production costs.

As you make your way toward the end of the street, pause to look at the red trolley parked in front of Sunset Market Ranch. The trolley has a clever hidden date on the front and the side. Sunset Boulevard opened on June 2, 1994, and the date is commemorated as the trolley's number, **694**. Just a few weeks later, on July 22, 1994, the screams coming from the Tower of Terror would begin.

Tower of Terror

When you reach the end of Sunset Boulevard, you can't help but notice Hollywood Studios' most easily recognized attraction. Tower of Terror is a massive edifice filled with secrets, some fascinating, some just downright creepy. The Imagineers meant for the attraction to be a horror story, but also a mystery; something scary, but also beautiful.

There is evidence all around you that the tower was quickly abandoned. Not only have all the clocks stopped at **8:05 p.m.**, the fateful moment lightning struck the building, but guests playing **mahjong** have abandoned their game, **luggage** has been left in the lobby, **unread mail** remains in the designated room slots behind the reception desk, and a

French visitor has left her **translation book** on a table near the sofa.

Why did Imagineers choose 8:05 p.m. as the time lightning hit the tower and stopped the clocks? Add up the numbers 8 and 5, and the resulting **unlucky number** gives you the answer.

If you have a sharp eye, you may see a **lipstick stain** on the champagne glass sitting on the table next to the wall, with a bottle of champagne next to it. If you can't see it with the naked eye, snap a quick picture with the zoom feature on your camera or phone.

The **bronze owl sculpture**, a highlight piece perched on the central stand surrounded by flowers in the tower's lobby, is a casting by nineteenth-century French sculptor Jules Moigniez, who was best known for his intricate detailing and dramatic depictions of birds. In another setting the sculpture might look majestic. Amid the hotel's cobwebs and spooky ambiance it acts as a vivid foreshadowing of menace.

The **folded newspaper** on the reception counter appears to have been left by the gentleman who also left his hat, his coat, and his room key. Notice the date on the paper: It's October 31, 1939.

Imagine That!

Eric Jacobson, producer–art director for *The Twilight Zone* Tower of Terror, talks about the decisions faced by WDI when creating an attraction based on a popular cultural icon: "We really had a challenge trying to figure out what the Fifth Dimension scene should be. That's the part of the ride where the elevator car goes horizontally through space. No one had ever realized what the Fifth Dimension was in *The Twilight Zone*; they had just talked about it. We took a lot of the elements of the opening of the show and some of the specific story points that we had created for our ride and mixed them up. We found another art director to help us realize what the mission should be, then we probably did four or five full-scale mockups of that scene. Each time we said, 'No that's not right,' until we got to the final one and said, 'Okay, now we've got it. That's what we're going to do.'"

Once inside the library, where Rod Serling tells you the story of the tower, you may recognize props representing various *Twilight Zone* show episodes. Above the bookcase next to the TV in the library you'll see the **demonic pop-up device** from "The Nick of Time" episode; the **metal robot** from "The Invaders" sits on the ledge above you; a pair of glasses with shattered lenses rest on a stack of books, recalling the episode "Time Enough at Last"; an **envelope** with the name Mary on the front from the episode "A World of His Own," on the writing desk in the library; and the book from the "To Serve Man" episode (during which the townspeople were horrified to discover the aliens' benevolent-looking book was actually a cookbook!) is lying face-up on a shelf at the back of the room on the right-hand side. Things do move, so look around if they mysteriously disappear.

There are other *Twilight Zone* references here too. The **trumpet** sitting on top of a page of sheet music in the library recalls the episode titled "A Passage for Trumpet," in which Joey Crown, convinced he will never amount to anything, throws himself in front of a truck after selling his beloved trumpet to a pawn shop. He ends up in limbo and has to make a decision between life and death.

But that's not the only interesting piece on this shelf. The sheet music you see underneath the trumpet is **"What! No Mickey Mouse? What Kind of a Party is This?"** written by Irving Caesar in 1932. The timing for this song is appropriate to the Tower Hotel, but another magical tie-up is that it was first recorded by Ben Bernie and His Famous Orchestra (aka The Lads), who, four years prior, had provided entertainment during the 1928 premiere of Walt Disney's cartoon short *Steamboat Willie* in New York's Colony Theater.

Behind the trumpet and the sheet music sits another appropriate detail for the time. Ouija boards—believed to create a direct connection to the afterlife through which spirits could spell out messages for the living—were popular in the 1930s, not only at Halloween but also during times of strife, as was the case on October 31, 1939, just a month after World War II began. While the odd "Goodbye" in the lower right-hand corner of the Tower Hotel's board and the inclusion of celestial bodies were standard features, this **Swami Ouija Talking Board** includes a get-out clause if users aren't getting a reply, compliments of the planet icon with the words, "Reception BAD." It might be a useful response in this particular instance too; the Swami board was first introduced in 1944, five years after the Tower Hotel's disastrous closing.

Just after you enter the ride elevator, look for the **safety inspection certificate** signed by Mr. Cadwallader, indicating the elevator is in good working order. The certificate is dated October 31, 1939, the day the Tower Hotel closed (and, of course, a spooky reference to Halloween night). The certificate commemorates an episode of the *Twilight Zone* titled "Escape Clause," in which Cadwallader, the devil in disguise, grants immortality to Walter Bedeker in exchange for his soul should he later choose not to live. The inspection certificate is number 10259, the numeric version of October 2, 1959, and refers to the date the first *Twilight Zone* episode aired. Now that you know the elevator has passed inspection, take your seat and venture into the terrifying unknown!

Besides highlighting the 1939 version of elegant dining (grapefruit with a maraschino cherry, anyone?), the menu on the wall to the right of the Sunset Room, just past the counter where guests can purchase pictures, holds a few hidden gems. Note the items **Whitefish Matheson**, **Rack of Lamb Johnson**, and **Polonaise Beaumont**. These refer to *Twilight Zone* screenwriters Richard Matheson (sixteen episodes), George Clayton Johnson (five episodes), and Charles Beaumont (twenty-two episodes). **Gateau Chocolate au Rodman** honors Rodman "Rod" Serling, creator, screenwriter, executive producer, and host of *The Twilight Zone*.

Rock 'n' Roller Coaster

Just around the bend lies another chance to scream for all you're worth. Rock 'n' Roller Coaster represents a bit of a departure from Disney's usual family-friendly style, and it brought more teen-appeal to the park when the ride opened in 1999.

Imagine That!

Just because an attraction is a big hit right from the start, that doesn't mean Disney can rest on its laurels when it comes to maintaining guest engagement, and such was the case with Rock 'n' Roller Coaster. How do you celebrate milestones for a high-octane screamfest through the streets of Los Angeles, compliments of the hottest band in town? With Corvettes, of course! The giant Stratocaster guitar outside the attraction was the inspiration for Rock 'n' Roller Coaster's first anniversary celebration, specifically its shape and its red-white-and-black coloring. Electric guitars are the icons of rock music, a genre that conjures up images of wild parties and hot cars, and what hotter car could there be than the Corvette? Cue Disney's invitation to eighty-five members of an Orlando Corvette club for the making of a promotional video. On the day filming took place, all eighty-five cars, arranged by color to form the Stratocaster's body, neck, and head, drove in perfect guitar-shaped formation across the empty parking lot at then-Disney-MGM Studios, creating a "moving tribute" to the coolest ride in the park. What were the Corvette owners paid for this stunt? A donut and a cup of coffee each, a free ticket into the park, and bragging rights forever.

The Rock Rack magazine dispenser next to the Parking Available sign contains the Central Florida tourism magazine *Enjoy Florida*. Which edition? The Walt Disney World edition, of course!

The delivery address for G-Force Records, just to the left of the light fixture on the building across the alley, reads, **1401 Flower Street**, which you'll recall is the address of Walt Disney Imagineering in Glendale, California.

You would think the name **Sam Andreas & Son** on the Construction Crew Only sign hanging on the fence just before the bend in the queue that leads to the loading area must be an Imagineer signature, right? But that would be "faulty" thinking. It's just a playful version of earthquake-prone San Andreas, California.

Buena Vista Fence Co has a sign on the chain-link fence, just before the turn toward the loading area. By now you know the phone number must mean something, and you're right. If you add the correct area code the phone number goes straight to the switchboard for Walt Disney Imagineering.

Lightning McQueen's Racing Academy

Lightning McQueen, seven-time Piston Cup champion and unwitting bearer of hidden Pixar references, sports his famed number **95**, an allusion to 1995, the year Pixar's mega-hit movie *Toy Story* debuted.

Just like in the Cars movies, part of Lightning's speed at the Racing Academy comes from his super-duper **Buzzard tires**, made by Lightyear. They're a Pixar mash-up of Goodyear tires and the name of a certain galactically popular Toy Story character.

When the honeycomb pattern comes on screen, look for the graphic of Lightning McQueen in the honeycomb directly above the Audio-Animatronic Lightning. Scanning to your left, look at the honeycomb above and diagonal to Lightning that contains the graphic of a blue car. Continue scanning left for two more blue cars, until you see a green vehicle. The green vehicle is the **Pizza Planet truck** from Toy Story, which finds its way into all Pixar movies and makes a hidden cameo here at the Racing Academy.

Shortly after the honeycomb pattern, Chick Hicks challenges Lightning McQueen to a race and promises rookie racers (you) a "huge pile of cash" if Chick wins. When the $100 bill with the image of Ben Cranklin appears on the screen, notice the serial number under each 100. It's **A11381818DC**. As you know, the inclusion of "A113" refers to the CalArts classroom where some of Pixar's and Disney's animators began their training. But this one is a double whammy. "1138," you'll recall, refers to *THX 1138*, the title of George Lucas's first feature film.

When Fillmore offers to help out during the race, notice his **license plate number, 51237**. It's a tribute to comedian George Carlin, who voiced Fillmore in the original *Cars* movie. His birthdate was May 12, 1937.

Fantasmic!

Hollywood Studios' nighttime spectacular, *Fantasmic!* showcases Mickey's struggle against the Disney villains, all with a happy ending and the chance to see many of the Disney movie characters. The riverboat ferrying the characters at the end of the show is a replica of the boat in **Steamboat Willie**. Notice who is up in the wheelhouse piloting the boat?

Imagine That!

Fantasmic! first appeared in the Disneyland park in California, and there were a few glitches to work out before its debut. Disney Legend Ron Logan remembers: "I was asked to create a spectacular for Disneyland, which had no big nighttime show. With seventy-five thousand visitors during the day, the parades weren't enough to absorb the crowds. We had water, and we had Tom Sawyer Island, so I thought, what can we put there? Walt Disney Imagineering said we couldn't change the island, so I said, 'Can we put a dock in front that blends with the island?' They agreed to that, so I said, 'What if we have speakers that come up out of the ground for the nighttime show and transition back into the island during the day?' That was okay too. At the same time, we were closing the *Golden Horseshoe Revue*, and the show's comedian, Wally Boag, happened to be good friends with Lucille Ball. We did a party for the last show, and Lucy showed up. I was wearing a new suit because I knew I'd be meeting her, and at one point she and I were making small talk when a technician came in and said to me, 'Is it okay to test the water cannon for that *Fantasmic!* show?' I went outside with him, and he said, 'Ready?' Well, he shot the cannon off and it threw water all the way to Pirates of the Caribbean! I was absolutely drenched. I said, 'I think we need to do a little work on that water cannon.' When I went back inside Lucy just looked at me and said, 'What the hell happened to you, honey?'"

At the end of *Fantasmic!*, just before the fireworks go off, there is a sudden dark segment. The characters are all out, waving, but when the lights go down Ariel covers herself with a **fireproof bag** so that the sparks from the fireworks don't burn her. After all, she doesn't have legs yet so she can't head into the enclosed portion of the boat with the other characters. If you're sitting on the far-left side of the theater you'll see her, covered up, when the scene brightens as the big fireworks go off.

And with that, it's a wrap!

Disney's Hollywood Studios Time Line

In April 1985, the Walt Disney Company announced plans to build a third gate at Orlando's Walt Disney World Resort. The $300 million park would be based on "the Hollywood that never was—and always will be." On May 1, 1989, Disney-MGM Studios welcomed its first guests, offering just five attractions, two theaters, one exhibit, a walking tour, a handful of "streetmosphere" actors, eight restaurants, and four shopping outlets.

The attractions that opened on May 1 were **The Great Movie Ride**, **Backstage Studio Tour**, **Superstar Television**, the **Monster Sound Show**, and the **Magic of Disney Animation** with the film *Back to Neverland*. Also open were the **Behind the Scenes Special Effects** walking tour, **SoundWorks** exhibit, and **Theater of the Stars** featuring *Now Playing*. Shortly after the grand opening, on August 25, the *Indiana Jones Epic Stunt Spectacular!* held its first performance, with audience members playing bit parts in the show.

On August 24, the excitement surrounding the **Star Tours** attraction, due to open at the end of 1989, cranked up a notch as the **Ewok Village** opened at the future attraction's entrance. Then, on December 15, the ride itself, based on the massively popular Star Wars films, blasted directly into thrill ride megahit fame.

1990: Muppets, Turtles, and Fireworks

The Broadway-style live musical *Dick Tracy Starring in Diamond Double-Cross* premiered in the Theater of the Stars on May 21, 1990, followed a day later by another new show, *Here Come the Muppets*, a stage performance with Kermit and Friends designed to generate interest in the Muppet attraction due to open the next year.

Five- to twelve-year-old boys everywhere were ecstatic when the **Teenage Mutant Ninja Turtles**, whose street show and meet-and-greet opportunities drew enormous crowds, arrived at Disney-MGM Studios. Youngsters were also the target market for the **Honey, I Shrunk the Kids Movie Set Adventure** (based on the 1989 movie *Honey, I Shrunk the Kids* starring comedian Rick Moranis), which opened on December 17, 1990.

But the brightest addition in 1990 was the visually spectacular **Sorcery in the Sky** nightly fireworks finale, an awe-inspiring pyrotechnics display with the Chinese Theatre in the foreground.

1991–1992: Frogs and Princesses

On February 16, 1991, less than a year after its first performance, *Dick Tracy Starring in Diamond Double-Cross* closed. It would be replaced by *Hollywood's Pretty Woman* show on September 24.

In May 1991, **Jim Henson's Muppet*Vision 3D** began serving up in-your-face laughs, both on screen and throughout the theater. The *Here Come the Muppets* show closed in early

September to make way for a new attraction, but having formally acquired the rights to use Muppet characters in the Disney parks after Muppet creator Jim Henson's death in 1990, Disney-MGM Studios unveiled the **Muppets on Location: Days of Swine & Roses** street show and meet-and-greet on September 16. Shortly after, characters from the television show *Dinosaurs* took over traveling stages originally intended for the Muppets when the **Dinosaurs Live!** parade rolled in on September 26.

Beginning on November 22, 1991, *Beauty and the Beast: Live on Stage* dazzled guests, young and old, as the characters from the movie of the same name were brought to life in the Theater of the Stars. The princess craze had begun.

Voyage of the Little Mermaid, a live musical extravaganza, started 1992 off on the right foot. Ariel and a host of puppet characters sang and danced their way through scenes from the 1989 blockbuster movie *The Little Mermaid*, while out in the streets of Disney-MGM Studios, the year ended on another high note as the characters from cinematic smash hit *Aladdin* marched along the parade route in **Aladdin's Royal Caravan**, debuting in December.

1993–1995: Towering Achievements

Things were quiet indeed as Disney-MGM Studios ran on autopilot through 1993. In honor of television's greatest actors, the **ATAS** (Academy of Television Arts and Sciences) **Hall of Fame Plaza** was unveiled, featuring busts of beloved entertainment icons from the 1930s to the present day. However, on the other side of the park the noise level was about to ratchet up by several decibels. Ground broke on May 28 for a massive new thrill ride, due to open in little more than a year.

Every park has a stampede attraction, and on July 22, 1994, Disney-MGM Studios opened the gates and the mad dash to the end of Sunset Boulevard began! *The Twilight Zone* **Tower of Terror** officially opened its doors and the enthusiastic screams have not stopped since. It would be another five years before the park welcomed a new attraction, but for now, the tower offered plenty to keep the thrill ride fanatics happy.

In 1995, the Backlot Theater played host to **The Spirit of Pocahontas** stage show, which opened in support of the big-screen movie *Pocahontas*. On November 22, heroes from the blockbuster movie *Toy Story* began marching down Hollywood Boulevard in the new *Toy Story* **parade**, replacing the lovable Aladdin and his friends. Over the years, guests had been asking for more character encounters, and Disney responded. Meeting beloved animated favorites had become an integral part of the theme park experience.

But the shining jewel in the 1995 crown had to be the premiere of the **Osborne Spectacle of Lights**, a dazzling nighttime presentation shown only during the Christmas season. Buildings along Residential Street were decorated with elaborate light displays, along with dancing vignettes, sculptures, vast archways, and seasonal slogans, all made with millions of multicolored lights.

1996–1998: The Quiet Years

Disney-MGM Studios coasted along with a few relatively minor changes from 1996 to 1998 as funds and attention were focused on creating Disney's fourth gate, **Disney's Animal Kingdom**. *The Spirit of Pocahontas* show was replaced in 1996 by *The Hunchback of Notre Dame: A Musical Adventure*, another live musical featuring characters, some in the form of puppets, from the movie *The Hunchback of Notre Dame*.

After a two-year run, the *Toy Story* parade was replaced by another movie-inspired offering, the **Hercules: Zero to Hero Victory Parade** in December 1997, and in response to the popularity of R.L. Stine's bestselling book series Goosebumps, the **Goosebumps HorrorLand Fright Show** brought the books' scary central characters to life along New York Street in a fiendish street show young boys seemed to love.

Later that year, the Osborne Spectacle of Lights was expanded and renamed the **Spectacle of Lights with the Osborne Family Light Display**, and was by that time a huge Disney fan favorite.

Hercules and friends marched in their final parade performance in May 1998. On June 19, Disney's *Mulan* **parade** arrived, with brand-new characters from the feature film *Mulan*, which premiered in movie theaters on the same day.

1998–1999: Fantastic? No, *Fantasmic!*

Sorcery in the Sky was no longer showing as of 1998, and the need for a new evening show was of pressing importance. On October 15, **Fantasmic!** premiered, a character fest starring Mickey Mouse as he battled the forces of evil and the show immediately drew record nighttime crowds. The 6,900-seat, purpose-built Hollywood Hills Amphitheater filled up nightly to standing-room-only crowds (to a total capacity of 9,900). *Fantasmic!* gave the park a huge boost in the form of much-needed evening entertainment.

The unusual audio adventure *Sounds Dangerous Starring Drew Carey* replaced the original Monster Sound Show, plunging visitors into darkness while Detective Carey bungled his way through a crime scene.

A year later, on July 29, **Rock 'n' Roller Coaster Starring Aerosmith** debuted, bringing Disney-MGM Studios firmly into the realm of theme park status. It was an odd fit, having nothing to do with Hollywood, the big screen, or the little screen, but it was welcomed enthusiastically nonetheless.

The park's youngest guests, most of whom would not make the new attraction's 4-foot height requirement, were not forgotten. In February 1999, television characters Doug, Skeeter, and Patti Mayonnaise from the show *Doug* delighted young guests with a new stage show, *Disney's Doug Live!*

In August, a second stage show—spun off from the beloved children's television show of the same name—*Bear in the Big Blue House: Live on Stage* worked its gentle magic, heralding a new emphasis that would permeate the parks over the coming years. Preschoolers and attractions that appealed to them were now very much on Disney's radar.

Disney-MGM Studios was a far cry from its humble beginnings. It now truly had something for everyone.

2000–2002: TV Takeover

The park remained quiet in 2000, but in April 2001, television's über-hit *Who Wants to Be a Millionaire* spawned the theme park equivalent in **Who Wants to Be a Millionaire—Play It!** The new attraction proved to be so addictive, at one point there were restrictions on how many times per day each guest could be a contestant. With a grand prize of a three-night Disney Cruise (with airfare!), the repeat factor was enormous. However, most hot-seat winners walked away with a pin or a hat.

On October 1, 2001, Walt Disney World also launched its **100 Years of Magic** celebration. Disney-MGM Studios honored its founder with a new attraction, **Walt Disney: One Man's**

Dream, featuring exhibits, artifacts, and a lovely ten-minute film showing the highlights of the great visionary's life.

The same day, *Bear in the Big Blue House* became *Playhouse Disney: Live on Stage* (starring Bear, with his television friends from *Rolie Polie Olie*, *Stanley*, and *The Book of Pooh*). The show would have several character changes over the years; characters from *JoJo's Circus* replaced those from *Rolie Polie Olie* in March 2005, and *Mickey Mouse Clubhouse*, *Handy Manny*, and *Little Einstein* characters joined JoJo and friends in January 2008.

The *Mulan* parade ended in March 2001 and was replaced on October 1 by a more general offering, Disney **Stars and Motor Cars**, featuring favorite Disney movie characters along with classic characters, some riding in appropriately themed cars. Mr. M. Mouse and company were in attendance, and even the Star Wars characters got in on the action!

2003–2007: High-Octane Thrills

The following two years, 2003 through 2004, were fairly quiet, though Residential Street underwent an extensive rerouting in 2003 to make way for a Disneyland Resort Paris import called *Moteurs...Action! Stunt Show Spectacular*. On May 5, 2005, *Lights, Motors, Action! Extreme Stunt Show* roared into Disney-MGM Studios, adding dynamic, high-octane energy to the far-left corner of the park. Real moviemaking had come to life!

C. S. Lewis's classic Chronicles of Narnia stories were made into a feature film, *The Chronicles of Narnia: The Lion, the Witch, and the Wardrobe*, in 2005. It would go on to win eleven Academy Awards and a place in Disney-MGM Studios. On December 9, 2005, **Journey into Narnia: Creating The Lion, the Witch, and the Wardrobe** opened in an empty soundstage on Mickey Avenue, a veritable winter wonderland of artifacts and costumes from the movie, storyboards, and walk-through exhibits, accessed through massive red doors resembling the famous fictional wardrobe.

Aimed at the preteen crowd, **High School Musical Pep Rally**, originally ill-placed in Magic Kingdom, found a new home as a mobile street show at Disney-MGM Studios on January 21, 2007. The East Side High Wildcats whipped the crowds into a frenzy of pep rally cheering. The show was revamped and renamed *High School Musical 3: Senior Year–Right Here! Right Now!* with less "you can be anything" preachiness, more song and dance, and a big high school helping of audience participation.

2008–2009: A Whole New Name

On August 9, 2007, the president of Walt Disney Parks and Resorts, Meg Crofton, announced an impending name change at the Studios, emphasizing the park's new focus on a broader range of entertainment. Then, on January 7, 2008, Disney-MGM Studios formally became **Disney's Hollywood Studios**.

In recognition of the merger between Disney and Pixar Studios, the Stars and Motor Cars parade was replaced on March 14 by the high-energy **Block Party Bash**, featuring a host of Pixar characters dancing and playing their way along the parade route, with a maximum of guest interaction.

Then, on May 30, the ambitious **Toy Story Midway Mania!** attraction debuted, placing a firm punctuation mark on the park's dedication to family entertainment, and guests of all ages were truly delighted. The Journey into Narnia walk-through exhibit was transformed into **Journey into Narnia: *Prince Caspian*** in June, and featured props from the second movie. In February 2009 **the *American Idol* Experience** debuted, bringing the popular television show to Hollywood Studios, adding even more live, hands-on appeal to the energetic Hollywood experience.

2010–2014: Show Shuffling and Final Curtains

A slow period followed the grand opening of Toy Story Midway Mania!, and it lasted until the big announcement of a reimagining of the Star Tours attraction. **Star Tours** closed September 8, 2010, as it received a new theme and new visuals. **Star Tours: The Adventures Continue** officially opened on May 20, 2011.

Disney-Pixar Block Party Bash had its final performance on January 1, 2011, and **Pixar Pals Countdown to Fun!** parade, which debuted on January 16, 2011, had a twenty-seven-month run, ending on April 6, 2013.

Journey into Narnia: *Prince Caspian* closed on September 10, 2011, to make way for **the Legend of Captain Jack Sparrow** show, which opened on December 6, 2012, and closed on November 6, 2014.

The *American Idol* **Experience** had its final performances on August 13, 2014, nearly five months ahead of its originally announced closing date of January 1, 2015, and **the Backlot Tour with Catastrophe Canyon** ended September 27, 2014, sparking rumors of a major expansion—or two!—coming to Hollywood Studios.

2015–2020: I've Got a Good Feeling about This!

Galactically popular **Star Wars Weekends** ended in 2015 to make way for something big. Really big. Like, planet-sized big. And when the boarding finally went up around Pixar Place, signaling seriously secret work was taking place,

Star Wars fans rejoiced. An entire land dedicated to a galaxy far, far away was about to become a reality.

Until then, a steady drip feed of Star Wars excitement took place. On December 1, 2015, Jedi Training Academy, the fun lightsaber battle that pitted young padawans against the menace of Darth Vader, morphed from the original 2006 version into **Jedi Training: Trials of the Temple**, with a more elaborate setting and the addition of the Seventh Sister, thrilling twice as many children per show.

December 1 also saw the opening of **Star Wars Launch Bay**, a massive themed gift shop with movie props and exhibits, which also featured interactions with Jawas, a ten-minute behind-the-scenes Star Wars documentary, and meet-and-greets with Chewbacca and Kylo Ren.

On April 2, 2016, *Honey, I Shrunk the Kids* Movie Set Adventure was another casualty of the march toward an outpost on the edge of wild space, as was *Lights, Motors, Action! Extreme Stunt Show* a day later. The loss of two attractions was softened by the debut of a Star Wars characterfest *Star Wars:* **A Galaxy Far, Far Away** live stage show; and **March of the First Order** Stormtrooper interactions on April 4, 2016, followed by **Star Wars: A Galactic Spectacular** nighttime pyrotechnics show on June 17, 2016.

But Hollywood Studios' transition wasn't just about Luke Skywalker and all things intergalactic. Animation was still part of the plan, with the upcoming Toy Story Land and the surprise closing of **The Great Movie Ride** on August 13, 2017, to make way for a new Mickey Mouse dark ride. Without its iconic movie-based attraction, there was no mistaking the park's move toward a different future.

Following the closure of Pixar Place, guests were invited to explore Andy's backyard from the perspective of a toy when **Toy Story Land** opened on June 30, 2018, with themed roller coaster **Slinky Dog Dash**, spinning ride **Alien Swirling Saucers**, the fun **Woody's Lunch Box** quick-serve dining, and meet-and-greets with Woody, Buzz Lightyear, and Jessie, as well as a new entry (and shorter name) for **Toy Story Mania!**, now minus the "Midway."

Audio-Animatronic show **Lightning McQueen's Racing Academy** opened March 31, 2019, but all eyes were firmly fixed on 14 acres on the other side of the park.

The land Disney fans had been waiting decades for finally came to fruition when **Star Wars: Galaxy's Edge** opened on August 29, 2019, with the chance to fly the most famous "hunk of junk" in the universe onboard **Millennium Falcon: Smugglers Run**, and the delicious anticipation of even more excitement for the spectacular **Star Wars: Rise of the Resistance**, which opened on December 5, 2019. Travelers to the planet of Batuu could actually walk through Black Spire Outpost, negotiate suspect dealings in **Oga's Cantina**, purchase Jedi and Evil Empire artifacts at **Dok-Ondar's Den of Antiquities**, build a droid at **Droid Depot**, and even create their own one-of-a-kind lightsaber at secret hideaway **Savi's Workshop**.

Mickey & Minnie's Runaway Railway opened on March 4, 2020, placing guests inside Mickey's wacky cartoon world, but a whole new concept in the Disney hotel portfolio was on the horizon, promising an unprecedented level of Star Wars immersion in the depths of deep space.

Disney's Animal Kingdom

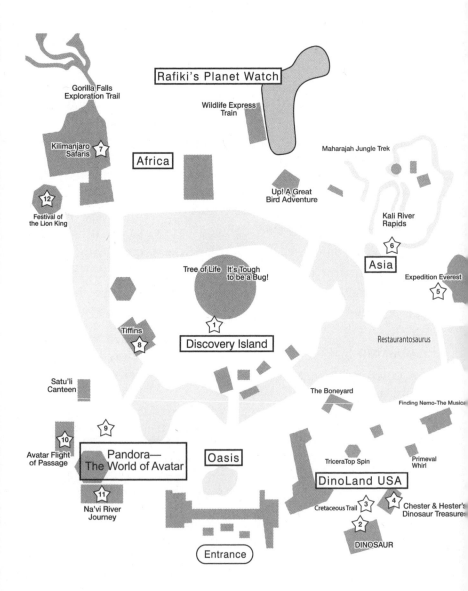

1. **Discovery Island:** Look at the long, low root "bench" to the left of the root featuring a carved chameleon. It's a crocodile, so you may not want to sit there!

2. **DINOSAUR:** Find a faded hidden Mickey under the lower jaw of the massive *Carnotaurus* painted on the wall behind the ride photo desk.

3. **Cretaceous Trail:** Take a look at the notice board at the start of the trail. There is a comical bit of duck-billed dinosaur evolution going on, compliments of the Last Sighting of Duck-Billed Creatures time line.

4. **Chester & Hester's Dinosaur Treasures:** That large, stylized dinosaur to the right of Chester & Hester's Dinosaur Treasures is made from found items, including a Cast Member one-year pin, awarded after a year of service.

5. **Expedition Everest:** The young man holding a cast of the yeti's footprint in a photograph in the Yeti Museum is Josh Gates, best known from his television series *Destination Truth* and *Expedition Unknown.*

6. **Kali River Rapids:** The shortcut leading to Kali River Rapids is bordered by two massive stone columns inspired by northern India and Nepal's ancient Pillars of Ashoka.

7. **Kilimanjaro Safaris:** Deep gashes in the savannah's termite mound are meant to be claw marks from aardvarks digging for their dinner.

8. **Tiffins:** The wood carvings outside Tiffins's front door honor each type of pack animal used by Imagineers as they traveled the world doing research for Animal Kingdom.

9. **Pandora—The World of Avatar:** The stream running alongside the pathway in Valley of Mo'ara is a remnant Imagineers kept from the former Camp Minnie-Mickey.

10. **Avatar Flight of Passage:** Dr. Jackie Ogden, head of the Pandora Conservation Initiative's science team and the person responsible for the technology that allows humans to link to an Avatar, is a tribute to Dr. Jacqueline "Jackie" Ogden, vice president of animal programs and environmental initiatives at Walt Disney World.

11. **Na'vi River Journey:** As you near the entry to the attraction, notice the footprints made by Na'vi adults and children. How do we know the smaller prints aren't from humans? Like all Na'vi, they only have four toes.

12. *Festival of the Lion King:* Immediately after entering the queue you'll see a plaque with the date 22-4-98. It's a reference to the opening day of Disney's Animal Kingdom, written in the day-month-year format used in Africa.

Chapter 4

Disney's Animal Kingdom

Jambo! Welcome to Disney's Animal Kingdom, where the message is clear: Observe and appreciate the intrinsic value of nature. The beauty of the living world surrounds you, but beware—there is an unmistakable element of danger around every corner too!

Several fundamental ideas influenced Imagineers as they were creating Animal Kingdom, among them the concept that not all adventures are physical adventures. When guests are called on to think deeply about an issue, such as deforestation or poaching, or they encounter nature in a way they hadn't before, or they simply immerse themselves in the story, they experience a "psychological adventure" and that experience can be transforming too. As you're exploring Animal Kingdom watch for moments that nudge you to pause and reflect. They're put there by design.

Imagine That!

Among the challenges faced by Imagineers was the animals' "refusal" to follow directions, because, well, that's what animals do. The beauty of their spontaneous nature means each time you experience an animal attraction in the park it's going to be new and different. The repeat value of attractions such as Gorilla Falls Exploration Trail and Maharajah Jungle Trek is immense and unending. Embrace the gentle chaos, as the Imagineers did!

Entrance

The ground under your feet holds a secret, and it starts just after you exit the tram. Those long, wavy red and green patterns embedded in the pavement form a **giant mural** of sorts. If you follow one of the flowing imprints, you may get the idea it's the branch of a tree, and you'd be right. The green pattern represents the Tree of Life, captured in cement. Can't quite make it out? Google Earth it when you return home!

The Oasis

Disney's Animal Kingdom follows a subtle evolution, beginning in the lush surroundings of the Oasis. There are no rides here and very little evidence of human impact on the environment, animal tracks crisscross the pavement, and there is a distinct and deliberate lack of human footprints. This is the world prior to the dawn of humankind, a peaceful haven before civilization sets in.

Be patient as you wander through the area. Animals move at their own paces, and the Oasis encourages you to follow suit. You may have noticed you are walking up a slight incline as you wind your way through the environment. The gentle hill you are climbing is intentional, prompting you to slow your steps and immerse yourself in nature's splendor.

April 22, 1998, was Earth Day, the perfect day to open a park honoring the world of animals and nature, Disney's Animal Kingdom. At the front of the Oasis you'll find the park's **dedication plaque** engraved in a large rock at the center of the landscaping under a light fixture, with opening-day comments from Michael Eisner.

Take the small cutout to your right, before you cross the bridge into Discovery Island, and you'll find a superb example of the way Disney uses sound to enhance their stories. The **recorded bird calls** here are unmistakable.

Discovery Island

The Tree of Life is an awesome achievement, standing 145 feet tall, carved with 325 reptiles, mammals, and birds, all designed to take your breath away the instant you walk from the Oasis into Discovery Island. The bridge between the two areas is wide in recognition of the fact most guests will stop dead in their tracks when they see it. While the view from here is astounding, one to be savored slowly as your eyes travel across its 160-foot expanse for the full impact, it is even more incredible up close, and you will get close enough to touch its roots in just a moment. Have cameras at the ready; your journey takes you underground shortly.

But first, take a look at the newest additions to the Tree of Life. **Two enormous roots** extending into the Oasis form a frame through which the tree is viewed, and they're covered in animals too. The root on the right includes large land mammals such as an elephant and a bison, along with the humble hermit crab, while the left root features a bighorn sheep and a chameleon. But there is another creature lurking nearby. Look at the long, low root "bench" to the left of the chameleon. It's a **crocodile**, so you may not want to sit there!

There is hidden magic in the Tree of Life that goes beyond the variety of animals. The tree's texture also represents a **variety of barks**, including cedar, oak, banyan, magnolia, and pine.

It's Tough to Be a Bug!

The last animal you see before you walk into the preshow area is the chimpanzee, and in this case, a very special chimpanzee. As the Tree of Life was being carved, Jane Goodall, the world's foremost authority on chimpanzees, was invited for a viewing. As the story goes, she asked where the chimpanzee was located, and because chimps were somehow overlooked, a carving of the chimp Jane named **David Greybeard**, the first chimpanzee observed making a tool in the wild (thus redefining the popular understanding of what it means to be human), now holds a place of honor on the Tree of Life. And he'll hold you, too, so climb up on his lap for a photo. Then, look to your left where you will find a small plaque on the wall telling Jane's story. As an interesting aside, David Greybeard is the only named animal on the entire tree.

Once the show starts, a brilliant piece of Disney Imagineering literally pops right up. The animatronic version of **Hopper** in *It's Tough to Be a Bug!* is 8 feet tall and is one of the most complex animatronics ever made. Hopper also plays a not-so-obvious role. His sudden, angry appearance signals the beginning of the end for many children viewing the show. When Hopper arrives, cue the crying! In fact, Disney itself cues the crying. That **first cry** you hear is actually a recording, designed to turn your attention to the audience, just as the bugs have.

Before you leave Discovery Island for adventures beyond, take note of a bit of hidden magic that's right in front of your eyes, though you may not have noticed it. Flame Tree Barbecue (on your way to DinoLand) and Pizzafari (on the opposite side of Discovery Island, near Pandora—The World of Avatar), both have a nature motif. Look closer and you'll realize the theme is really about the conflict between **predator and prey**. You're surrounded by one species bent on making a meal of another, and you symbolically become part of the act as you devour lunch or dinner.

While you're looking for predator-and-prey combinations at Flame Tree Barbecue, notice the **rhinoceroses** that appear to be charging from under the restaurant's roofline. They have birds on their heads, and while rhinos don't eat birds and birds don't eat rhinos, they do have a symbiotic relationship that still works within the theme. The end result of a rhino's meal ultimately provides a meal for the birds.

The pathway to the left of Flame Tree Barbecue doesn't just lead to a restful location for a nap or a meal; it also features a **Balinese reflection pool**, an architectural feature traditionally used to cleanse both body and spirit.

DinoLand U.S.A.

Pass under the Olden Gate Bridge (groan!) and the world of dinosaurs opens up in front of you. You're not actually visiting during the time of the great beasts, though. Instead, you're working with a group of scientists and student paleontologists who have unearthed a treasure trove of fossils. But there is a distinct feeling that the two groups may not be completely in harmony. For the students, it's all about fun. The scientists, however, are on a serious mission, and the divide in their territory (and in their thinking) is symbolized by the changes in the pavement. The area's red pavement is the realm of the scientists; the dirt-like pavement is the paleontologists' stomping ground and the location of their dig sites.

Although most of the dinosaurs referenced in DinoLand did exist at one time, that isn't the case when it comes to one particularly adorable version of a *Smilodon*. As you're roaming around the land, see if you can find the round sign that reads, **Smilodon Sez "Have A Nice Day!"** If you can't find it, check out Solution 5 in Appendix: Solutions to Hints.

The Boneyard

One of the first areas you come across after you pass under the Olden Gate Bridge is the Boneyard Dig Site, a great place to let children loose while adults take a much-needed break. But even the most tired tourists will find some of the Boneyard's hidden secrets entertaining enough to get up off their crates and take a look (or a listen).

Before you enter the Boneyard, notice the wrapped **stegosaurus shoulder blade**. It is a real casting, but it's in the shape of Animal Kingdom before Asia and Pandora—

The World of Avatar were added. The orientation mark "N," for north, and the arrow show which side is up.

The **bulletin board** across from the entry to the Boneyard further enhances the difference between the prankster students and their long-suffering professors. But another conflict is revealed here too. Read the **Notice section** printed in the Dino Institute's newsletter, at the bottom left corner of the right-hand panel. Security has issued a plea for help in reporting those pesky relatives of Chester and Hester, who have been hanging around the dig site and are certainly up to no good.

Just under the notice is a second plea in **A Word from Dr. Dunn**, which details one of the pranks the students have played on their professors.

Dinosaur fossils aren't the only treasure in DinoLand. Tacked to the upper right-hand corner of the bulletin board just across the pathway from the dig site is a **hand-drawn map of DinoLand** as it existed when the park first opened.

Restaurantosaurus

It's not a ride, but it certainly is an attraction. Restaurantosaurus is filled with fabulous little gems that make DinoLand feel like a real working environment, but it does have at least one foot in reality. You can't miss the big silver **Airstream Travel Trailer** sitting right outside the restaurant, which, in real life, belonged to the grandmother of Imagineer Todd Beeson.

The student paleontologists may be just a bit too laid back, if the **basketball** left to decay above the hoop on the front of Pterodactyl Pterrace is anything to go by.

The students bunking down in the attic of the Restaurantosaurus are definitely out to cause trouble too.

They have been shooting makeshift plunger arrows at the **water tower** from a lawn chair on the roof of the restaurant.

The **dinosaur painting** to the left of the four dinosaur heads on the left-hand wall in the counter service area was created by none other than Joe Rohde, lead Imagineer for Disney's Animal Kingdom. Look closely at the bottom right-hand corner just under the fern leaf and you'll see his signature.

Look for the newspaper clipping titled **Mammoth News!** on the bulletin board below the dinosaur heads. Dr. Marsh is promoting the Time Rover as the latest and greatest innovation in archaeology, but that isn't the most interesting part of this clipping. Notice the dateline, which reads, **Bisby, AZ**. Although there is no Bisby in Arizona, there is a Bisbee, and it includes the paleontologist-named Bisbee Quadrangle in southeast Arizona's Mule Mountains, site of fossil finds from the Cretaceous period.

Head around the corner to the opposite side of the dino-head trophy wall and you'll find a genuine treasure of Disney memorabilia. A set of **four pen-and-ink drawings** from the 1940s Disney film *Fantasia*, in which the drawing's scenes were set to Igor Stravinsky's *The Rite of Spring*, depicts the creation of the planet and the rise and fall of the dinosaurs.

Exit Restaurantosaurus by the side door across from the DINOSAUR attraction and pause a moment to look at the first window on your left. A careless student has left a **dinosaur bone** on the window ledge. Why hasn't it been moved (or stolen)? Go ahead, try to pick it up. It seems to have fossilized to the ledge.

Before you head to DINOSAUR, take a quick look at the notice board along Cretaceous Trail. There is a comical bit of duck-billed dinosaur evolution going on, compliments of the **Last Sighting of Duck-Billed Creatures** time line.

Standout moments include Bubba the Cave Duck (a character in Disney's animated television program *DuckTales*); Huey, Dewey, and Louie's 1987 encounters with a baby hadrosaur (recalling the 1987 *DuckTales* episode "Dinosaur Ducks"); and finally, Donald Duck, who was sighted only "Yesterday."

DINOSAUR

It's pretty hard to miss a 40-foot-long, 20-foot-high meat-eating Tyrant Lizard King, so it is unlikely you will overlook the *Tyrannosaurus rex* charging out of the foliage on the right-hand side of the pathway leading up to the DINOSAUR attraction. She is an exact replica of Sue, the largest, most complete, best-preserved *T. rex* ever found.

Walking through the Dino Institute as you queue for DINOSAUR, you enter the rotunda area, where it feels as if you have not only gone back in time, but also underground. Strata along the walls give a clue to how far you have traveled into the earth. That dark layer running beside you, about halfway up the wall, represents the **K-T boundary**, the scientific demarcation point between the age of dinosaurs and the age of mammals.

The **meteorites** you see in the queue are the real deal, and each of the artifacts is either genuine or a cast of the authentic item.

Imagine That!

Describing what Walt Disney Imagineering does, Eddie Sotto, senior vice president of concept design with WDI, beautifully captures the department's intensity and excitement when he says, "WDI is the perfect storm of imagination, technology, and design that transforms impossible dreams into timeless realities. To me, the thrill ride formula is pretty simple; it's: Fear minus death equals fun."

If you aren't too frightened about your impending trip back in time, pay attention to the name of the scientist who is about to send you on your search-and-recovery mission. His name is **Dr. Grant Seeker**. (Another groan!)

Because DINOSAUR is a popular ride drawing long lines throughout the day, you should have plenty of time to look at the scenery as you wind your way down to your Time Rover. While standing on the stairway just above the loading area, take a look at the pipes running down toward the track. The **chemical formula** painted across the red pipe is the chemical makeup of ketchup, the yellow pipe displays the formula for mustard, and the white pipe is, of course, the formula for mayonnaise.

After you board your Time Rover, notice the indication **Vortex Capacitor Sector WDI CTX AK 98** on the right-hand wall. There are several references here, including Walt Disney Imagineering (WDI); Countdown to Extinction (CTX), which was the name of the attraction when it first opened; and the name and opening year of the park (AK 98).

You're in for one wild ride, and it isn't long after you make the jump back in time that it all goes haywire. Dr. Seeker provides instructions on which way your Time Rover should duck and dodge, but pay attention to which way you really go when he shouts, **"Veer left!"** and **"Veer right!"** It's a hint that this may not end well.

What caused your Time Rover to lose its tracking? Those bright lights streaking past are **meteorites**, and one of them has just crashed nearby.

Sure enough, it didn't end well, at least for Dr. Seeker. Watch the **security camera screen** across from the ride photo screens. The Iguanodon is wandering the Institute's halls and Dr. Seeker is desperately looking for a quick exit!

Before you move on, take a look at the massive *Carnotaurus* painted on the wall behind the ride photo desk, specifically at the flap of skin under his lower jaw. It's hard to see, because it's faded, but the hidden Mickey just under the three knobby bumps where the lower jaw meets the flap of skin definitely reveals this meaty carnivore's softer side.

Your knees may be shaking when you exit the attraction, but you can recover from your trip in relative peace and quiet if you take the shady trail between DINOSAUR and Chester and Hester's Dino-Rama, just to the left of the attraction's entrance.

Chester & Hester's Dino-Rama

Chester and Hester Diggs, the eccentric proprietors of Chester & Hester's Dino-Rama, are definitely the local yokels, with a sense of style that is seriously kitschy! But they do know a great opportunity when they see one. They turned their little plot of land into Dino-Rama, a garish roadside carnival, after their dog unearthed a bone that turned out to be a dinosaur fossil. The Diggs saw dollar signs, refusing to sell their land when the Dino Institute caught wind of the geological treasure trove beneath their feet, instead adding to their empire with Dino-Rama.

Every good roadside attraction has its gift shop, and you'll enter Dino-Rama's just past the shady trail you took from DINOSAUR. Chester & Hester's Dinosaur Treasures recalls the tacky roadside souvenir shops dotted across America and, some would say, still prevalent in the Kissimmee/Lake Buena Vista area today.

There are all sorts of wacky dino-related decorations in the shop, all of which reflect the low-budget nature of the place. Watch for homespun decor, including a **set of golf**

clubs (probably Chester's) on a shelf to the right of the front door, whose heads have been painted with dinosaur faces.

Chester and Hester aren't just cheap. That **random mess of painted-over nails** in the doorjamb below the golf clubs indicates they're lazy too.

Most of the **phone numbers** scribbled on the walls near the pay telephone weren't put there by naughty tourists. They were added as part of the atmosphere, with the inactive prefix "555." Read them and you'll discover some are competing companies for Chester and Hester's former service station.

The sign on the roof of Dinosaur Treasures indicates Chester and Hester are having a **Going Out of Existence Sale**, but the real gems here are the names on the drawing of the planet. The bottom one reads **Gondwanaland**, and it isn't a made-up word. Gondwanaland existed 570 million years ago and was one of two supercontinents that fused to form Pangaea before splitting apart again during the Jurassic era. The name on the land mass above Gondwanaland is **Euramerica**, also known as Laurussia, which was the second "half" of Pangaea.

On a billboard at the back of Dino-Rama, to the right of Primeval Whirl, you'll see **498**, referencing April 1998, the opening date of Disney's Animal Kingdom. It's just over the right shoulder of the cartoon dinosaur.

That large, stylized dinosaur to the right of Chester & Hester's Dinosaur Treasures, made from various bits of debris pressed into concrete, holds a real treasure. Stand facing the dinosaur's left side and look for the small gold pin, just below the fourth scale on his back. It's a **Cast Member one-year pin**, awarded after a year of service.

Remember, Imagineers aren't allowed to sign their work, but occasionally an exception is made for an outside artist, and the cement dinosaur does, indeed, feature a signature.

On the front of the piece, written in small white stones, are the words **By Mr Imagination**. Mr. Imagination is folk artist Gregory Warmack, known for his works assembled using found objects. You'll see another of Mr. Imagination's distinctive pieces in the form of a freestanding archway outside House of Blues at Disney Springs.

Primeval Whirl

You can't miss Dino-Rama's main attraction, just outside Dinosaur Treasures. Primeval Whirl packs a real punch, and it's Chester and Hester's less costly time-travel answer to DINOSAUR. But it also pays homage to another Walt Disney World attraction. See those three **dinosaurs hitching a ride**? Do they remind you of another Disney classic? If you thought of Haunted Mansion's Hitchhiking Ghosts, you'd be right!

Chester and Hester either have a bad case of Dino Institute envy or they'll do anything to make a buck. Either way, Primeval Whirl is their version of a journey back in time. Without the funding the institute has, the creative couple has resorted to using **common household items** to create their time machine.

Before you exit Dino-Rama and head past the giant orange "concreteasaurus" toward Asia, pay attention to **Highway U.S. 498**, which runs around the carnival, creating a subsection of sorts within DinoLand. Highway U.S. 498 is another reference to Disney's Animal Kingdom's opening date.

Asia

Welcome to Anandapur (pronounced "Uh-NON-duh-pour"), the "place of delight"! As its name implies, enchantment awaits at every turn, capturing the essence of Asia in minute detail. The pavement beneath your feet shows an evolution that not only includes the imprint of human feet, but also a great feat in the evolution of transportation. People are not just walking in Asia; they're also riding bicycles, a popular mode of transportation in these parts. However, at the base of the mountains you will only see human prints and hoofprints. You are now too high up for bicycles, and pack animals are the transportation of choice.

The **foliage imprints** in the mud pathway also change as the symbolic elevation changes, going from palm fronds in front of Trekkers Inn, to long pine needles on the pathway outside the Yeti Museum, to pin oak leaves in the courtyard of Serka Zong Bazaar.

As you think about the name of the attraction, an interesting detail may occur to you right away. Although you are on an expedition to climb Mount Everest, the legend here is really about the **Forbidden Mountain**. The train ride will take you to a base camp on the Forbidden Mountain, where preparations for the ascent will take place. However, there is something standing in the way, and it's a big, angry something!

Fascinating Fact

The fictional village of Serka Zong was inspired by several locations in Nepal, chief among them Upper Mustang's Kagbeni village, and the Annapurna Conservation Area and its Kali Gandaki River gorge, the deepest in the world. The conservancy, located on Nepal's northern border with Tibet, is hugely popular with trekkers. Its diverse landscape includes waterfalls, rural villages, and, of course, the Himalayas. The area's population has embraced the need to protect their natural resources while also making a living through tourism, with numerous tea houses, family-owned guesthouses, and the ability to hire local guides for mountain treks. Sounds familiar, doesn't it?

Serka Zong is old. Really old. As you wander, notice age indicators such as the **sagging windows** on the left-hand side of Himalayan Escapes and **three exposed layers** of wall at Thirsty River Bar & Trek Snacks. You may have noticed there is a lot of **paint** throughout Serka Zong, on the buildings, statues, signs, and other artwork. Red is considered a color of protection, a magic spell of sorts that keeps evil spirits at bay. **White paint** represents the underworld, **black** is the "spirit maker," and the totems ward off evil spirits. The village's inhabitants are paying close attention now that the yeti has been angered.

Fascinating Fact

Everything in Serka Zong has a symbolic meaning, including the three stripes on shrines, which represent three spirit worlds. These worlds have various regional names, including Svarga, the upper world where gods live and humans reside until their reincarnation; Prithvi, the middle world of people and all known things; and Patala, the underworld, home to demons.

The long **red and black stripes** cascading down the exterior of Serka Zong Bazaar indicate that the family who owns the shop and lives above it is rich, has old money, and has ties to the monastery.

What is that bright red building to the right of Serka Zong Bazaar? It's a **gompa**, a Buddhist religious-learning fortress. Gompas may be nunneries, homes to monks, or retreat centers. It's no wonder the inhabitants here have covered the building in protective red paint.

Why is there **no snow on Everest**? Because the sun can be fierce at the summit and the winds are so powerful they often blow the snow away, exposing sheer rock.

What's with the waterfall tumbling down the Forbidden Mountain? It represents **melting glaciers** pouring down the mountainside, setting the seasonal time frame between May and September. Sir Edmund Hillary and his Sherpa guide Tenzing Norgay summited Mount Everest in late May, making the time frame appropriate to their historic climb. Also in honor of their climb, the **Hillary Step**—a treacherous 39-foot wall of ice along the final push to the summit—is represented in the view of Everest from Serka Zong.

Fascinating Fact

How did Anandapur's Himalayan mountain range get its sharp, menacing look? Imagineers used an array of carving tools, but added an extra layer of cragginess by pressing aluminum foil into the wet concrete.

Expedition Everest—Legend of the Forbidden Mountain

Your journey up the mountain and into the lair of the yeti begins in the village of Serka Zong, progressing through Norbu and Bob's booking office for Himalayan Escapes, past the Yeti Mandir, into Tashi's Trek and Tongba Shop, and finally making your way through **Professor Pema Dorje**'s Yeti Museum, which was once an old tea warehouse, before you begin your trip into the unknown.

The banner stretched across the boulder to the left of the ride's height ruler reads, "Expedition Everest," the name most guests use when referring to the attraction. But look closer. There is a Beware notice peeking out from behind the banner that includes the words, **The Legend of the Forbidden Mountain**. This notice and others scattered across the boulder are the land's only place-making elements that include the attraction's full name. Within Serka Zong's story, legends about the mountain are common, but not specifically in connection with expeditions up Mount Everest. In reality, the full name simply guides guests to the attraction's entry.

Fascinating Fact

The "short" itinerary for hiking to the summit of Mount Everest takes forty days. It starts with twenty-eight hours of hiking from the airport in Lukla, Nepal, over the course of a week, plus two rest days during that week to acclimatize, and that's just to get to Everest's base camp. Then it's another day at base camp to acclimatize, followed by twenty-five days of difficult hiking to reach the summit (hopefully!) and return to base camp. But there is no climate-controlled limousine waiting to pick hikers up for the return journey, so they're on their feet three days later for another seventeen-hour hike back to the airport. Why so much shorter on the way back? Hikers are used to the altitude, allowing for faster movement in fewer days. To summit Everest properly—and safely—with more time to acclimatize, requires up to two months!

Take notice of the photographs as you walk through the queue. With the exception of the man holding a sword, all of the photos were taken by Imagineer Joe Rohde during various travels. Each photo is a narrative in miniature, and because they have no captions, you get to imagine your own stories around them as you make your way toward Everest's base camp. To spark your creativity, take note that the **man in the orange cape** in the framed photo to the left of a coin purse is a member of Nepal's Gurung tribe, who gather honey from high cliffs in the Himalayas, often using just a rope ladder, a basket, and a long bamboo pole.

Enter Norbu and Bob's, where the name of their tour company, **Himalayan Escapes**, has the double meaning of an escape *to* the Himalayas and an escape *from* them.

Sir Edmund Hillary and his Sherpa guide Tenzing Norgay, the first two people to summit Mount Everest, are honored with the inclusion of the book *Tenzing Norgay and the Sherpas of Everest*, which sits on a shelf in Norbu and Bob's office. It was written by Tenzing's grandson, Tashi Tenzing, whose first name happens to be the same as a certain trek and tongba shop here in Anandapur. Sir Edmund Hillary and His Holiness the Dalai Lama wrote the book's foreword.

The trek part of Tashi's Trek and Tongba Shop is obvious. But what does "tongba" mean? It's a millet-based alcoholic drink popular in Nepal, with a sour, yeasty flavor. It is traditionally served hot, making it a good warmer on a cold Himalayan night. Tashi's has everything trekkers could need to make their journey more comfortable, but if it is uncomfortable, at least the beer will take the edge off. Look for a tongba mug on the table in Tashi's, and several for sale on the shelves, complete with specialized drinking straws.

The large cabinet you come to just after you make the first turn in the queue inside the Yeti Museum holds an important piece of Mount Everest research material. The faded blue book behind the propane stove recalls the speech **"Observations on the Rocks and Glaciers of Mount Everest"** given by N.E. Odell to the Royal Geographical Society on May 18, 1925. The presentation covered Everest's geography in great detail, including maps and photographs taken during a five-month expedition during which Odell, a geologist, served as the climbing party's oxygen officer.

You will find two more references honoring Tenzing Norgay and Sir Edmund Hillary in the Yeti Museum. One is a **picture of Norgay,** in the second large cabinet you come to as you're walking through the queue. The shorter case to its left holds a copy of the July 13, 1953, edition of *LIFE* **magazine** featuring the explorers' summiting of Mount Everest.

The young man holding a cast of the yeti's footprint in the photograph on the wall above a door in the Yeti Museum, and in a cabinet with the cast itself, looks like an authentic scientist, although he isn't. He is **Josh Gates**, an adventurer best known from his television series *Destination Truth* and *Expedition Unknown*. That "yeti footprint" cast isn't one Disney Imagineers cooked up; it's a cast Gates took during his own expedition to the Himalayas, then donated to Serka Zong's museum. While it fits beautifully into Disney's story line, it also has one very big foot in reality—at least from the standpoint of the cast itself being real.

Fascinating Fact

The sense of realism is immense due to the Imagineers' attention to detail and the fact that there are more than two thousand authentic items throughout the attraction that were handcrafted in Asia. Many everyday items were purchased in Nepal to ensure authenticity. Even the nails holding up pictures on the wall were purchased from locals. They look like the real deal because they are the real deal.

Norbu and Bob are on a mission to **convince tourists the yeti doesn't exist**. Notice the sign on the wall to your right just before you exit the Yeti Museum. It's obvious they don't want you to cancel your upcoming trip.

Read the letter Professor Dorje has received from **Russell A. Mittermeier, PhD**. Mittermeier was the president of Conservation International from 1989 until September 2014, and he is considered one of the most important wildlife conservationists in the world. In 1999, he was named one of *TIME* magazine's Heroes for the Planet.

While you are waiting to board, notice the **boiler at the back of the train**. It isn't practical to have a full load of water onboard this particular steam train, so Imagineers employed a little magic. Watch closely, and you'll see the steam actually comes up through the train from the tracks below shortly before it sets in motion. Where does the steam originate? It starts in the boiler you see to the right of the boarding area. You'll pass it as you begin your journey.

Why is the Forbidden Mountain's yeti brownish-orange, when most of the yeti toys in the gift shop are white? Yeti sightings have historically included the description of **brown or orange-brown fur**, so Expedition Everest's yeti honors those oral histories. White yetis fit well with Westernized images of an "abominable snowman" and are, apparently, deemed cuddlier.

Imagine That!

Animals adapted to cold, snowy climates have a few things in common, so Expedition Everest's yeti had to be huge and hairy, with very little facial skin exposed. Although yetis must be herbivores due to the lack of mammals as a food source in wild areas of the Himalayas, they would also need strong jaws and big canine teeth, useful tools when eating fibrous plants. When it comes to a structured nose, forget it. Primates adapted to cold environments have nasal openings, but no tissue or cartilage that forms what we think of as a nose. Throw in a heaping helping of attitude and you've got yourself a yeti! Those were the decisions Imagineers made when they created Expedition Everest's starring creature.

As you exit the attraction, dazed but unharmed, your newfound appreciation for the sanctity of the mountain may inspire you to send up your own prayer of thanks for a safe return. And the place to do it would be the **prayer wall** you see off to the left as you are walking up the stairs to the main pathway. Common in Tibetan culture, carved mani (prayer) stones are often piled up near mountain passes, temples, lakes, and other outdoor areas, providing a sacred place for the faithful to pray.

But the biggest secret of Everest is this: The yeti *isn't* feared as an evil, destructive creature. He is honored, in every way you have just observed and in real life among the Himalayan people, as the spiritual **Protector of the Mountain**. Sure, he's going to chase you away as soon as you reach the summit, causing your train to careen wildly down the mountain. But hey, he's only doing his job. You dared to enter the realm of the yeti!

As the blue signs at the front of the building insist, **Gupta's Gear** carries backpacks, boots, oxygen tanks, and first-class mountaineering equipment, but there is a rather grim side to how Gupta might get his gear. His shop is closed, which indicates he might be out on the mountain stocking up on supplies. One wonders if he's getting them at rock-bottom prices (free), hoovering up the debris left behind by eager summit seekers or those who gave up and went home.

The real Mount Everest is rarely the tallest mountain you see because it is usually viewed from a distance, making closer mountains appear to be larger. With that in mind, Imagineers created a **peekaboo moment** (a quick glimpse of something interesting from other areas in the park) for

Anandapur's Everest, with the telescope you see next to the shrine as you leave the Everest area heading farther into Asia. Look through the telescope and you will see it is focused on the mountain to the right of the highest peak. That's Everest. The highest mountain you see is the Forbidden Mountain, and its placement in front of Everest giving the illusion of height is another form of forced perspective.

While you're admiring the shape of the shrine, pay attention to the **small yeti**, the mountain range he is holding in his right hand, and the way his right leg is bent. You'll see his bronze twin when you visit the Trek Gallery at Tiffins later in your tour.

The shortcut leading to Kali River Rapids, to the right of the gibbon's temple, is bordered by **two massive stone columns** capped with stylized lions and cobras. They were inspired by commemorative pillars found throughout northern India and Nepal, the most famous of which are the Pillars of Ashoka. Emperor Ashoka's pillars were much simpler, with a relatively plain inscribed column and an elephant, a lion, or a bull at the top.

Fascinating Fact

Emperor Ashoka ruled India's Mauryan empire from 265 B.C.E. to 238 B.C.E., at first as a cruel tyrant, but in his later years, after viewing the aftermath of the massacre he ordered against the region of Kalinga, he had a change in consciousness and began following a righteous path. When you reach Maharajah Jungle Trek the stories' similarities will be unmistakable. However, in Emperor Ashoka's case, rather than using his newfound knowledge to live in harmony with nature, he erected 50-foot-high stone pillars across the Magadha region of northern India, carved with the wisdoms he gained from his new life in Buddhism—along with an apology for his massacres, an assurance he experienced an awakening, and a fair bit of humble-bragging about his good works.

Drinkwallah beverage outlet, across from the Yak & Yeti Restaurant, is rather unassuming, but its proprietor has gone out of her way to embellish her establishment with all sorts of unusual touches. Notice the metal hood over the slushie machines, made by Anandapur Sheet Metal Company, and the disproportionately large poster of her favorite celebrity. She wasn't overly creative with her business's name, however. *Wallah* has several meanings in Hindi, but in this case it refers to a seller, so "Drinkwallah" translates to "**drink seller**."

The proprietor's boat is in the waterway below Drinkwallah's lower garden, and her bicycle is parked next to her shop. Their purpose fulfills another meaning of the term "wallah." The proprietor is also a **delivery-service provider**.

Enjoy a drink at one of the covered tables, and while you're sitting there, look up. The **painted storytelling boards** that make up the slanted roof prove recycling is alive and well in Anandapur.

Interested in doing a bit of trekking while you're in the area? Check out the **notice board** inside Drinkwallah, where trekkers and tour companies have left notices.

Kali River Rapids

Kali, the Hindu goddess who lends her name to the river in Animal Kingdom's Asia, is the goddess of time and of the transformation that comes with death. She is the ferocious incarnation of the Divine Mother and is believed to create the fear of death in the ignorant while removing that fear in those who seek knowledge. With that little tidbit in mind, are you ready for a ride down her river?

The **Trekking Guide of Anandapur Township** sign, just off the main path between the Siamang temple and the outdoor dining area of the Yak & Yeti Restaurant, lists a certain **Seven Summits Mt. Trekking**, recalling the Seven Summits Expeditions window on Main Street, U.S.A. honoring Frank Wells, president of Walt Disney Company from 1984 until 1994, who was an avid mountaineer.

Another feature of the Trekking Guide is that all the locations listed in blue are places you can actually visit in Anandapur, while those listed in red are fictitious. **Chakranadi Chicken Shop** falls somewhere in between; it was a real dining spot in Anandapur, but it closed in 2006 to make way for the Yak & Yeti Restaurant.

The building on stilts on the left side of the pathway leading to the queue for Kali River Rapids is someone's home, and they're not the wealthiest people in the village. Notice the **floral curtains** at the windows. One of them is a shirt.

The beautiful paintings on the ceiling of the temple just after you enter the covered portion of the queue are based on a vast body of Buddhist literature called **Jatakas**. Similar in style to the old European fairy tales, the Jatakas are stories of the Buddha's lives, which offer moral guidance to his followers.

A sign posted on the wall just before Mr. Panika's Shop gives tourists an idea of what they can expect from the nearby hotel. Take note of the warning, **"mattress and toilet paper just a little extra."**

As you walk through Mr. Panika's Shop, notice how he has employed his best English to attract more tourists. He didn't get it exactly right, but his signs reading "**looking looking is free please you kom in our store**" and "**spesial prices for tourists**" show he's making an effort.

Mr. Panika will do just about anything to make a sale. The sign above his desk reads, **Antiks Made to Order**, and it doesn't mean "antics," it means "antiques." Want to take home a special souvenir of your visit to Anandapur? Mr. Panika will assemble something quickly and you can tell your friends it's ancient. They'll never know the difference.

Kali Rapids Expeditions keeps a close eye on what their raft excursions are up to, and the Manaslu Slammer raft hints at a problem. The chalkboard listing each of the **expedition rafts and their current disposition** indicates the Slammer was due back yesterday. But don't worry about your rafting trip. What could go wrong?

Look for the **canoe paddles** with names and comments on them hanging on the walls as you walk through the Kali Rapids Expeditions office. Some of them are the signatures of the attraction's Imagineers and designers. Cast Members who work at Kali River Rapids are also allowed to sign a paddle when they leave so that they are always a part of the attraction.

Once you are settled in your raft, look at the rockwork on the left side of the river as you approach the top of the first lift hill. If you have a sharp eye, you'll see the **face of a tiger** carved into one of the rocks. In the planning stages, the attraction was called Tiger Rapids Run and the face carved here is a nod toward its former name.

Imagine That!

Realistic environments are a key element in the parks, but one of the main goals is to bring guests fully into the story in ways beyond the visual. Immersing guests in evocative sights, sounds, textures, and scents is of primary importance, as Imagineer Joe Rohde explains: "It's got to feel like nature, not just look like nature. If you feel the naturalness, then you're going to feel the threat all the more, which is, of course, the threat to harvest out the value of nature and turn it from intrinsic value to monetary value. Therein lies the conflict that is at the source of almost every story at Animal Kingdom."

When your raft careens over the edge, you're not going over a waterfall, though that seems like the obvious circumstance. Instead, your drop indicates **the land has been decimated** and is now giving way beneath you.

Maharajah Jungle Trek

After your harrowing journey down Kali River Rapids, you're probably ready for a more relaxing adventure along Maharajah Jungle Trek, which winds its way through the Royal Anandapur Forest.

Why have newspapers been stuffed into the ceiling of the building at the entry into Maharajah Jungle Trek? They're an **inexpensive form of insulation**.

Nature has taken over what was once the Royal Hunting Palace of the Maharajahs, but the villagers make use of the abandoned rooms too. Notice the **movie camera** suspended from the ceiling in the fruit bat enclosure. This is a community room, where films are shown and special events take place. If you look at the **calendar** on the wall just after you exit the enclosure you'll see what's on the agenda for this month.

When you leave the bat enclosure, look to your right and you'll see a series of interesting pictures in the hallway. The **photographs** are of real caves in Asia that were inhabited by bats, though they were not the bats you see here. Even better, the man in one of the pictures with his back to the camera is none other than Animal Kingdom's lead Imagineer, Joe Rohde.

Murals along the jungle trek tell the story of the maharajahs who once lived here. The first prince you see on the left was a hunter who felt it was his right to control the natural world, while the prince on the right cared only for the material world. As the balance between man and nature broke down, the third prince attempted to regain order, and the fourth prince, surrounded by birds, allowed nature to take over as he left the palace and found peace among the animals.

As you walk along the pathway, notice details such as the **black and white floor tiles** of the former ballroom, **support columns** that no longer hold up a roof, and **walls** that once separated rooms in the hunting palace. They are partially obscured by foliage, telling a story of nature's retaliation over man's indifference.

As you browse the shops before leaving Asia, notice the picture of the **Royal Couple of Anandapur**. Every shop will have one, not only to honor Their Highnesses, but also to show how wealthy the shop owner is. The bigger the picture is, the wealthier the owner.

The more mundane reason for the display is to prove the business is **licensed by the government**. Even the owner of the rickshaw that parks in various places around Serka Zong displays their picture on the front of his rig to show he's an official form of transportation.

Africa

You have finally reached Africa, the cradle of civilization. Hoofprints dot the pathways, leading off into the lush underbrush. Human influence is evident, but there is a sense of cooperation between people and animals, a feeling of balance, with neither overpowering the other. Enter the village of Harambe and you'll find a bustling settlement full of music, wildlife, and some fascinating hidden gems. Of all the lands in Walt Disney World, Africa is the one that most closely resembles the real thing. Every building you see here is an exact replica of an existing building in Africa, right down to the cracks and crevices.

Imagine That!

Imagineer Eric Jacobson, senior vice president of creative at WDI, describes the meticulous process of moving a concept from rough idea through to the "cracks and crevices." "We like to say—and we follow this extensively—it all starts with a story. In everything we do, we have a story that we're following so that the entire team knows what the goal is and what story we're telling. Then, all that layering from the initial outline to the script to the physical building to all the detail supports the story line that we developed in the beginning. We may modify it or massage it along the way, but basically we all follow that one path. Just by doing the detail and those extra things, it brings the story to life in a way that people really appreciate."

The time period is post–British rule, with evidence of the occupation (such as the iconic British **mailbox** near the restrooms across from Tusker House) and of East Africa's subsequent freedom.

Take note of the directional sign next to Tamu Tamu Refreshments as you approach Harambe, and in various other locations around the village. The date you see on the sign's base, **1961**, signifies the year the Republic of Kenya began its road to independence, when Jomo Kenyatta won the presidency of the Kenya African National Union. That date ties Disney's fictional Harambe to Kenya's real town of Harambee. But another important event took place in 1961 too. Tanganyika (later called Tanzania) in East Africa became fully independent of British rule on November 1, 1961. Because Animal Kingdom's Africa is a blending of many African nations, that political change is also relevant, and is honored through the motto **Uhuru**, the Swahili word for "freedom," which you will find in various locations throughout Harambe.

Even Dawa Bar has a hidden meaning. In Swahili, *dawa* literally translates to "medicine," but in connection with a bar it means something along the lines of "**party medicine**," inviting guests to have a drink.

You may not notice anything particularly intriguing about the Hoteli Burudika, just past Dawa Bar as you walk toward Kilimanjaro Safaris, but take a look anyway. See that notice posted on the wall with the peculiar word **Jorodi** on it? Say it slowly. It's a hidden Imagineer signature, and by now you can probably figure out whose!

The address for Jorodi Masks and Beads is **Ushaufu Way**. *Ushaufu* has several meanings in Swahili, including "frivolity," "something misleading," "something disappointing," and "vanity." However, it does have another meaning: Translated as "pendant," it is an appropriate reference to Joe Rohde's signature earrings.

Fascinating Fact

Thatch is a near-perfect roofing material. It's fire resistant and highly insulating, and it lasts up to forty years. Thatched roofs in Animal Kingdom's Africa section, with the exception of those near Harambe Theater, were made by thatchers from Zululand in South Africa.

Festival of the Lion King

The story of Harambe Port revolves around a former fort, which has been repurposed as a theater for traveling entertainment.

But the theater isn't the only business in town. **Bars on the windows** above the theater's exit reveal that this part of the fort has been turned into a jail. Next to the theater's exit is the **Ubongo Center of Learning**, while several other businesses, including an artist, a hairdresser, a silversmith, a traditional healer, and a local offering computer classes have taken over the former **Customs & Clearance center** and the building formerly occupied by **His Majesty's Imperial Protectorate Mail Service**.

Imagine That!

Many of Disney's special effects, such as the dancing ghosts in Magic Kingdom's Haunted Mansion, are fairly high-tech, but some are decidedly low-tech. The short wall just outside of Harambe Theater looks as if it has been there for fifty years, but the aged effect was created by an artist flinging handfuls of concrete against the wall to give it texture, then painting on algae and other details.

Just as the visitors to Hoteli Burudika while away the hours above the Dawa Bar, those who work in the theater district enjoy their break time on the roof of the Customs and Clearance Center. There is even a **satellite dish** on the roof, supplying television service to the area.

Flyers on telephone poles advertising the theater's show read, **"Maonyesho ya mfalme simba. Utendaji mizuri. Inafunguliwa siku zote. Kiribu nu Harambee Beach."** They translate to, "Performances of *Lion King*. Good performance.

Opening all day. Synergy Beach closed now." In Swahili, *harambee* means "let us all pull together," or "synergy."

Take time to read the signs posted along the queue as you make your way toward the festival. Immediately after entering the queue you'll see a humorous reference to **rascally baboons**, and a plaque indicating you are in an **Official Harambe Heritage Site**, with the date 22-4-98. Although it states Harambe Fort was built in 1498 rather than 1998, by now you know the date is a reference to the opening day of Disney's Animal Kingdom, written in the day-month-year format used in Europe and Africa.

Just before you enter the theater, notice the sign to the extreme left of the doors. It advertises the **Mpira Tyre Company**. In Swahili, *mpira* means "tire" (spelled "tyre" in Africa), "rubber," and "ball," making it a fitting name for the company.

Kilimanjaro Safaris

There is no mistaking Animal Kingdom's message of conservation as your safari takes you to the African savannah, and the power of being directly immersed in the animals' natural habitat brings that message home in a real and immediate way. Although the environment is closely controlled in some ways, this is one of the few attractions in Walt Disney World where almost anything truly can happen. You never know where the savannah's residents might be at any given time and you never know what you might see. Every journey is different, and in this place the animals dictate where the magic will be found.

Although flatbed trucks were modified to look like jumbo versions of authentic safari vehicles, the **lattice-like**

bumper on the front of the truck isn't found on an actual African safari. Mickey doesn't want his friends to get into trouble, so Disney installed "bird guards" that ensure smaller animals won't accidentally find themselves under your jeep.

Imagine That!

Kilimanjaro Safaris presented a unique problem for the Imagineers, who recognized the unpredictability of the show environment. Designer Joe Rohde describes how they dealt with the challenge: "Unlike a scene in a ride where you can direct people to 'look over here,' we knew two things: One, you can look wherever you please, and number two, we will never know where the focal object is going to be, which is an animal. The animal could be anywhere and you can look anywhere. So when we did our storyboards, we drew a line on the ride track estimating the average speed of the vehicle, made a dot every thirty seconds, and we drew 180-degree storyboards that we would hold up in front of our faces and go, 'Okay, that's at second number seven hundred, we're here, seeing something like this.' The wildebeests might all be over here, they might all be here, but they're going to be in this scene. We'd pick up the next one, bend it around our head and, all right, this is the next scene. So we could get some sense of what is this going to be like to progress through this environment because, of course, back then we couldn't do a digital ride-through. No such thing existed."

When you reach the savannah look at the termite mound to your left, just as you round the first right-hand bend in the road. Those deep gashes are meant to be **claw marks from aardvarks** digging for their dinner.

Fascinating Fact

For the animals' safety, many of them must return to a shelter for the night. How do they know when to return? Each species responds to a specific sound. Out on the savannah, zebras return when they hear a cowbell, giraffes return to the sound of a sports whistle, most of the hoofed animals respond to a horn, and the Thomson's gazelles have the most unusual signal—they come running when they hear a goose call.

Animals are not the only ones making use of the savannah. Just after your tour passes Flamingo Island, look at the **outcroppings** on either side of your Jeep. The local tribe has added an artistic touch to the rocks.

There is more to explore, this time on foot. Your next adventure waits just around the bend, to the left of the exit for Kilimanjaro Safaris, in the form of a walking path, providing a respite from Africa's hustle and bustle.

Gorilla Falls Exploration Trail

At the beginning of the trail you'll pass through an **archway** that is, literally, a piece of Imagineer handcrafting. The simple mud structure became a work of art when the designers applied their bare hands to the job, leaving their prints on the arch as they applied its rough surface. Even Executive Designer Joe Rohde and Concept Architect Tom Sze left their imprints on the walls, re-creating a timeless building technique while adding their own silent signature to the work.

The original family group of gorillas that inhabit this area, formerly known as Pangani Forest Exploration Trail, came from the **Lincoln Park Zoo** in Chicago, Illinois. The group's dominant silverback (who originally hailed from Denmark, then Chicago) has since fathered fourteen offspring who went on to produce twenty grandchildren. From them came ten great-grandchildren and counting!

Fascinating Fact

Gorilla Falls Exploration Trail's newest troop member is Grace, born on May 1, 2019. She takes her name from the Gorilla Rehabilitation and Conservation Education Center, or GRACE for short, a sanctuary in the North Kivu Province of the Democratic Republic of Congo, which rescues and rehabilitates orphaned lowland Grauer gorillas before reintroducing them into the wild. These gorillas are critically endangered, in large part due to poaching for bushmeat, and each life saved is precious. Interested in knowing more about how you can help? Visit GRACEGorillas.org.

The shipping crate next to the chalkboard drawing of a lowland gorilla, on the left side of the first gorilla viewing window you reach, is addressed to **Dr. William Coway, New York Zoological Society**. It's a slightly skewed reference to Dr. William Conway, former president of the New York Zoological Society, which later became the Wildlife Conservation Society and with which Disney has partnered for more than fifty years.

On the shelf next to Dr. K. Kulunda's desk in the scientific research station you'll see a large book with the title *Animal Kingdom*. While it is about animals of the world, it's an obvious reference to both the name and the theme of the park.

Fascinating Fact

If you're inspired by what you're experiencing in Animal Kingdom and you want to support animal conservation, here's a hidden gem just for you: The Visitor Information board just after you exit the trail features a letter to the Harambe Research Team, with a list of eight organizations Disney supports. Take a picture or jot them down, and become a genuine member of the research team once you get home.

Harambe Market

The names Harambe's entrepreneurs have given their marketplace enterprises follow a general pattern in African countries: They're chosen with a specific meaning in mind. **Kitamu Grill** stems from the Swahili word for "tasty." *Mwanga* in **Chef Mwanga's** means "light" in Swahili, and it's also a town in Tanzania. *Wanjohi* is a town in Kenya, but it has a second translation that fits here. As a given name, traditionally for a male child, its meaning is "brewer" in the Kikuyu dialect in Kenya, and you can purchase that very beverage (beer) at **Wanjohi Refreshment**. **Famous Sausages**? Well, that's just the optimistic entrepreneurial spirit shining through.

There are lots of humorous signs around the market, but one comes with a warning all visitors should heed. A green sign on the right-hand side of the archway into the market reads, **Clean Hands Means Clean Food**. Reinforcing that crucial message, the sign below it reads, **Wash Your Hands** in Swahili.

Your next adventure whisks you away to another planet, but the issues caused by imbalance with nature continue. Take the pathway out of Africa via the bridge near Tusker House rather than using the wooden walkway beyond *Festival of the Lion King*. You may want to experience that pathway later, but for now visit Pandora through its main entrance. You'll make one stop before your journey to the home of the Na'vi.

Tiffins Restaurant

Tiffins isn't an attraction in the traditional sense of the word, but it's certainly an attraction when it comes to immense storytelling presented through artwork and detailing. Take time to look around this gorgeous venue, and as you do, watch for representations of rhinos, tigers, elephants, tamarin monkeys, sharks and rays, coral reefs, butterflies, cranes, great apes, and sea turtles. They are the **ten living things** that the Disney Conservation Fund's program "Reverse the Decline, Increase the Time" has been set up to help save.

Tiffins is named for the **metal, multilevel container**—called a tiffin-box or tiffin-carrier—used by workers and travelers in India to carry a light meal. The word "tiffin" actually refers to the contents of the container, but became synonymous with the lunch box itself. Its layers keep wet items, such as pickles or yogurt, from turning bread or other dry items into a soppy mess, and prevent the pudding from mixing with the vegetables and rice. They also serve as bowls from which to eat each item. With a locking lid that keeps all the layers together and a handle with which to carry them, tiffins are a clever solution for ensuring a healthy, economical meal is ready to go. But the word "tiffin" isn't an Indian word. Instead, it originated during the British colonial era in India, from the slang word "tiff," which refers to the delightful tradition of sipping (or "tiffing") a wee dram of alcohol with one's afternoon tea.

Imagine That!

Emily O'Brien, Walt Disney Imagineering executive show producer for Disney's Animal Kingdom, remembers how Tiffins got its name: "When you go on animal-back adventures and you carry food with you, it's typically in a metal lunch box of some sort, so when it's bouncing against the side of the animal, or in the jeep, it doesn't destroy your food. They're called 'tiffins,' and there are several in the display cases that we've gotten from around the world. It's a mess kit, but it's a global thing. They're in almost every culture [so] it was the perfect culmination. Once somebody suggested 'Tiffins' as the restaurant's name, it was like, 'Oh, of course! It has to be that. There is nothing else it could be.'"

Before you enter the restaurant, look up at the peak of the canopy over the door. See that **yak carving with big, curly horns**? A few of its details are a bit unusual, unless you're a Tibetan yak herder. What's up with the **red tassels** hanging from its ears? Domesticated yaks in Tibet have their ears pierced, and tassel "earrings" are hung from the piercings as a means of decoration and good luck.

Tiffins's yak also has a **bell around its neck**, and while the music that bell would make isn't meant to be beautiful, it is certainly meant to be useful. Work animals in the Himalayas each wear a bell or string of bells around their necks, and as they plod their way along steep, narrow, gravelly trails, people also using the trails know an animal is coming their way before they're able to see it. It's especially helpful to know a herd of yaks is headed toward you, as they can be panicky animals who don't like surprises.

Also notice the other wood carvings as you're walking toward Tiffins's front door. They honor each type of **pack animal** used by Disney's exploration teams as they traveled the world doing research for Animal Kingdom.

That gorgeous wooden wall art you see behind the check-in desk isn't just a stunning **map of the world**; it's also a map of all the places Imagineers visited when creating Animal Kingdom. Notice the dinosaur bones in the American Southwest, the temple in Asia, and the safari truck in Africa. DinoLand, Anandapur, and Kilimanjaro Safaris should come to mind.

Surely the Imagineers didn't seek out palaces when creating a park dedicated to animals, so why are those **charming little castles** on the map? They're placed over locations where Disney has resorts, and although Disney did not request them when they commissioned the map, the artist decided they were a nice feature to include.

Explore the **field note sketchbook pages** near the check-in desk, in the left-hand hallway leading to Nomad Lounge and in the right-hand hallway leading to the Grand Gallery and Safari Gallery. They are the original reference drawings done by Imagineers during their travels.

You'll also find **photographs and sketches** pinned to corkboards hanging in each of the hallways, which were taken during the Imagineers' travels.

Best prop in the whole place? The **photo of Joe Rohde with a singing bowl on his head**. It's in a cabinet on the left, next to the singing bowl.

Among the striking elements in the Grand Gallery are the **five carved pillars** that separate the large room into two smaller, friendlier sections. When Animal Kingdom first opened it featured six of these "totems," each topped with a box kite–style flag and used to guide people through different areas of the park. Later they were relocated to the pathway leading to Camp Minnie-Mickey. When that land closed to make way for Pandora—The World of Avatar, artists working on Tiffins stripped off the totems' pink paint to enhance the beauty of each animal carving, and placed them in the Grand Gallery. What happened to the sixth pillar? It was too damaged to use. Happily, these five survived.

The totems aren't the only items that were reimagined. The **beaded headdress** on the front wall of the Grand Gallery is from the *Festival of the Lion King* show, and the **artwork featuring an elephant, a monkey, a gorilla, a rhino, and other animals** is backed by fabric remnants from the original Rivers of Light storyteller shamans' costumes. They're illuminated as a nod toward the glowing animal Spirit Guides in the show.

The square box covered in electrical wires, circuit boxes, and photos in the Safari Gallery honors the ingenuity of citizens in small villages in Africa, who have to be creative with their resources. It isn't unusual to see homespun tents along the roadside advertising services, or wires leading from a home to the nearest power grid point. Tiffins's version is a nod to communities' cobbled-together methods of **sharing electrical hook-ups**.

Each of the **wooden panels** at the back of the Safari Gallery are pieces that were used as molds or left over from building the Africa section of the park.

By now you can probably guess that nondescript, yet somehow compelling, work of art in the Trek Gallery, made from **wooden blocks carved with yeti faces**, is composed of pieces of wood originally intended for use at Expedition Everest—Legend of the Forbidden Mountain.

Imagine That!

Emily O'Brien shares insights into a sentimental favorite that represents storytelling in the truest sense of the word. "Around the perimeter of Nomad Lounge are questions about travel—why do you travel, what's the craziest thing you ever ate—and the banners are artists' renderings of answers that came from people who went on these trips. There is one with a drawing of an octopus, and that inspired the octopus on the menu." Although Tiffins is dedicated to the Imagineers' travels, it's really about the human journey and its wonders when we dare to leave the confines of home.

Also in the Trek Gallery is a beautiful wooden **Sumatran rhino**, carved in Bali and displayed against a white background. The letters on the background are the gene sequence of this magnificent animal. Notice how the bottom line of lettering is nearly gone? The Disney Conservation Fund, and others like it, are working to ensure that isn't the fate of the Sumatran rhino.

It would be difficult to miss the rearing horses and horse head carvings on each end of the ceiling beams on Nomad Lounge's outdoor deck, but you may miss a subtle reference to the Imagineers' travels on the woodwork below the rearing horses. **Carvings of footprints, animal hoofprints, and tire tracks** are reminders of the various ways Imagineers got around.

Exit Nomad Lounge from the deck rather than through Tiffins, watching the walkway as you go. Not only is there a transition from human-created wooden decking to nature-made "mud;" you'll also see **animal prints** of all kinds, with a few hiking boot impressions mixed in for good measure. The big round prints that butt up on the garden and look like bubbles? Elephant feet!

Pandora—The World of Avatar

As you cross the bridge into Pandora you get your first hint at the blending of past and present. The lampposts are beautiful now, but they were once surveillance locations for the Resources Development Administration, or RDA. You can still see the **rusted security cameras**, no longer in commission. They have been left to corrode for so long, one of them has nearly broken off. All over Pandora you'll find this nod to restored balance, and symbols that indicate the brevity of human work and the timelessness of nature.

Also take note as you wander: Items and structures abandoned by the RDA are typically rusted, but those put up by **Alpha Centauri Expeditions** (ACE), the tour company that brought you to Pandora, are new and well maintained.

Although you may be tempted to walk right past the sign installed by ACE that reads "Welcome to the Valley of Mo'ara Pandora," on the left-hand side of the pathway leading into the valley, pause for a moment and read the **Visitor Information**. Much like the great national parks on Earth, there are warnings visitors should heed, and (fictional) hints that you may not be safe if you leave your common sense behind.

The sign also hints at another overriding theme in the valley: Cooperation now exists between the **Pandora Conservation Initiative** and ACE. Each of their names appears on the sign, an indication of the tenuous balance between conservation and exploitation.

There is no mistaking Pandora's other-worldly nature when you reach the gigantic **Flaska Reclinata** plant on the right-hand side of the pathway. Although its Latin-sounding name suggests its shape (a reclining bottle), the real magic can be seen farther along. A toxic plume the Reclinata spews out contains spores that have taken root, and baby Reclinatas are happily growing in the stream paralleling the walkway.

You'll recognize them by their dramatic, red, sword-like leaves, pointing upward.

After you pass the Reclinata, keep an eye out for a crashed **twin-blade RDA helicopter**. It's partially obscured by the plant life around it, but you'll see it on the opposite side of the stream, just beyond the short cut-out pass off the main walkway. Stand by the first lightpost after the Reclinata and look across the stream.

The **Valley of Mo'ara's stream** is a remnant Imagineers kept from Camp Minnie-Mickey. If you remember that now-extinct land, you'll recall Daisy Duck, Huey, Dewey, and Louie hiking alongside this stream while Donald Duck, Mickey Mouse, and Goofy were fishing, with faithful dog Pluto waiting patiently nearby.

How are you able to breathe on Pandora without proper equipment? Thank those veiny yellow-green pods you'll see all around the valley, and the large, leafy blue globes along the riverbank. They're **Vein Pods** and **Puffball Trees**, and along with the Reclinata, they help keep the air free of methane and other toxic gasses. How do the Na'vi breathe in this newly purified atmosphere? Disney magic!

Valley of Mo'ara

Once you get your breath back after seeing the Valley of Mo'ara spread out before you, pause for a moment and look at the floating Hallelujah Mountains. If you think they look like a **humanoid figure** with two heads (the small floating mountains that are higher than the others) and outstretched arms (the long vines that connect to the mountain to their left), you're right. The effect is quite dramatic if you keep your eyes fixed on the mountains as you walk toward the drum circle and stop near the queue entry for Na'vi River Journey.

One of the floating mountains that looks like a head is much bigger than the other, with a broad, flat face and nose. The other is smaller, with more angular features. **Na'vi and human**, side by side?

As you're looking at the "heads," allow your eyes to scan down the vine "arms" over to the mountain to the left. Much of that mountain is covered in foliage, but there is a long vertical strip of bare tan-and-beige rock, with yellow-green staining to its right, and diagonally to the left and above the higher waterfall. Fix your eyes roughly in the middle of the bare rock and you'll see a teeny-tiny head that stands out against the flatness of the mountainside. Keen eyes will notice this one looks just like a **smiling face**! If you can't make it out, take a zoom photo and look for it that way.

By design there is **very little signage** in the valley, because you're supposed to be exploring. But while you're meant to be an adventurer, your real goal is to get to Flight of Passage as quickly as is humanly possible, so think like a Na'vi and look for something natural and symbolic. (Hint: It's banshee-shaped.)

The RDA expats living and working in the valley often use Na'vi phrases when they interact with ACE tourists, and the Na'vi have borrowed words directly from English, French, German, Italian, Greek, and Mandarin, giving visitors a peek at the **diversity within the RDA**. In a supreme example of hidden meaning, **Pandora's name and cautionary message** harken directly back to Greek mythology, and what happens when you metaphorically open Pandora's box.

Fascinating Fact

After fiddling around with words based on the Maori language for his upcoming film *Avatar*, James Cameron enlisted the help of linguist Dr. Paul Frommer, who created an entire language for the Na'vi, including the word "Na'vi." However, it's not a new language word at all. It's from ancient Hebrew, and it means "prophet" or "seer." "Na'vi" isn't the only Hebrew-based word, either. Swap the "s" for a "z" and the "h" for a "d" in the Na'vi word *Tsahik* (clan spiritualist) and you've got *Tzadik*, which is "righteous person" in Hebrew. *Eywa*, meaning "world spirit," is also in Dr. Frommer's dictionary, but if you think it sounds familiar, you're right. It's a phonetic transposition of the word "Yahweh," the Hebrew word that translates to "I am" or, roughly, "creator of all that exists," but was commonly used as a reference to God.

Much of Pandora has been left in its natural state, but you'll come across a few locations where roots, vines, and other organic items have been woven into totems. Watch for the Ikron (Mountain Banshee) at the entry to Flight of Passage, and the Shaman of Songs covered by a giant wood sprite (a seedling from the sacred Tree of Souls) at the entry to Na'vi River Journey. These **woven pieces of art** act as signage for their respective attractions.

Pandora is one of the few places on Walt Disney World property where you won't find Disney characters. It's also the only land in the park where there are no live animals, though there are "live" animals in the fantasy sense of the word. Watch for **Blue Reef Ticks** (beetle-like bugs) in the pond where you see the Sagittaria—those squirting, alien squid creatures that invaded conch shells—and **Cerebellis Scapularis** (green bugs with two big black eyes) on the shore nearby. Unlike the conch-squids, the bugs are stationary.

But don't worry; you'll hear them even if you don't see them right away.

As Pandora transitions from day into night, pay attention to how the plants and animals react. Listen for the **symbiotic relationships** some species have, with one calling out as a means of alerting others to the presence of invaders (you!) or dangerous nighttime stalkers.

Pandora is a place of great conflict as well as deep harmony. Animals are animals, and some, just like on Earth, won't survive the night. You'll hear this timeless **predator-and-prey drama** unfold in the forest at night, so be sure to stay on the path!

During the day, Pandora's "sacred place of song" connects visitors to Eywa through music, but all is not well here, either. On the flowing roots used to create the bench to the right of the drum circle you'll see **deep, slashing claw marks**. Considering the predator sounds coming from the surrounding forest once the sun goes down, you may want to be careful at night.

Na'vi River Journey

As you near the entry to the attraction, notice the **footprints** made by Na'vi adults and children. How do we know the smaller prints aren't from humans? Like all Na'vi, they only have four toes.

In a supreme act of cooperation, the Na'vi have agreed to allow ACE guests to journey along a sacred river that runs through a hidden cave system and into a bioluminescent forest, for an encounter with the Shaman of Songs. The area you pass through to reach the river (the outdoor queue) is filled with weavings and built entirely of items found in nature, including the enormous weaving above you, whose blue vines create a **map of the Kaspavan River**, which you're about to traverse. Notice how they lead directly to the shaman? That's a nod toward what you'll experience during your journey.

See that **Na'vi warrior** standing guard near the entry to the sacred river? He isn't there by chance. He's making sure you're part of the ACE group, and when he decides you are, he gives verbal permission to continue down the river.

Although you don't get close enough to see the **frog-like creatures** hopping from leaf to leaf above you, their shadows reveal they have six legs. Most animals on Pandora are hexapods, so watch for this curiosity as the viperwolves, hexapedes, and direhorses trot past in the background or come down to the riverbank to check you out.

Imagine That!

Guests who enjoy exploring every facet of a land in minute detail will find the outdoor queue at Na'vi River Journey almost overwhelming, and that is by design. There is so much going on it's hard to take it all in, and Imagineers' intent was to dissuade over-analysis and guide the viewer toward immersion in the environment as if it were real, rather than using their analytical minds to figure out how it was created.

As you move away from the Na'vi's domain, where the ground is imprinted with Na'vi footprints, animal tracks, leaves, and organic matter, toward the area formerly occupied by the RDA, the pathway turns to **prefab cement slabs** with manhole covers that look like an airlocking system.

A mundane item that serves a dual purpose is the **metal wall** just beyond Pongu Pongu, which separates guests from Disney's backstage area. The wall makes it clear ACE tourists aren't allowed access to the road that, within the story, once led to the quarry where the RDA mined for Unobtanium.

Satu'li Canteen

The dining outlet's name is a blend of English and Na'vi. *Satu'li* means "heritage," and *canteen*, of course, means "mass-market meals in a cavernous setting." Happily its **Pandoran-Earthling fusion** cuisine is as interesting as the restaurant's wonderful place-making details.

Once the RDA's commissary, Satu'li Canteen is the Pandoran equivalent of finding a 1950s American diner in Tibet; the idea is there, but it's probably not what the Na'vi have on their dinner tables each night. Stand in the courtyard in front of the canteen and you'll see the **mash-up of cultures** through the metal Quonset hut and the more nature-based front patio. After you enter the queue to order food, pay particular attention to the photo of Marshall Lamm among the first set of letters and photos on the wall after you make the first left-hand turn. It's really **Jon Landau**, producer of the movie *Avatar*.

Next you'll see a photo of **six humans with giant blue shovels**. From left to right in the original photo, and in their roles at the time the photo was taken, were George Kalogridis, president Walt Disney World; Meg Crofton, president parks and resorts operations; Tom Staggs, chairman Walt Disney Parks and Resorts; Jon Landau, producer of *Avatar*; Bruce Vaughn, chief creative executive Walt Disney Imagineering; and Joe Rohde, creative executive Walt Disney Imagineering.

On the ordering area's far-left wall you'll see a photo of two Na'vi in front of the **Amplified Mobility Platform** (AMP) suit outside of Pongu Pongu, posing with some humans. The man wearing sunglasses is **Zsolt Hormay**, vice president creative and the Imagineer responsible for the land's place-making.

Pongu Pongu

Step up to the window between quick-serve Pongu Pongu and Windtraders gift shop and look up. See those black and orange **military dog tags** on ball chains, hanging between two crossbars? Those were once ID tags for RDA personnel, and the photos they contain weren't chosen for no reason. Look for a black tag on the left-hand side of the right-hand crossbar, with the photo facing forward. That's Joe Rohde, lead Imagineer for Pandora and Animal Kingdom. He's surrounded here by other Imagineers and designers.

Take a closer look at the **Order Here and Pick Up Here signs** over the ordering window. The words have been hand-painted, which is your cue that something interesting has happened. These two signs have been recycled for the convenience of visitors to Pandora. The Order Here sign used to be a warning about unauthorized use of AMP suits, and the Pick Up Here sign formerly indicated an entry to Level 3, location of the laboratory in the former RDA building. Other metal, such as the light fixtures, has been recycled too.

Why is that enormous AMP suit parked out front? It belongs to Pongu Pongu's owner, who used to be a mechanic for the RDA but stayed on Pandora after the RDA departed. His neighbor, Windtraders gift shop, is also run by former RDA employees, as is the Colors of Mo'ara kiosk. This insight helps set a time frame around which the experience is based. You're visiting within one human lifetime from the transition.

That gorgeous **painting on the ceiling** above the Ikron rookery in Windtraders is more than an eye-catching decoration. It's also a representation of Pandora and the celestial bodies that surround it.

Avatar Flight of Passage

The queue for Flight of Passage is one of the most immersive feats of storytelling Disney has ever created, starting with the scenery outdoors. When you reach the bridge over the stream, turn to your right and face the twin waterfalls. See that **series of three arches**, the first of which is broken? In the movie, stone arches similar to these formed an open canopy over the Tree of Souls, and while it is worrisome that one is broken here, it is hopeful that two remain intact.

Cross the bridge and stop in the small cutout just before you reach the woven banshee on your left. Look at the bare face of the floating mountain closest to you, specifically just inside the cavernous opening between the top stretch of green foliage and the stretch of green foliage below. Those blue things you see clinging to the rock aren't flowers. They're **stingbats**, an aggressive and prolific Pandoran predator with an alarming inability to make life-saving decisions. You can also see them if you stand in front of the pond to the left of Flight of Passage's entry to the queue. Scan the underside of the sharp ledge at the bottom of the light-colored center mountain. They're the blue things hanging by their feet.

Once you reach the indoor queue you're immediately surrounded by **cave paintings**. Notice how some are much older than others, with more primitive designs that have chipped away over time, or are partially covered by newer paintings.

The primary focus of these paintings is the Na'vi's coexistence with banshees, but there is plenty to suggest the Na'vi's spiritual relationship to the universe as well. Along with symbols that clearly represent Eywa, dozens of circular images are based on **Polyphemus**, the planet around which Pandora orbits. Look at the painting below the gigantic red leonopteryx on the ceiling. You'll see blue Polyphemus just below its left wing.

Fascinating Fact

Polyphemus's name comes from Greek mythology's cyclops Polyphemus, son of Poseidon, for its characteristic "eye," also reminiscent of the Great Red Spot on Jupiter. A fitting name, both for the eye-like feature and the fact mythology's Polyphemus was a man-eater. The RDA didn't stand a chance with that thing looking down on them.

As you go, watch for **Na'vi handprints** on the walls. Some have a human handprint over them, which speaks to the cooperation that now exists, but many go even deeper than that. Some Na'vi handprints have three fingers and a thumb, and some have four fingers and a thumb. Why? Because the four-fingered prints represent Avatars created when human and Na'vi DNA blend.

The natural aspect of the cave is disrupted by the results of a boring machine that has carved out a large round passage leading to a series of man-made walls and doorways. Exposed rebar, stress fractures, mold staining the walls, and rusting utilities boxes set the time frame during which you're visiting. You're entering a **former RDA building**, now long out of service.

Walk through the third airlock door and look at the wall to your right. You'll see **JC Shoring** painted in white, with the number 08.016.54 painted below it. This is a hidden signature for James Cameron, whose birthdate is August 16, 1954. What does "Shoring" refer to? The retaining wall is assembled from metal shoring, so perhaps JC Shoring is, jokingly, James Cameron's fallback company in case the whole filmmaking thing doesn't work out. You'll see more of these as you walk through this forest.

You may be tempted to think the number beneath Cameron's birthdate is a **telephone number**, and you'd be partly correct. As you proceed through the queue, set yourself a little task. Using the dialing keypad on your cell phone, see if you can work out which city in Ontario, Canada, those numbers spell out. They are a cryptogram for the name of James Cameron's city of birth. Pay close attention, though; the second to the last number isn't what it appears to be. Compare it to the previous number 8, and notice it's just a bit different. You'll find the answer in Solution 6 in Appendix: Solutions to Hints.

A startling transformation takes place as you move into the eerie, forested section. The pathway changes from concrete to "dirt," and bioluminescent plants are swallowing up all signs that the RDA once had a **toxicity testing zone** here. From the skull-and-crossbones sign that will soon be covered by plant life, to the safety instructions and biohazard records on the walls, in another hundred years it will all be hidden.

The path becomes concrete again as you move from the "outdoors" into a human-made structure. The cooperative results of nature-versus-industry open up before you as you enter the **scientists' laboratory**, which was once part of an RDA bunker and is now home to the Pandora Conservation Initiative and its Mountain Banshee Project.

Once you're inside the lab, the story goes into hyperdrive. Everywhere you look there are details that make you feel as if you're really in a working research center. Along with experiments and reference manuals, watch for **employees' personal effects**, such as crayon drawings from their children; sci-fi author Douglas Adams's posthumously released book, *The Salmon of Doubt*; H.G. Wells's *The War of the Worlds*; and even a small Japanese Maneki Neko "waving kitty," a symbol of good fortune.

The **spikey ball** swimming around in an experiment container in the enclosed section of the lab is part of a research program geared toward cleaning contaminated water. A second, blobby version is one container over, and a third, blobby-spikey incarnation is just beyond, with notes that indicate each variation in the experiment is more successful than the last. Why is this water conservation project so prominent? All living things depend on a food chain that begins with a healthy water ecosystem.

The book *Pandoran Botany* by Dr. Grace Augustine stands out for its vivid front cover featuring bright green plants against a purple background. In *Avatar*, Norm introduces Jake to his new boss, though she's still in her psionic link unit, by saying she heads the Avatar Program, she's a legend, and she literally wrote the book on Pandoran botany.

To the right of the *Pandoran Botany* book is an entity that looks like moving magnet shavings. It's a **velocivirus**, inadvertently brought to Pandora on a space transport. While it's mesmerizing to watch in the confines of a containment unit, its darker personality as an invasive species is a reminder of the need for extreme caution when dealing with delicate ecosystems, including ACE tourists' home planet of Earth.

It will be difficult to pry your attention away from the floating Avatar as you get closer to him, but take one final look at the enclosed lab. Dr. Jaclyn Ogden has left copies of her book ***Ikron, My Connection, Life with the Banshee***, along with a note stating they're for the Chem-Gals Pen-

Pals. You'll soon learn why Dr. Ogden is important to the Flight of Passage story, as well as who she is in Disney history.

The instruction board, **From Link to Flight**, to the left of the desk, tells visitors how the process of linking to their Avatar happens, including the step of linking "psionically." Although it sounds like a made-up word, it actually means "using psychic powers."

See that **signed baseball** in a protective case on the bookshelf to the right of the desk, just before you leave the lab? It's a memento from a game Team Banshee played. They aren't the best team in the universe, as evidenced by the encouraging notes pinned to the bulletin board to the left. As a consolation prize, each member of Team Banshee gets a coffee mug.

The books to the right of the ball also tell a tale. Two titles are *Reason for Hope* and *Hope for Animals and Their World* by Jane Goodall, along with *The Everglades: River of Grass* by Marjory Stoneman Douglas, and *The Na'vi* by Phred Palmer. Placing them together, with a nod toward Florida's fragile habitat and its preservation, is a quiet indication that balance on Pandora is being restored, and another warning about ecosystems on Earth.

Once you're inside the Genetic Matching Room, Dr. Stevens, who addresses visitors via video feed, mentions **Dr. Jackie Ogden**, head of the Pandora Conservation Initiative's science team and the person responsible for the technology that allows humans to link to an Avatar. You'll meet Dr. Ogden when you move on to the pre-boarding room. She is clearly important within the story, and that's your hint she's someone special in real life too. Dr. Jacqueline "Jackie" Ogden in her Earth-bound incarnation is an experimental psychologist and the vice president of animal programs and environmental initiatives at Walt Disney World.

Imagine That!

Fictional Dr. Ogden is clearly a collector of artifacts, some from Pandora and some from Earth. Many of the Earth relics she displays are, in reality, from the Pacific island of Papua New Guinea. Mining operations in New Guinea, much like the RDA's mining on Pandora, resulted in the catastrophic destruction of the population's water quality, sanitation, financial viability, and personal safety, as well as the indigenous flora and fauna. The items in Dr. Ogden's office are a stark reminder of the devastation irresponsible mining has on a community and its land.

Although Dr. Stevens in the video feed is a man, his surname appropriately honors **Beth Stevens**, Disney Worldwide Services' senior vice president of environmental affairs.

As you're leaving the attraction after your breathtaking soar over Pandora, you'll walk past **three red handprints** on the wall, with the initials JC, JR, and JL under them. You've probably guessed they are the handprints of James Cameron (writer and director of *Avatar*), Joe Rohde (lead designer of Disney's Animal Kingdom), and Jon Landau (*Avatar*'s producer). A set of not-so-hidden signatures!

As you wind your way out of the park at the end of a long, rewarding day, let your pace slow to a meander and pause to enjoy the small details that add an extra element of depth to the stories unfolding around you.

Imagineer Joe Rohde summed it up best when he said, "Just as we hope to bring joy and inspiration to our guests, we hope that they take that inspiration out into the world. See it every day in the living world around them and act upon that inspiration. That is the heart of Animal Kingdom."

Disney's Animal Kingdom Time Line

Forty years after Walt Disney's first theme park in Anaheim, California, opened, the Walt Disney Company announced their intention to build what would arguably be their most unique and challenging park yet. It would take another three years of development, but finally, on April 22, 1998, Disney's Animal Kingdom swung the gates wide and welcomed its first guests.

Attractions open that day were **the Boneyard** dinosaur dig area, **Countdown to Extinction**, **Cretaceous Trail** walking paths, **Discovery River Boats**, *Festival of the Lion King*, **Flights of Wonder** exotic bird show, **Gorilla Exploration Trail**, *Journey into Jungle Book* stage show, **Kilimanjaro Safaris**, *Pocahontas and Her Forest Friends*, **Rafiki's Planet Watch**, and **Wildlife Express Train**. There were six distinct areas on opening day: the Oasis, Safari Village, Africa, DinoLand U.S.A., Camp Minnie-Mickey, and Conservation Station. A seventh area, Asia, was due to open within a year, with the mythical **Beastly Kingdom** also on the drawing board.

Beastly Kingdom would cover the "animals of myth and legend" portion of the park, a land of fire-breathing dragons and gentle unicorns, of *Fantasia*'s fauns, centaurs, and dancing hippos; the world of fantasy and fairy tale brought to life. It was an incredible concept, but it has yet to be realized.

1998–1999: First Expansion

By the end of 1998, Gorilla Exploration Trail would be renamed **Pangani Forest Exploration Trail**; the Discovery River Boats would close, reopening two months later as **Discovery River Taxis**; and, a month later, Discovery River Taxis would make its final run—sort of. It would reopen in March 1999 as **Radio Disney River Cruise**, a jaunty music- and banter-filled boat ride to nowhere (that also closed down before the end of the year, another formula that just didn't work). The March of the ARTimals also paraded for the final time in 1999.

However, there was something new to enjoy, and it was substantial. The new section of Asia opened on April 22, 1999, with the soak-you-to-your-skin river-rafting experience, **Kali River Rapids**, and the peaceful **Maharajah Jungle Trek** walking trail. Kali originally went by the conceptual title Tiger Rapids Run and was intended to showcase animals from Asia as guests floated past in circular rafts. But these things have a way of changing, and Kali River Rapids ultimately became a whitewater saturation-fest loosely wrapped around a mild lesson about the dangers of logging.

2000–2001: Time for a Parade

Animal Kingdom sailed along happily for two more years before adding any new attractions. The beautifully artistic **Mickey's Jammin' Jungle Parade** then made its first run on October 1, 2001 (as part of the Walt Disney World 100 Years of Magic celebration), with stylized animal puppets, stilt walkers, and Disney characters riding safari vehicles. The puppets were worn by humans and were designed by Disney's *The Lion King* Broadway show puppet creators, Michael Curry Design.

There was more on the horizon, though, as Disney was aware there still wasn't enough here to keep eager fans happy and to make it more than a half-day experience in many guests' minds. The first part of it arrived in DinoLand in November 2001, and it finally gave preschoolers a ride tailored just for them. **TriceraTop Spin** was another variation on the Magic Carpets of Aladdin in Magic Kingdom (which were themselves a spin-off of the popular Dumbo ride), but they added a tried-and-true favorite, with baby triceratops ride vehicles instead of flying carpets or big-eared elephants.

2002: Dino-Drama

The full development of this new area came in April 2002. **Chester and Hester's Dino-Rama** "roadside carnival" in DinoLand was certainly big all right. At least, the towering yellow brontosaurus framing the entrance was big!

As well as TriceraTop Spin, Dino-Rama consisted of a handful of paid-for carnival games, tacky (intentionally, said Disney) gift shops, and the area's saving grace, **Primeval Whirl**. Though it looked like a cheap (but again, intentionally tacky) "wild mouse" coaster with a cartoonish prehistoric theme, it was actually a dynamic, spinning coaster that packed a gut-wrenching wallop!

Many fans felt the area was the theme park equivalent of "throwing them a bone," no better than the seasonal fairs that spring up all over small-town America. But they still waited for an hour just to ride Primeval Whirl.

2003–2005: A Lucky Strike

Even that wasn't enough to keep guests coming back in droves, as the area was intended to do, since most guests still considered Animal Kingdom a half-day park. But Disney's response was slow. When it did come, in April 2005, it was in the form of a green, cart-toting, free-roaming, self-contained Audio-Animatronic baby brontosaurus with personality plus! Lucky the Dinosaur was a first in Disney's animatronic world. He could walk on two legs, pulling a cart behind him; he could grab objects in his mouth; he had a degree of vocal expression; and he could fully interact with his "handler" in a most convincing way. However, Lucky's stay at Animal Kingdom was short. By the end of July 2005, he had moved on to Hong Kong Disneyland.

Cries for a new land—ideally, Beastly Kingdom from the park's conceptual stage—grew louder. Although Animal Kingdom had begun to increase in popularity, it lacked the kind of draw that kept guests coming back again and again. But a new day was about to dawn in Animal Kingdom. The yeti was about to arrive.

2006: Enter the Yeti

On April 7, 2006, **Expedition Everest—Legend of the Forbidden Mountain** careened into Asia with a Himalayan train ride on the fast track toward the mountain's protector, the fearsome yeti. The coaster's precarious journey put riders face-to-face with the angry beast before making a breakneck escape down the Forbidden Mountain.

Walt Disney Imagineering had a new megahit on its hands and had fulfilled, at least to some degree, the park's original intent to include mythical creatures in the animal lineup. Attendance soared.

2007: A Musical Note

Things were going along swimmingly at Animal Kingdom, and on January 24, 2007, a new attraction officially debuted at Theater in the Wild, replacing *Tarzan Rocks*, which closed in January 2006. *Finding Nemo: The Musical* offered a charming human-puppet show featuring Nemo, Marlin, Dory, Crush, and their friends in an artistic pageant the whole family could enjoy.

Because the blockbuster movie *Finding Nemo* did not have any songs, adapting it into a musical was left to husband-and-wife team Robert Lopez, cocreator of *Avenue Q*, a Tony Award–winning Broadway hit, and Kristen Anderson-Lopez, cocreator of a cappella musical *Along the Way*. The duo wrote fourteen original songs for the new show.

Actors dressed in costumes similar to their character handled larger-than-life puppets, but they were fully visible to the audience. While Disney had employed this technique in EPCOT's parade Tapestry of Nations and Mickey's Jammin' Jungle Parade, it was unique to an onstage, in-park musical. *Finding Nemo: The Musical* would also mark the first time Disney Creative Entertainment, a division of Walt Disney Imagineering that was created in 2001, produced a major musical show for a Walt Disney World park.

2008: Ten Years After

On April 22, 2008, Disney's Animal Kingdom celebrated its tenth anniversary with a special rededication ceremony featuring renowned primatologist Dr. Jane Goodall, who was there at the beginning of this "new species of theme park" and was happy to mark the park's milestone birthday with her own signature chimpanzee vocalization!

2009–2014: Goodbye Campers, Hello Aliens!

The land that was once earmarked for Beastly Kingdom but became an area of meet-and-greet trails underwent a major overhaul when **Camp Minnie-Mickey** closed on January 6, 2014, to make way for the new *Avatar* land due to open in 2017. **Festival of the Lion King** went on hiatus when Camp Minnie-Mickey closed, and the building was moved, lock, stock, and barrel, to the Africa section of the park. It reopened on June 1, 2014.

Mickey's Jammin' Jungle Parade ended May 31, 2014, leaving Animal Kingdom with no afternoon parade but with the tantalizing prospect of all-new entertainment in the form of a **Rivers of Light** show on the park's waterway, and spectacular nighttime entertainment on the Tree of Life and throughout Discovery Island.

2015–2020: Opening Pandora's Box

Projection mapping found its way to Animal Kingdom on May 27, 2016, with the wonderful **Tree of Life Awakenings**, which transformed the park's central icon through a projection show playing several times nightly. While the Tree of Life's animals seemed as if they had come to life, the much-anticipated Rivers of Light show was causing Disney a bit of a headache. As its challenges were being addressed, the temporary lagoon show *Jungle Book: Alive with Magic* stepped in on May 28, 2016, to fill the gap. Finally, on February 17, 2017, **Rivers of Light** made its grand debut.

Animal Kingdom was moving in the direction of a day-into-night park in anticipation of a major new land, through enhancements including **Kilimanjaro Safaris Nocturnal Encounters** and **Harambe Wildlife Parti**. Other minor tweaks included a name change from Pangani Forest Exploration Trail to **Gorilla Falls Exploration Trail**, and the December 31, 2017, closing of Flights of Wonder for a new story in **UP! A Great Bird Adventure**, which opened on April 22, 2018.

But the headliner change the park had been waiting for came on May 27, 2017, when **Pandora—The World of Avatar** whisked travelers away to the Valley of Mo'ara, beautiful by day and spectacular by night. As captivating as its bioluminescence was, and as lovely as its gentle **Na'vi River Journey** turned out to be, the **Avatar Flight of Passage** attraction, a breathtaking soar over Pandora on the back of a banshee, blew visitors away, fulfilling Animal Kingdom's quest for equal billing with its three sister parks. And the crowds poured in.

An all-encompassing experience is at the heart of each of the Walt Disney World theme parks. You are meant to participate, becoming part of the story rather than acting as a passive observer. Let *The Hidden Magic of Walt Disney World, 3rd Edition* inspire you to seek out the finer points and allow yourself to be totally immersed in the heart of the magic.

Solutions to Hints

The Magic Kingdom

Solution 1: The reassembled blocks read, DISNEY.

Solution 2: Who killed whom?

- Uncle Jacob's icon is a flower, and he died first. He was killed by Bertie.
- Bertie's icon is a bottle of poison, and he killed Uncle Jacob. He was killed by Aunt Florence.
- Aunt Florence's icon is a gun, and she killed Bertie. She was killed by The Twins.
- The Twins' icon is a dead bird, and they killed Aunt Florence. They were killed by Cousin Maude.
- Cousin Maude's icon is a hammer, and she killed The Twins. She died in a house fire, possibly set by herself, given the three matchsticks you'll see tucked into the top of her hair.

Solution 3: The Open Sectors at Space Mountain are:

- FL-MAWP: Fantasyland—The Many Adventures of Winnie the Pooh
- AL-AFC: Adventureland—Aladdin's Flying Carpets
- FL-MPM: Fantasyland—*Mickey's PhilharMagic*
- FRL-SM: Frontierland—Splash Mountain

- TL-BLSRS: Tomorrowland—Buzz Lightyear's Space Ranger Spin
- TL-MILFaFt: Tomorrowland—Monsters, Inc. Laugh Floor…with a mysterious postscript that is not part of the attraction's name

Closed Sectors are:

- FL-20K: Fantasyland—20,000 Leagues Under the Sea
- FL-MTWR: Fantasyland—Mr. Toad's Wild Ride
- TL-SK2FL: Tomorrowland—Skyway to Fantasyland
- MSU-SB: Main Street, U.S.A.—Swan Boats
- FL-MMR: Fantasyland—Mickey Mouse Revue
- TL-M2M: Tomorrowland—Mission to Mars

EPCOT

Solution 4: FN2BFRE stands for "It's Fun to Be Free," the peppy little tune from the former World of Motion attraction.

Disney's Animal Kingdom

Solution 5: *Smilodon*'s sign is on the roof at the back of Chester & Hester's Dinosaur Treasures.

Solution 6: The name of the city James Cameron was born in is Kapuskasing.

Acknowledgments

I would like to thank Imagineers Eric Jacobson, Asa Kalama, Scott Mallwitz, Ron Logan, Ron Rodriguez, Emily O'Brien, Eric Baker, Eddie Sotto, Laura Neiderheiser, J. Daniel Jenkins, Brian Piasecki, Alex Grayman, Dave Minichiello, and Chrissie Allen, and author Christopher Lucas for generously sharing his story. I would also like to thank the Walt Disney World Cast Members for their unfailing dedication to providing a magical experience to all their guests.

Thank you to Brendan O'Neill, Julia Jacques, Peter Archer, and Sarah Armour at Adams Media, an imprint of Simon & Schuster.

And a very special thank-you to Gene Columbus, not only for sharing his time and his stories but also for being the wonderful mentor and inspiration he has been to the next generation of entertainment industry professionals.

Index

Index

About the Author

Susan Veness is an international travel writer, researcher, online content provider, and itinerary planner specializing in Florida, Disney, Orlando's theme parks, and cruising. She is the author of five books in the Hidden Magic of Walt Disney World series; *Walt Disney World Hacks*; and she is also the coauthor of the *Brit Guide to Orlando* and the biography *Defying Expectations*. She has been visiting Walt Disney World since it opened in 1971, and with a home just minutes from the Mouse, she continues to tour the parks on a regular basis.

Experience the Magic of the Disney Parks Right in Your Kitchen!

100
Easy and Delicious Recipes Inspired by Walt Disney World!

Your Guide to the Happiest Kitchen on Earth!

The
Unofficial
DISNEY PARKS
COOKBOOK

From Delicious *Dole Whip* to Tasty *Mickey Pretzels*,
*** 100 Magical Disney-Inspired Recipes ***

ASHLEY CRAFT

PICK UP OR DOWNLOAD YOUR COPY TODAY!